The World of the French Revolution

The World of the French Revolution

R. R. PALMER

LONDON · GEORGE ALLEN & UNWIN LTD

Ruskin House Museum Street

To my wife

First published in Great Britain in 1971

ISBN 0 04 944009 8 Cased
0 04 944010 1 Paper

This work was first published in French under the title
1789: *Les Révolutions de la liberté et de l'égalité*
© Calmann-Lévy, 1967

Printed in Great Britain
by Compton Printing Ltd
London and Aylesbury

Contents

Preface

THE PRESENT BOOK, though wholly new, is also largely an abridgment of the second volume of my *Age of the Democratic Revolution*, published in 1964 by Princeton University Press. Hence there are occasional similarities of language which a careful reader might discover. Some parts, especially the first and last chapters, have no equivalent in the earlier work.

The book was first written at the request of the French publisher, Mr. Robert Calmann-Lévy, for translation into French and inclusion in his series Great Waves of Revolution. It appeared in Paris in 1968 under the title *1789: Les Révolutions de la liberté et de l'égalité*. Though now published later than the French version, the present book is in fact the original. It is adapted to the purpose of the French series, in which each volume was to stress not only its own revolution but the "wave" of international repercussions which accompanied it or into which it merged.

I should like to express my thanks to the Centre International Universitaire in Paris, which provided me with the pleasant accommodations in which the book was written. Most of all I am indebted to my wife, who bore with the writing of this book at a time when we might have enjoyed, and perhaps even needed, a more carefree leave of absence.

New Haven, Conn.
June, 1970

R. R. P.

THE WORLD OF
THE FRENCH REVOLUTION

Preliminary Observations

THERE ARE DATES ON WHICH HISTORY seems to turn, and which become symbols loaded with meaning. Such for the English is 1066, the year of the Norman Conquest. The Americans have such a magic number in 1492, marking the "discovery" of America—that is, the beginning of its Europeanization. The date 1789 provides as great a symbol for the French, and indeed the world. It is the dawn of Liberty and Equality, or more prosaically the point of transition between the Old Order and modern society. One of the purposes of this book will be to explain why this transition took the form of revolution. Revolutionary it was, however, and in fact one of the most portentous consequences of the upheaval was the "invention" of revolution itself, the launching of the belief—or, as some would say, "myth"—that human problems will be solved by a vast phenomenon in world history known as "the revolution." No one had made any such supposition before 1789, not even those Frenchmen who, in the course of events, became revolutionaries.

The shock of 1789 produced waves that spread in all directions—through society, through space, and through time. Socially, while the movement of 1789 was initiated by the upper and educated classes, it soon imparted itself to the whole population of France. It aroused to political action, and to political purpose and consciousness, deeper levels of society, on the farms and in the workshops, in a way never seen before on so large a scale. By

1792, for the first time in an advanced country of 25 million people, the world saw a republic that its leaders called democratic.

In space, the explosion of 1789 sent immediate tremors through Europe and those parts of the world with which Europe then had close connections. The violence in France merged with lesser eruptions, or more local revolutionary developments, which had already begun independently of French influence in Holland and Belgium, at Geneva in Switzerland, in Ireland, and in Poland. The French Revolution of 1789 absorbed and soon surpassed the influence of the American Revolution of some fifteen years before. After the great war came in 1792 between revolutionary France and the European powers, and after the French Republic began to win victories, new revolutionary states were set up: the Batavian Republic of 1795 in the Netherlands; the Cisalpine, Ligurian, Roman, and Neapolitan Republics in Italy from 1796 to 1799; the Helvetic Republic in Switzerland in 1798. During the same war the reform movement in Poland turned into the unsuccessful revolution led by Kosciuszko. The United Irish rose in a vain attempt to create an independent republic in Ireland. England and Scotland were full of active sympathizers with the French Revolution, who demanded far-reaching changes in the institutions of Great Britain. In the United States, where the new federal constitution was just going into operation, the political character of the new country was profoundly shaped by conflicting attitudes toward the French Revolution. In the West Indies, in the French sugar colony of Saint-Domingue, events led to the proclamation of the independent republic of Haiti; it was the first example in which a black population overthrew and expelled its white masters. Lesser agitations in Spanish and Portuguese America anticipated the independence that came a generation later. After 1800, with the continuing victories of the French under Napoleon, reforming administrators in Germany, Italy, the Netherlands, Switzerland, Poland, and to some degree even in Spain, welcomed the opportunity to cooperate with the French in the modernizing of their own countries, along lines laid down by the French Revolution of 1789.

But in politics, if not in hydrography or physics, waves are accompanied by counterwaves, and strong currents of antirevolution or conservatism gathered strength in these same years. It was conservative resistance in France itself, in large measure, which both precipitated the Revolution and drove it forward to lengths not originally foreseen. European governments came to the support of the displaced representatives of the Old Order in France. The traditional governing class in Britain, after a long struggle not only against revolutionary France but against English and Scottish malcontents and Irish rebels, was so strengthened in its position that not all the parliamentary reform of the following century seriously undermined it. In Germany there grew up a deeply anti-French habit of mind, which became very critical of the liberalism, the individualism, and the constitutionalism of the West. In Eastern Europe, which was then embraced by the Hapsburg, Hohenzollern, and Romanov monarchies, counter-revolution prevailed as early as the 1790s. Government and society in this Eastern region, fearful of a French Revolution which spread so rapidly in Western Europe, and jointly concerned to hold down revolution in Poland, took on the character of military and agrarian conservatism, which they retained until the three monarchies themselves collapsed in the First World War. The line between a liberal West and an autocratic East in Europe in effect dates from the events symbolized by 1789.

Waves also rolled on through time. There were many moments at which the Revolution of 1789 was supposed to be "over," its achievements completed or at least fully formulated and launched. For some, the Revolution, properly speaking, was "over" in 1791, for others in 1795. Napoleon supposedly ended it in 1799, while preserving its most substantial innovations. It was "over" in 1815 with the return of the Bourbons, and again in 1830 when the Bourbons were again driven out. Nevertheless "the Revolution" persisted. Or rather, revolutionary discontents and revolutionary purposes persisted, to break out over much of Europe in 1848, in France in the Paris Commune of 1871, and sporadically elsewhere.

The truth is that in Central and Western Europe there has been no revolution of large magnitude since 1848, and no revolution both large and successful since the tumultuous decade that followed 1789. The Paris Commune was abortive and localized; the Weimar Republic was characterized by the absence of revolutionary enthusiasm; the disorders and new creations that followed both world wars, in Central and Western Europe, were not the products of true revolutionary upheaval. The great Revolution of Western civilization—or what has also been called the Atlantic Revolution, since the American Revolution of 1776 entered into it—occurred at the end of the eighteenth century. There has been nothing like it in the Western countries since.

What persisted in the nineteenth century was not so much the fact as the idea or ideal of revolution. It was organization, planning, writing, and philosophizing for and about revolution in a way scarcely known during the real Revolution of 1789. For some, notably persons of assured income, or those who possessed property either large or small, the Revolution was either a glorious memory or an unfortunate necessity of the past. It was like a war that had been won, to be followed by peace. For others, however, the war was not over, there was as yet no social peace, and revolution was a necessity of the future. Of this opinion were certain intellectuals, journalists, political leaders, and spokesmen for the laboring classes, together with many of the laboring classes themselves, for whom the Revolution of 1789 had aroused hopes that it could not fulfill. Divisions of this kind, between those who worked for stabilization and those who saw the Revolution as unfinished, appeared among the revolutionaries of 1789 within a few months after the fall of the Bastille. They contributed to the radicalizing of the Revolution at least until 1793.

After the Revolution of 1830, by which the great gains of 1789 (but not of 1793) were believed to be secured, the same divisions reappeared. Once again the more comfortable members of society, including those who had most fully benefited from the changes of 1789, wished to regard the Revolution as at most a historical fact. Others were still dissatisfied, and with good reason, for the early years of industrialization, which became evident in France about 1830, were a time of severe trial for the laboring classes, both those who attended the new power machinery and those whom it deprived of their old skills and employments. There was bound to be a renewal of social thinking in any case. Very large groups of people had yet to be integrated into society. If social thought, for many, took the form of belief in "the revolution," a kind of future miracle by which the world would be transformed, this could not have happened except for the great remembered example of 1789. Or, more specifically, what excited the new leaders was the memory, somewhat idealized, of a great democratic republic under Robespierre in 1793.

The flaming words of 1789, as of 1793, were "the constitution," "the people," "the nation," "the rights of man," "the law," "the citizen," and "the patriot." The new revolutionary movement after 1830 made use of a new vocabulary, which it applied to current social diagnosis, to forecasting the future, and retrospectively, to interpreting the past, and which included such words as "socialism," "bourgeoisie," "radicalism," "conservatism," and "reaction." It is a surprising fact that none of these words was used in the actual revolutionary decade from 1789 to 1799. The terms "left" and "right," "capitalists" and "proletarians," though not unknown in French in the 1790s, were hardly ever heard. The men who really made the French Revolution, as well as those who opposed it, went through the whole experience never employing the language without which any discussion of revolution now seems impossible. In fact, it was precisely during the French Revolution that the old French word *bourgeois* went out of use. It returned after 1830 and passed from French into other languages. Its new meaning was never wholly distinct or agreed upon, but at least in classical Marxism the "bourgeoisie" came to refer to the class of people whom Marx saw as the chief agents and beneficiaries of the French Revolution, especially of the arrangements of law and property that came out of that Revolution, but who would disappear in the revolution of the future.

Neither in France, nor in any of the other industrialized countries of the West, did this revolution ever come. From Marxism the idea passed to Lenin, who reinforced a revolutionary movement native to Russia with an ideology built upon the study of Marx and of the French Revolution. The French Revolution remained, until Lenin's own successes in 1917, the great precedent and example of what a true revolution was and how it should be conducted. Since the Russian Revolution the importance of the French Revolution, for those favoring the liquidation of existing society, has somewhat receded. The waves generated in the great storm of 1789, as they lap upon distant shores almost two centuries later, have been much altered by intervening tempests and configurations of the land. But the effects of that great storm in midocean, or at the heart and center of Western civilization—for such were France and Paris in 1789—are still present and still felt.

The purpose of the present book is to set forth not so much the history of the French Revolution in France itself as the revolutionary "wave" to which it gave rise, mainly the impact of revolution in Europe and America at that time, but with some attention to the continuing power or explosive charge of the French Revolution in later times.

Vast though it was, the French Revolution, as Tocqueville remarked, was entirely unforeseen. It took the world by surprise. That the splendid monarchy at Versailles should collapse, that a Constituent Assembly should sit in Paris, that the peasantry throughout France should rise in rebellion, and shopkeepers and artisans in the cities become politically militant could hardly have been imagined a few years, or even months, before they happened. This lack of foresight can be partly understood by the fact that the social sciences, and the close empirical observation of contemporary society, were undeveloped. Social classes lived in considerable ignorance of each other. Nor was there any revolutionary party before 1789, either publicizing the virtues of a coming revolution or working secretly to bring it about. That some frightened conservatives soon after 1789 saw the Revolution as the product of years of clandestine conspiracy, like Barruel in France or Robison in Great Britain, is evidence of their own surprise and consternation at the event and of their inability even after the event to perceive any adequate causes for it. It was not revolutionaries who made the Revolution of 1789. It was the Revolution that made the revolutionaries. Perhaps the same is true of all the really great revolutions.

The unexpectedness of the Revolution suggests two paradoxical lines of thought. First of all, if it was so far outside the realm of reasonable expectation, it may have been in the nature of a historical accident, or at least due to incidental and short-run causes. If only the French government had not faced a financial crisis in 1786, if only certain other choices had been made, if only certain concessions and compromises had been granted, there need have been no revolution. This seems to be true, but upon reflection it becomes evident that the reasons for the fiscal crisis and the reasons why the concessions could not be made go deep into the nature of the French monarchy, the structure of French society, the relationships between classes, and the thought patterns and purposes of divergent social groups. In short, and fortunately for the rationality of human events, while allowing for the importance of existential and momentary considerations, we are soon driven for an understanding of the Revolution to a review of basic causes operating over a long period of time.

The second observation is that, though what happened in 1789 was unplanned, the participants in the Revolution had from the beginning an amazingly distinct idea of what they wanted. The deputies called together by King Louis XVI, essentially to assist him in balancing his budget, proceeded to redefine the royal job, overhaul the tax structure, reorganize the whole government on new principles, and remake the whole country in a new image. In that sense they were indeed already "revolutionary." To understand this phenomenon we must refer not only to the negative effects of disaffection but also to the positive impact of an intellectual revolution, which was provided by the Enlightenment of the eighteenth century. From the Enlightenment came the expectation not indeed of revolution but of a civilization of the future soon to be realized, and more rational, more progressive, more efficient, and more equitable than existing arrangements in church and state. In addition, the peasants who revolted in 1789, and whose revolt surprised the Revolutionary Assembly, which it both strengthened and frightened, also knew quite distinctly what they wanted. They wanted to get rid of the seigneurial, or manorial, system, to stop the payments of money or goods to their lords, to improve their economic and social position by their own action. Here again we must deal with basic causes.

There remains the problem of the sensational, universal, and sudden appeal of the French Revolution in other countries. What accounts for the wave, or as was then said, the "contagion"? The answer lies in the uniformity and intercommunication of Western civilization at the time. The social and political conditions, the level of economic development, and the intellectual preparation of the Enlightenment, while not the same as in France, were sufficiently similar to make French development relevant elsewhere. To understand the waves of revolution—and of counter-revolution—we must examine the European world as a whole before 1789.

[1]

The Old Order

THE OLD ORDER WAS NOT "OLD" until it was superseded. It was a young man's world. Not only were the revolutionaries of 1789 predominantly young men—Robespierre being only thirty-one when he came to Paris in that year, and Mirabeau and the Abbé Sieyès seeming elder statesmen among them at forty— but those reaching power through legitimate channels were often also surprisingly young: Joseph II was co-emperor with his mother at twenty-four, William Pitt was prime minister of Great Britain at the same age, half the members of the conservative Parlement of Paris were under thirty-five, and Louis XVI and Marie Antoinette, having reigned for almost twenty years, were both dead before their fortieth birthdays.

The Old Order abounded in new developments and new ideas. Population was growing substantially for the first time since the Middle Ages, but since it apparently grew about as much in China as in Europe, and as much in southern Italy as in France or England, it is hard to see it as a specific determinant of events. Combined with other conditions, however, the increase in human numbers can have serious consequences. If on the one hand it produces more customers for trade and more taxpayers for governments, it might also, through swelling the younger age groups, make it more difficult for young men of the educated classes to

11

find suitable careers, and could impoverish many of the agricultural population by heightening the pressure upon the land. City life was becoming more common, with all the increased awareness that it brought with it. London had a million inhabitants, Paris about 600,000. As centers of culture, fashion, serious thinking, government, and business, both cities overshadowed their respective countries more than they ever had in the past. More important, however, than such huge agglomerations (Constantinople was probably even larger) was the network of smaller cities throughout Central and Western Europe. As administrative, judicial, educational, commercial, and residential centers they possessed more vitality, in comparison with the capitals, than under the more centralized conditions of later times. Communications were improving, a few of the main roads were paved, and the road system, though still rudimentary, was the best seen in Europe since Roman times. Regular mail service had recently been introduced, and coaches now served the public on regular schedules.

Much that still stands and now seems old was new in the generation before the Revolution. Cities such as Bath and Mannheim had recently been built or reconstructed. St. Petersburg, the Russian capital (now Leningrad), was no older than Philadelphia. French provincial towns were adorned with handsome new government buildings and townhouses of leading landowners, merchants, and lawyers. It was estimated in 1788 that 10,000 new buildings had been put up in Paris in the preceding thirty years. There was some talk of tearing down the ancient Bastille, and at the opposite edge of the city the architect Gabriel built the Ecole Militaire and laid out the vast Champ-de-Mars (now the site of the Eiffel Tower), which was to be the scene of many revolutionary celebrations. Churches were built or improved despite the secularism of the Enlightenment. While Mont-Saint-Michel and Notre Dame de Paris were neglected even by their own clergy because they were old-fashioned, new churches were erected in the classical or modern taste, such as Ste. Geneviève, now the Pantheon. Versailles itself, when abandoned by the royal family in 1789, was less old than the United States Capitol today. The "royal squares," such as the magnificent Place Louis XV (now the Place de la Concorde) and similar works of urban planning in Nancy, Turin, and elsewhere, testified to the vigor of the institution of monarchy.

All this new growth was made possible, in general, by the changes summarized as the commercial revolution, which for several centuries had been shifting Europe to a money-and-market economy. It is not enough to speak of the rise of capitalism, still less of a "bourgeoisie," if only because the rise of the money-and-market economy was as much a part of political as of economic development, depending as much on state power as on the incentives of trade, and because the owners of "capital," or of wealth valued for the money income it might produce, were an extremely heterogeneous lot, among whom the differences were more important than the resemblances. The old landed aristocracies were much affected by the need for money, which was the more desirable because of the increasing array of luxuries and services it could buy. They tried to obtain it from their tenants. The poor were affected; there was a difference in the potential behavior of a peasant on a subsistence estate, who in time of bad harvest simply starved, and one whose problem, in a time of falling prices, was that he could not obtain enough cash to pay his rents and taxes. City populaces were sensitive to variations in the price of bread. Governments were voracious consumers of money; the kings were great builders, and the style of life at court had become very costly. Wars, though less destructive than in the past, were more expensive, for soldiers now had to be carefully drilled, kept in service for years, paid a wage, and housed in new barracks. Navies also had to be maintained; the whole structure of the American and Asian trade was won and kept up by sea power as much as by commercial enterprise or investment. Taxes increased but were never sufficient. Governments borrowed incessantly, and then had to carry the debt. Nothing was more common in the eighteenth century, from the American colonies to the Hapsburg empire, than for constitutional and political crises to arise out of problems of government finance.

The rise of the money-and-market economy, over a period of several centuries, had produced four recognizably distinct zones in the area of European civilization. One was England, the second was the general region of Western Europe, to the north of Spain and central Italy; the third was Eastern Europe; and the transatlantic region of European settlement or exploitation may be considered a fourth. The four zones were to react very differently to the French Revolution.

England was the most advanced and successful country under eighteenth-century conditions. It had had its great revolution a century before, the Puritan revolution, in the course of which a king had been put to death; but these events were hardly remembered and when remembered were called a rebellion, not a revolution. In England the "revolution" referred to the proceedings by which Parliament had replaced James II with William and Mary in 1689. Important constitutional liberties had been won, such as freedom from arbitrary arrest, and toleration, though not equal rights, for Protestants outside the Church of England. The most important consequence of the English seventeenth-century troubles was that Parliament became supreme over the Crown, and that the British landowning aristocracy (Scotland having been joined with England in 1707) became supreme in Parliament. Though the House of Lords was hereditary (except for the bishops), and the House of Commons was in principle elective, the difference between the two was not very great; both were based on the ownership of land, and members of the same families sat in both houses. Lords and Commons were subject to the same taxes; and the landowners who governed the country, though they increasingly threw the burden upon others in various ways, accepted in principle the direct taxation of their own incomes from landed rents. In these circumstances there was an aristocracy in the true sense of a mainly hereditary governing class which actually governed, but there was practically no nobility as known on the Continent. It was possible for landowners to work with men enriched by commerce, especially if the latter bought landed estates and adopted or respected the manners of the aristocracy.

In England, through the institution of Parliament, economic and political power coincided, and the elites of wealth and government were the same people. This fact, peculiar to England, had many very important consequences. It made the government financially very strong. The Bank of England was founded in 1694, chiefly to provide a channel by which private wealth could be made available to William III in his wars against Louis XIV. Men of means would more readily lend to a government whose policies and finances they could control. The government, in sharp contrast to France, could draw on the full resources of the country. The credit of the British government, seemingly inexhaustible, became a puzzle to the rest of the world, where the mechanism of credit was not so well understood. It was widely expected, during the French Revolutionary wars, that England would soon collapse in a pile of worthless paper, but the truth is that British credit, as much as anything else, defeated not only Louis XIV but also Napoleon.

The wealthy in England, and those hoping to become wealthy, having a strong voice in Parliament, could use political power effectively for economic advancement. They built up an unparalleled colonial empire in the long series of wars against France. They built a navy to police and extend the empire. The volume of trade with America, with Asia, with Europe, increased rapidly, and with it the supply of liquid wealth seeking further investment. At the same time the landowners, through acts of Parliament, were able to extinguish old common-law rights in the land, convert common fields to private property, enclose the old open fields, and buy up the smaller owners, until England became a country in which most of the land was owned by a few thousand families. The owners leased it to a relatively small middle class of farmers, while converting the bulk of the rural population into wage laborers. There was no landowning peasantry or mass of small farmers cultivating small parcels, as in neighboring parts of the Continent. Large landowners, having the necessary capital, open to new ideas, and susceptible to motives of future profit, carried through an agricultural revolution by which the productivity of the soil was greatly increased and the number of necessary agricultural workers were greatly reduced. Thus the food supply was enlarged while men became available to seek other employments, in new factories or in growing cities, to which they were more willing to move because neither property nor tradition held them in their rural homes. Capital, labor, food, new ideas, enterprise, and the profit motive produced a readiness to finance and support problematical new devices such as the steam engine; the elements were present by which England was the first country to enter, with no previous model, upon the process of industrialization, the famous Industrial Revolution, which was evident about 1760 or 1780.

Obviously these beginnings of industrialization were of the utmost importance for the future. In the period of the French Revolution they showed their effects indirectly. Both the owners and the employees of new factories were few in number, and they played no distinctive political role. There was no revolution in transportation or communications until well after 1800. Ships continued to be made of wood, in England as elsewhere. Except for improvements in cannon, in which the French excelled, the firearms in all armies were much the same in the Revolutionary and Napoleonic wars as in the War of the Spanish Succession. Indeed, no century since the introduction of gunpowder has seen such stability in military technology as the eighteenth. It was essentially only in textiles, and above all in cotton, that the use of new machinery and of steam power was lowering costs and enormously increasing the volume of production in England. This meant an astronomical increase in the export of British cotton goods for several generations after about 1760. Profits from the export of cotton were now added to those from agriculture and from the older international trade, such as the resale to Europe of American sugar, tobacco, and coffee and Asian tea. The economic advantage of England, in comparison to the most developed parts of the Continent, still lay in the greater productivity of its land and hence the affluence of its upper classes, and in the institutions of banking, sea power, and foreign trade, which increased the wealth on which the British treasury could draw.

But precisely because of its great successes—its wealth, its empire, its toleration, its high level of life for the upper classes, its identification of economic and political elites, its revolution enshrined in the past—England in the eighteenth century was a highly conservative country, somewhat like the United States two centuries later. The British constitution was a source of great self-satisfaction. Economically flexible and expansive, Britain was politically rigid.

It was unable to meet the demands of its American colonies, which it lost in the American Revolution. Toward Ireland it was more accommodating, but really satisfied only the Anglo-Irish and Anglican "ascendancy" in that island. English reformers, even William Pitt when he became prime minister, were unable to broaden the basis of selection to the House of Commons. English Dissenters, or non-Anglican Protestants, were again refused equal political rights in 1789, at the very time when non-Catholics were receiving them in France. Not even the game laws could be relaxed. British conservatism was to be a constant factor in the world of the French Revolution.

The second zone comprised France, Germany as far east as the Elbe river and the Bohemian border, northern Italy, and the intervening Dutch, Belgian, and Swiss regions. As in England, there was a good deal of commercial and urban development, especially in the seaports from Hamburg and Amsterdam down through Nantes and Bordeaux to Marseilles, and hence a large merchant and professional class. There were two great differences from England. Politically, in this area the French were the only people who had arrived at a national unity on a large scale, and they had done so under a so-called absolute monarchy. The rest of the zone was politically fragmented into small states susceptible to influences from outside. The United Provinces (the Dutch) were very wealthy but in many ways were dependent on England, in which much of their wealth was invested. The Belgian provinces (or Austrian Netherlands), like the duchies of Milan and Tuscany, were associated with the Hapsburg empire, within which they enjoyed varying degrees of autonomy. Genoa and Venice were patrician republics, Piedmont a compact little monarchy with its capital at Turin. Germany west of the Elbe was a mosaic of heterogeneous jurisdictions—free cities like Hamburg; small monarchies like Hanover, which belonged to the king of England, and Bavaria, which was usually allied to France; bishoprics and archbishoprics, where the prelates were the temporal rulers, together with much else, all gathered into the Holy Roman Empire, an obsolescent and almost nonfunctioning organization of which the reigning Hapsburg was usually the head.

The distinctive characteristic of this second zone, however, regardless of political forms, was in its land use and land tenure. Here the rise of the money-and-market economy had left a strong peasantry in occupation of the soil, from which, at the same time, a class of lords, or seigneurs, drew an income by the collection of miscellaneous dues, fees, and rents. The peasants, or rural laboring population, were legally free, not serfs as in Eastern Europe, nor were they predominantly wage laborers as in England. Some peasants owned parcels of land, in the sense in which their property was then legally understood. They could inherit, bequeath, buy, sell, or lease out these parcels as they wished. They owned and marketed the product and received the income, subject to the payment of customary and perpetual dues to the seigneur, which if paid in money might be quite insignificant, because of the decline in the value of money since the Middle Ages, but if paid in kind would be more of a burden. Other peasants, or indeed the same ones, worked pieces of land on modern leasehold terms, for periods of about nine years, at money rentals subject to rene-gotiation upward or downward upon expiration of the lease. Others worked on shares, dividing the proceeds of cultivation with the landlord. And many were landless, obliged to seek employment from other peasants, or from the lords, or in the weaving and other handicraft industries which were still located in the country though managed from the towns. In any case the actual cultivation or management of agriculture was in the hands of the peasants either as individuals or as village communities. It tended therefore to be traditional and relatively unproductive. The investment and experimentation which were revolutionizing agriculture in England were, though not unknown, much less common on the Continent. On the other hand, the countryman in this second zone was a more socially sensitized being than the British or Irish agricultural laborer or the East European serf. He made visits to town to sell his produce. He might have legal business, or rights to defend against the seigneur. He was directly exposed to, and could himself perceive, the fluctuations of agricultural prices and wages, the level of rents, and the mounting burden of taxes. Peasants were still mostly illiterate, and hardly shared in the glories of eighteenth-century civilization, but in this second zone they were not insulated from the social forces around them.

The lords, or seigneurs, in this agrarian system, drew their income less from direct exploitation of their estates than from the collection, sometimes in large total amounts, of a variety of small dues and rents. Since the whole system had originated in the medieval manor, the lord also had certain vestiges of legal jurisdiction. He could hold a court for the settlement of legal disputes, presided over by his agent and so usually favorable to himself; or he had a monopoly right to maintain a village mill or oven, which could be leased to a miller or baker for the money income it would produce. Characteristically the lord was a noble— in his own eyes descended from the chivalry of the Middle Ages— but in truth the whole system had become a system of property, valued not only for the amount of the income but for its quality or status, since income of this kind conveyed more prestige than the profits of trade or the earnings of the professions. In France, anyone who could afford it, such as a new noble, a bourgeois, or an occasional rich peasant, could purchase a manor and enjoy a seigneurial income. In places where nobles were rare or unimportant, as in Holland, Switzerland, and some of the German free cities, well-to-do townspeople received incomes of substantially this same kind from the surrounding rural population. Church bodies, dioceses, convents, universities, schools, and hospitals might also be manor lords. But the manorial, or seigneurial, system, though a form of property, was economically no longer functional. The recipient of the income played no role in production; he made few decisions and provided little or no capital for improvement. Often he was an absentee. To the peasants the whole arrangement came increasingly to seem a useless superstructure. It was generally to be abolished in the Revolution, with no immediate loss to production, though in the long run the economy of small holdings, and of peasant proprietorship or cultivation, presented problems for the modernization of agriculture.

In the short run, for the period of the Revolution itself, the significance of the land system in the second zone was twofold. It provided a basis, especially in France, for cooperation between townspeople and peasants. And the older aristocracy, being less firmly fixed on the land, was in a far more precarious position than in either England or Eastern Europe. It was more dependent, to sustain its income, on certain privileges in taxation, or on appointments in church or state (preferably sinecures), or on squeezing more revenue out of the peasants while taking no corresponding measures to increase productivity, which is to say exploitation of the poor by the rich, under circumstances in which such exploitation could be resisted. It was in this second zone, and not merely because of proximity to France, that the most powerful waves of revolution were to be felt.

The third zone, for present purposes, may be taken to mean Eastern Europe except for the Balkans, which belonged to Turkey, and except for Scandinavia, whose history was different. Here, too, as in Western Europe, there had been great changes, though in an inverse direction. Formerly, in medieval times, Poland, Bohemia, and Hungary had shared in the general life of Latin Christianity. With the reorientation of commercial activity which followed upon the opening of the Atlantic trade routes, and by which Western Europe had greatly prospered, the towns of Eastern Europe fell into relative decay. Towns were far apart, few in number, and with a few striking exceptions very small. Often they were of different nationality from the surrounding country; many towns in the Baltic provinces of Russia, in Bohemia, and in Hungary were ethnic islands of Germans, and in Poland and Russia many individual merchants, shop owners, architects, or government employees were German, French, English, or Scottish. Between town and country there was little communication; indeed, outright hostility and suspicion were more common. In the political assemblies, or diets, of Bohemia and Poland, where the towns had been represented until about the year 1500, they were now virtually excluded, in part because of old religious and ethnic quarrels, but mainly because of the triumph of an agrarian and antimercantile mentality in the landed gentry and nobles.

For the rise of a money-and-market economy in Eastern Europe had been more favorable to landowners and governments than to burghers, and it had been ruinous to the peasants. The governments—that is, the Prussian, Russian, and Hapsburg monarchies—so far as their machinery of state and the territories they ruled in 1789 were concerned, had all grown up rather rapidly since the beginning of the preceding century, and in developing their systems of taxation, their armies, and their policies of expansion they had obtained the loyalty of an unruly nobility by sacrificing the peasantry. The noble had accepted the higher authority of a new kind of government on the understanding that this authority stopped at the borders of his estate, where he retained full jurisdiction over his "subjects." The noble, in contrast to his counterpart in the second zone—and in this respect somewhat resembling the British landowner—lived on the income of an estate that he managed himself. He differed from the British landowner in using unfree, or forced, labor.

In short, in Eastern Europe the peasantry had sunk into serfdom, which in the eighteenth century was still expanding in Russia, though in the Hapsburg empire the government was trying to restrain it. The peasant, with the usual exceptions, worked under the direction of the lord, often as much as six days a week, without wages, under a system of compulsion that could be enforced by flogging or imprisonment. Though lacking secure tenure of any particular piece of land, he was attached to the estate; that is, the purchaser or seller of the land bought or sold the village and its inhabitants as well. In parts of Poland and Russia the serf could be sold apart from the land, or sent off by the owner to work in town or in a mine, so that his legal condition approached that of slavery in America. Normally, the peasant might not leave the estate, nor marry off it, nor learn a new occupation except with the consent of the lord. If he fled, he could be legally pursued. His geographical and social mobility were zero, or entirely dependent on the lord's wishes. And as capitalism began to show itself in Eastern Europe, as it did when an occasional landowner wished to increase his money income by rational development of agriculture for export or of the timber or mineral resources of his estate, it did so with a noble playing the role of entrepreneur, in a patriarchal atmosphere of servile labor.

In these circumstances the barriers between the three basic social classes—landowners, peasants, and townspeople—were incomparably greater than in Britain or Western Europe. Neither peasants nor townsmen had the legal right to own rural estates, which were the proper domain of the nobles; or conversely, anyone allowed to own an estate was considered noble, so that the proportion of "nobles," reaching as high as a twelfth of the population in Poland and Hungary, was much higher than in Western Europe, and the nobles swamped the bourgeoisie by sheer weight of numbers. Such nobles, however, were divided between a few very rich magnates and a mass of lesser gentry, some of whom were very poor, hardly different from peasants except in the consciousness of superior status. Upper nobles and magnates in Poland and Russia had become very Westernized, speaking French in the home, using French tutors, gardeners, and cooks, reading French books, importing luxuries from the West, and becoming addicted to foreign travel. They patronized the lesser nobles, by whom they were often resented; greater and lesser nobles both scorned the burghers, or tradesmen; landowners and townspeople both looked upon the peasants as brutish, beyond the pale of civilized living; peasant serfs, isolated from the currents of society outside their villages, viewed both nobles and burghers as distant and alien beings. With the rural masses so abject, and the middle and town classes so small and undeveloped, only the nobles could have much influence upon government, but their influence tended to be unconstructive and negative, setting a limit beyond which even a reform-minded monarch could not go. The waves of revolution, when they reached Eastern Europe, were lacking in force; the counterwaves were to prove much stronger.

The fourth zone, the overseas regions of European settlement and exploitation, though weeks or months distant from Europe by the ships of the time, played an important part in its affairs. Its direct connections were with the Atlantic peoples—Spanish, Portuguese, French, Dutch, and British, and the Danes also had a few small islands. The chronic wars between England and France, from 1689 to 1815, were fought in part for control in these regions, and as the British won out over the French in India and America, the Dutch and Spaniards also lived in fear of losing their possessions to Britain—a fact that was to have its importance during the wars of the French Revolution. The zone comprised the trading stations east of the Cape of Good Hope and the coasts of West Africa, where Europeans obtained African slaves from the interior, through the mediation of African chiefs, for transportation to the Americas. India and the East Indies, though they took few European exports, were great sources of profitable activity, and towns like Liverpool and Bordeaux owed much of their growth to the African slave trade. But the Americas were far more important.

From Brazil and Mexico a flow of gold and silver came into Europe, increased in the eighteenth century by the opening of new mines and the use of new scientific devices in the processing of the ores. The augmentation of the money supply had a gradual inflationary effect, which not only enhanced the profits of trade but even benefited, until about 1770, those peasants who, as in France, sold their own products at prices that rose more rapidly than their rents or seigneurial dues. The increasing use of foods originating in America, such as Indian corn, which was fed to poultry, or the potato, which was used for human consumption in the less-favored regions, was one cause of the general rise of population, which brought prosperity in places offering a variety of new employments, but only aggravated a bad social situation in places like Ireland and southern Italy. Coffee brought from America may have had, as a stimulant, some imponderable effect on European temperament and behavior; at least it produced, in the coffeehouse, or café, an institution in which people came together, talked, and developed opinions on public questions.

In the West Indies were the sugar islands, operated by Europeans using huge gangs of African slave labor. Under preindustrial conditions, sugar was one of the most important articles of international commerce. The chief producer was the French island of Saint-Domingue; the British island of Jamaica and many smaller islands followed in importance. The biggest plantation owners often returned to live in England or France, where their wealth, luxurious tastes, and arbitrary demeanor gave them a certain prominence. Facing the West Indies were the southern colonies, later states of the United States, from Maryland through Virginia and the Carolinas to Georgia, where export crops were also largely produced by the labor of African slaves, under supervision of an agrarian gentry. The main crops were tobacco and indigo, but cotton was increasingly planted, in direct relationship to the new industrial development in England. It is obvious that without these American plantations, including their slave labor drawn from Africa, the Industrial Revolution as we know it could not have occurred in England.

North of the plantations, from Pennsylvania through New England, was an area unique in the world in that, while not in Europe, it had a large population almost exclusively of European whites, mainly English, with mere handfuls of Indians and Negroes. It must be added that in Virginia and the South the small white farmers were so numerous that the southern part of the mainland, for all its distinctiveness, had more in common with the North than with the West Indies. These "Americans"—that is, emigrated Europeans—were discovered by the European Continent at the time of the American Revolution. It was found that, although clearly somehow related to European civilization, they lived without benefit of certain European institutions, notably the seigneurial or manorial system, hierarchical churches, royal courts, titled nobility, or professional armies. The American Revolution, occurring just at the time when Louis XVI became the king of France, had a powerful and immediate impact in France and much of Europe, partly because it was a rebellion against the British but also because it announced its program with a philosophy that Europe could understand and to which many could respond with enthusiasm. In addition, the participation of France in the War of American Independence, which became another of the Anglo-French wars fought in the West Indies and in India as well as America, overburdened the French treasury and contributed to the fiscal crisis from which France itself fell into revolution.

After the establishment of American independence, divisions began to trouble the United States. The North, characterized by busy seaports, inland towns, small property-owning farmers, commercial fishermen, shipowners, and merchants, resembled Western Europe. The South, almost without towns or a commercial middle class, dominated by owners of great estates who were also the masters of servile labor, who lived by the importation of manufactures from Europe in return for a staple crop, and who felt a contempt for business activities and a strong dislike for centralized government, had more resemblance to the third zone in the present classification, perhaps most especially Poland. The two regions reacted differently to outside events, so that under the stresses imposed by the French Revolution and the Napoleonic empire the infant United States was almost to be torn apart.

More generally, the existence of the two American continents, in view of British command of the sea, was an incalculable advantage for Britain in the struggle with France that accompanied the French Revolution. Using raw cotton from the United States, while excluding it from the Continent, the British were able to carry forward their industrialization. When the French tried to defeat them by blocking their exports to Europe, the British made up much of the loss by expanding their markets in Spanish America. And Continental Europeans proved very unwilling to do without American sugar and coffee, obtainable through British channels, when Napoleon imposed his Continental blockade. The resulting disaffection and smuggling were among the reasons why a French ascendancy in Europe, carried on the waves of the French Revolution, proved impossible to establish.

In an overall view, the institutions of Europe in the eighteenth century can be described under three headings—monarchy, the church, and the arrangements of social stratification suggested by the idea of "estates." They were interconnected; one could begin with either of the three and proceed to the two others. Let us begin with monarchy.

Although the most spectacular of the three, monarchy was actually the least universal. It is easy to forget that many places in Europe before 1789 recognized no king; that it was *after* the French Revolution, at the Congress of Vienna, that republics were said to be "out of fashion." Before the upheaval there were various republics of a traditional kind, considered quite as legitimate as any monarchy—the Republic of Venice with its mainland territories, the Republic of Genoa, the republican states of the Swiss Confederation, the Dutch Republic, or United Provinces, and the anomalous Republic of Poland, comprising the "kingdom" of Poland, where the king had no power, together with the grand duchy of Lithuania. Other regions lived, so to speak, under a monarchy twice removed, well cushioned by local liberties against assertions of royal power, as in the ten provinces of the Austrian Netherlands, the Milanese, the Anglo-American colonies, and the numerous church states and the fifty free cities of Germany. In Great Britain the role of the monarch had become very attenuated. The real monarchs of Europe, as they were before 1789, can be counted on the fingers of two hands—the kings of France, Spain, and Portugal; the kings of Sweden and Denmark (which then possessed Norway); the kings of Sardinia and Naples; and the three great rulers of the East: the emperor of Russia (actually the Empress Catherine II), the king of Prussia, and the king of Hungary, Bohemia, Dalmatia, Croatia, and so forth, archduke of Austria, and so forth, who rejoiced also in the title of Holy Roman Emperor.

Monarchy, however, outside England, was the dominant as well as the most dynamic and progressive institution of government. It offered the model that dukes and "electors" in Germany (the Kurfürsten, or nine princes, having the right to elect the emperor) assiduously tried to follow. Among the Dutch, the stadtholderate, formerly an elective office in the several provinces, had become hereditary in the House of Orange, which was something like a constitutional monarchy, though it did not become one until 1814. Only the monarchies (even the British Parliament took care to work through His Majesty's government) raised powerful armed forces or played a significant part in international struggles.

Monarchy was hereditary and absolute. That is, where the monarch was not hereditary, and where more ancient practices of elective kingship still prevailed, as in Poland and the Holy Roman Empire, the office was entirely ineffectual; and the king of Great Britain and Ireland, being hereditary but not absolute, was a monarch more in a social and legal sense than in the realities of his power. The hereditary monarchies were called dynasties, a royal word for the family. The kings considered their possessions as family inheritances, to be guarded, developed, or extended like the estates of any well-to-do family, by ingenuity, patience or marriage—or by force, the *ultima ratio regum*. Wars, at least on the Continent, were interdynastic rather than international. There were as yet no nations in a modern political sense. Wars could be easily stopped as well as started. Peace could be concluded by a facile trading of territories in which no pretense was made of consulting the wishes of the inhabitants, as when the Bourbons and Hapsburgs, in 1738, made peace by an arrangement in which the king of France took Lorraine, and Tuscany was added to the miscellaneous Hapsburg holdings. The monarchs, especially in the eighteenth century, also regarded themselves as public person-ages, charged with the welfare of their peoples and of the state; but in their own eyes they were so charged only by God or by the station to which they were born; they accepted no delegated authority. Most rulers, even Louis XV at times, took their royal duties very seriously. The confusion between private patrimony and public authority was characteristic of society as a whole, not only of monarchs but of lesser officeholders, seigneurs, and even the masters of guilds.

"Absolute monarchy" is a term more used by historians than by the kings themselves or their subjects. Only when pressed very hard, as Louis XV was before the Parlement of Paris in 1766, would a ruler emphatically assert his absolute or divinely appointed power. West of Russia, all rulers recognized the importance of law and of lawyers and conceded at least in principle the existence of liberties for their peoples. In fact, the whole history of mon-archy since the Middle Ages, and never more so than in the eighteenth century, was the record of a struggle of kings with groups of nobles, the church, or autonomous provinces, each insisting on its own historic rights. Nevertheless, and as a result of these struggles, to achieve social peace, and to have a level at which final and binding decisions could be made, the royal power in the eighteenth century was generally held to be legally "abso-lute"—that is, not in the end dependent upon the wishes of any other person or body within the state. Two centuries of political theory since Bodin, two centuries of public opinion since the horrors of the Wars of Religion (1560–1648), had combined to produce the conception of sovereignty—a final lawmaking, war-making, and peacemaking power—which was attributed to the kings before its transfer to the nations or peoples.

Royal absolutism was limited even in theory. As Bossuet had said, the legitimate power of the king of France was absolute but not arbitrary. The king could not do simply as he wished or claim to embody some historic destiny or national will; he was a Christian monarch, operating within the laws of religion and of the church. The royal power was even more limited *de facto*, not only because even the ablest ruler depended on associates and advisers, but also because each monarchy was a composite construction of different classes and provinces, each with its separate status, legal system, or privileges, on which the royal authority had been superimposed. There was no such internal unity, or common citizenship, as later came to characterize the modern state. In this respect, also, England was the most advanced country. If it had a "common law" and no "provinces," it was because the English crown in earlier times had been exceptionally strong.

The role of kings everywhere had long been to subjugate a formerly feudal nobility, to turn them into subjects against whom law and public order could be enforced. In imposing himself, however, the king had to make concessions, which in the end left him dependent on these same nobles. He might, like Louis XIV, build vast palaces and gardens and develop an elaborate ritual at court, with a view to overawing and pacifying his *grands seigneurs*. He would live lavishly, because among the rich the king must be known as the richest. The result was that, surrounded by courtiers, he could not escape from the charmed circle that he himself had created. Or, tacitly or explicitly, the kings won acceptance by granting special advantages to those strong enough to extort them. An extreme case in point has already been noted in Eastern Europe, where the rulers left the lords with full jurisdiction over their peasants, who remained "subjects" of the lords and, in fact, serfs. In France both nobles and nonnobles were subjects only of the king. But everywhere, and especially in France, the nobility enjoyed certain privileges, including exemptions from taxation. There were similar privileges for whole areas within the several monarchies; Brittany and Alsace paid far less in taxes than the interior provinces of France; Belgium, Lombardy, and Hungary paid far less than Austria proper. Such exemptions were a great advantage for those who enjoyed them, but a great *de facto* limitation, if not fatal weakness, for the monarchy as such.

On the other hand, under the monarchies, the lineaments of

the modern state as known to Western civilization were taking form. In the eighteenth century, organized private warfare was a thing of the past. In the professional armies the officers were under discipline as well as the men. Taxation, though unequal, was accepted as normal. Law courts, lawyers, and habits of settling disputes by legal action, all gained in strength under the royal justice. Roads, bridges, and harbor works were built under the direction of central governments. Civil services, bureaucracies, ministries, and councils of state grew up as agencies of the royal power. They were staffed in part by nobles, who thereby became functionaries of the state instead of merely lords, but they were also extensively staffed—especially in the middle and lower levels —by men of the middle classes, which, on the Continent, grew in strength and numbers more by association with government than by purely economic activity. This development of government services, with trained and salaried lifetime personnel, or what in a negative way may be seen as bureaucracy, went much further in the great monarchies—France, Prussia, the core of "hereditary provinces" of the Austrian empire—than in nonmonarchical but otherwise more advanced countries like England and Holland, where amateur or episodic participation in public life was more common.

The church offers another dimension in which the society of the eighteenth century can be seen. As a spiritual power, the church always insisted that its realm of concern, the care of souls, was in no way subordinate to government. But since the last centuries of the Roman Empire, the Christian religion had been associated with public power. Since the great conversions that ended in the eleventh century, all Europeans (except Jews, to be sure) were supposed to be Christians. There was thus built into European life a homogeneous element of a kind that the great civilizations of India or China never had. It was built in, however, at a certain cost, since it carried with it the principle of compulsory membership in a body of believers. The body was now somewhat broken, for some Europeans were Catholic, others Lutheran, Reformed (Calvinist), or Anglican; but every state, large or small, monarchy or republic, absolutist or constitutional, was associated with its own official or established religion. The

church in return gave its blessing to the state, taught the duty
of obedience to lawful authority, supervised morals, and sought
at best to Christianize the exercise of power and at worst to
preserve its own worldly interests. In England the Anglican
bishops sat in the House of Lords. In Hungary and Poland the
Catholic prelates sat in the upper houses of the diets. At Amsterdam and Geneva the Reformed pastors had a great influence, since
only Reformed laity could belong to the governing councils.
The clergy were traditionally the first estate, a conception that
still had vitality among Catholics, especially in France. The relation
of church to state was symbolized in the monarchies by the corona-
tion, called the *sacre* in French, a religious solemnity in which
the new ruler took an oath to defend religion and to do justice to
his subjects. Society and government were supposed to be "Christian." The French monarch was officially the *roi très chrétien*,
the ruler of Spain was the *rey católico*, and the king of England
stuck to a title once granted by a pope, *Fidei Defensor*.

In Britain, the United Provinces, and parts of Germany there
was a legal toleration of religious differences, but it was everywhere the belief, or at least the practice, that only persons of
the officially recognized religion could be entrusted with public
power. It was a practice carried over from the days of the religious
turmoil a century or two before. In the eighteenth century it was
reinforced less by religious zeal than by social distinctions, for
with the passage of time the religious minorities tended to form
a subculture of inferior social standing. Dissenters in England,
Mennonites and Roman Catholics in the United Provinces, and
Protestants in France were generally regarded as stubborn eccen-
trics. In England only Anglicans could legally hold office in the
armed forces or in the upper management of the Bank of England
or the East India Company, or belong to a borough corporation,
or take a degree from Oxford or Cambridge. In the United
Provinces similar safeguards protected the Dutch Reformed. At
the free city of Frankfurt persons of all religions lived in peace,
but only the Lutherans could take part in city affairs; a saying
has it that the Lutherans governed, the Catholics prayed, and
the Calvinists made money, an apothegm which ignored the

numerous Jews. In France, where Henry IV had used his absolute power to impose the toleration of Protestants in 1598, and Louis XIV had used it in 1685 to enforce conformity to Catholicism, Protestants in the eighteenth century had no legal existence, and hence no rights of marriage and inheritance, though they formed about 5 percent of the population. Everywhere, however, after about 1750 religious animosities were dying down. The famous Calas case of 1762, in which Jean Calas was convicted of the murder of his son to prevent his conversion to Catholicism, was seized upon by Voltaire as a means of attacking the Catholic church, preaching toleration, and reforming the procedures of French criminal justice. There is reason to believe, however, that the conviction of Calas was due more to social fear than to religious excitement—fear felt in Toulouse for the aroused Protestant peasantry outside the city, in time of war against the Protestant powers of England and Prussia. In fact, from about this time, the French courts contrived means of recognizing Protestant marriages and property, until they were confirmed by the monarchy in 1787. Nowhere before 1789, however, was there any full legal equality between persons of different religion in the same state.

There were other ways—though generalization is difficult—in which Protestant and Catholic countries were alike. Marriage was everywhere sanctioned by religion. There was no civil marriage and no divorce. Orphanages and hospitals were usually conducted by religious people. Churches attempted to control thought and morals, and Rousseau's writings were as vehemently condemned at Protestant Geneva as in Catholic France. Education was mainly under religious sponsorship. In Italy and Germany the universities were more independent, but the French universities were Catholic institutions, and Oxford and Cambridge were Anglican. In both England and France the government in effect appointed the bishops, and the designation of parish clergy was often in the hands of lay patrons or local landlords, not of the church. The functions of the parish overlapped with those of local government. In France the parish clergy were usually of peasant stock, while in England the village curates were closer to the gentry; but in both countries, as the eighteenth century went on, the trend was for the bishoprics to be filled by members of the upper classes, so that the Anglican episcopate by 1789 was highly aristocratic, and all the hundred-odd French bishops were nobles.

Institutionally, the church was stronger in Catholic than in Protestant countries. In the Protestant world, the churches possessed far less real property, having lost it during the Reformation. Protestant churches were also more dependent on their respective governments, and the fact that Protestant clergy were married family men, sometimes the sons of clergymen themselves, made them less differentiated from the rest of society in behavior and opinions. The Protestant churches also suffered from repeated fragmentation; in England there were Quakers, Congregationalists, Presbyterians, and Baptists alongside the Anglican church, within which the Methodists were beginning to develop; on the Continent there were Moravians, Mennonites, and other evangelical sects alongside the older Lutheran and Reformed establishments. Such religious pluralism, of which British America already had given the extreme example, made for more tolerant attitudes, at least on theological questions, in the Protestant than in Catholic countries.

The Catholic church, while free of such sources of institutional weakness, had other sources of strength as well as weaknesses of its own. It had a powerful hierarchy, rising to its apex in the pope, whose infallibility in matters of faith had not yet been made a matter of dogma but to whom the bishops in various countries could always appeal to strengthen themselves in conflicts with governments. Everywhere the bishops were important public figures. The bishop of Rome, or pope, was also a temporal sovereign, ruling the central part of Italy as the Papal States. He likewise possessed Avignon, an enclave in southern France. In the Germanies also the prelates were territorial rulers, notably the three great Rhineland archbishops of Cologne, Mainz, and Trier, but including the archbishop of Salzburg and many others.

In the Catholic world, in addition to bishops and parish priests, there were "regular" clergy in the religious orders of men and women, some installed in abbeys or convents, others such as the Jesuits more active in the world or in maintaining systems of schools. The clergy collectively owned a great deal of property. As a result, some bishops and abbots enjoyed large incomes, while the mass of the clergy lived in poverty. Its wealth involved the church in all kinds of financial transactions, so that some of its leaders were men of affairs without much religion. The property of the church was generally tax-exempt, and its amount was sufficient to make such exemptions a subject of dispute. To protect its property, control its own clergy, and guide the laity in such matters as marriage, the church had its system of canon law and ecclesiastical courts. It was more aggressive than the Protestant churches in the censorship of opinion, the suppression of books, and the enforcement of orthodox belief, though the extreme case under this heading, the Inquisition, was of no importance except in Spain.

These very advantages, however—wealth, power, organization and corporate spirit, and independence—were at the same time a cause of weakness, involving the Catholic church in everlasting conflicts with governments and public opinion. Anticlerical and antireligious feeling became far more heated in Catholic countries than in the Protestant ones. Parish priests, living close to the common people, whose poverty they shared, became very critical of an increasingly aristocratic upper clergy. France and Italy were racked by Jansenism, a complex movement shared in by a few bishops who opposed the papal power, a few Augustinian theologians, and many morally aroused lesser people who believed the church to be too wealthy, too worldly, or too corrupt. The fact that Jansenism was officially pronounced a heresy by the bull *Unigenitus* in 1713 only added to the acrimony of the struggle; and the measures taken to enforce the bull in France, continued for fifty years, probably did as much as Voltaire or the *Encyclopédie* to undermine the prestige of Catholicism. Partly as a result of Jansenist pressures, the Jesuits were expelled from France in 1763. Their order was dissolved for the whole Catholic world in 1773, by the pope himself, at the instigation of the Catholic governments. In Germany the archbishops battled with the pope in the movement known as Febronianism. In the Hapsburg empire Joseph II carried on an anti-Catholic campaign that closely anticipated the French Revolution. Everywhere the role of the church in society had become a problem, and the stronger the church the more acute the problem was.

As widespread as the church, and more universal than monarchy, was another complex of institutions found in one form or another in all parts of Europe. They are hard to understand because they were precisely what the Revolution was to sweep away. They are suggested by a variety of interrelated ideas—feudalism, inter-mediate powers, constituted bodies, estates, *Stände*, privilege, rank, status, and liberties.

What a later generation would call inequality was built into the fabric of society. It was seen in a positive light as a beneficial distribution of roles in a hierarchic order. Persons at each level showed deference to those above. All persons in principle had rights recognized by law or custom, but their rights were different. Rights depended on the social category to which one belonged. Rights were concrete and specific. Differences of religion gave different rights. So did differences of occupation. Nobles could not be members of guilds or engage in retail trade or shopkeeping, from which they were barred by their own tastes and by burgher dislike of competition. It was thought that nobles were more suited for positions involving the leadership of men, as in military com-mand and the higher offices of state and church. A peasant had no right to open a mill in his own village, since the right usually belonged to a lord. Only members of guilds had the right to pursue their respective trades; unless he was a guild member, a man could not open his own shop as a mason or a tailor. The dissolu-tion of such barriers in England in the seventeenth century was one reason for its superior economic activity in the eighteenth. Rights to real property were subject to qualitative variations. England still had its freeholders and its copyholders, only the former having the additional right to vote for a member of Parliament; in France the peasant proprietor and the seigneur had different rights in the same field; in Eastern Europe the property rights of burghers and nobles were different and noninterchange-able.

Sir William Blackstone, in his *Commentaries on the Laws of*

England, analyzing the "rights of persons," listed about forty status levels from laborers to dukes. French lawbooks before the Revolution, while varying from one province to another, made similar classifications, which they summarized under the conception of three estates: clergy, nobility, and "third." When the codification of Prussian law, begun under Frederick the Great, was published in 1791, it gave separate chapters to the rights of nobles, townsmen, peasants, clergy, government servants, and others. In the language of the Prussian code, which in this respect was characteristic of most of Europe, a person's rights depended on "his birth, destination or principal occupation," and persons alike in these respects and hence enjoying equal rights among themselves made up an estate within the state. But the rights of the several estates were unequal.

Rights could be granted, or indeed even sold, by monarchs or governments. But for the most part, in prevailing theory, they were inherited. It was normally expected of everyone, as of kings themselves (except for the clergy) that a man's estate, status, station in life, rank, or occupation would be that of his father. The theory was of course put to a strain in places strongly marked by change, money economy, and social mobility, such as England or most parts of France, or great cities like Amsterdam or Vienna. It was not at all suited to the development of new social roles in journalism, literary work, the learned professions, science, finance, or new forms of economic enterprise. Nor was the idea of inheritance of position consistent with ideas of quality and efficiency of performance, even in such older activities as government and agriculture. The incompetence of hereditary kings was the subject of much ridicule, and some exaggeration, by critics of the existing order.

Everywhere there were different levels of people who participated differently in public affairs. Geneva, an independent city-state of 25,000 people, had its *citoyens,* who had the right to hold office; its *bourgeois,* who had only the right to vote; its *habitants,* who had the right to carry on certain trades but no political rights; its *natifs,* whose rights were even more limited; and finally its peasant *sujets* outside the city walls. In the United Provinces the ruling families were called regents. The governing council

of Amsterdam consisted of thirty-six men who sat for life and
who chose their own successors. In Venice, with a population of
130,000, only "nobles" could hold office, and there were only
111 noble families in 1796, less than half as many as in the great
days of the Middle Ages. In Württemberg, noted among German
states for the activity of its political life, since an assembly still
met, only about 1,500 persons out of a population of 600,000
chose the deputies. At Frankfurt am Main an ordinance of 1731
divided the population of 30,000 into five estates, of which the
highest was composed of a few families that had sat on the town
council for a hundred years.

The patrician republics and oligarchic city-states were more
exclusive and less favorable to the rise of new men than either
England or the great monarchies of the Continent. Those who
took part in public life in England were very few, probably fewer
than in Hungary; Arthur Young estimated the entire British
electorate at 250,000, and Richard Price in 1776, after careful
study, announced that half the House of Commons was chosen
by 5,723 persons. These were mainly of the aristocracy but
included new men also. William Pitt himself, though the son
of the famous Earl of Chatham, was the great-grandson of a self-
made adventurer in the East. In the civil services of the absolute
monarchies the duties of office were less parochial than in Frankfurt or Geneva, so that personal competence was likely to be
valued as well as family background. Bureaucratic organizations
like the French *Ponts et chaussées*, by requiring trained personnel
and moving men from one part of the country to another, offered
many opportunities for the growth and education of the middle
classes. It was the increasing difficulty of making use of such
opportunities, as will be seen, that alienated the French middle
classes from the existing order.

The great difference was between the nobleman and the person
not noble. Nobility in the eighteenth century was a complex and
by no means decadent institution. The word itself was used only
in the Latin countries, and the French *noblesse*, numbering
between 1 and 2 percent of the population, including men, women,
and children, provides the classic example. Some nobles bore titles,

such as duke or count, but many more were known only by the particle "de" or "von." In England only the two hundred peers, heads of families and members of the House of Lords, enjoyed what might be called privileges of nobility, but any landed gentleman of substance in England considered himself the equal of a French *chevalier*, not to mention a Spanish *hidalgo* or German *Junker*. On the Continent, there was a trend to regard as somehow noble all upper-class families no longer actually engaged in money-making through trade or the professions. In France itself, the members of the superior law courts, or parlements, whose great-grandfathers had been of the solid bourgeoisie, were now noblemen and leaders of the nobility. The Dutch regents, the patricians of Bern and Basel, the *nòbili* of Venice, the ruling families of Nuremberg—who forbade all citizens but themselves to wear feathered hats and swords and regarded the public funds as a source of dowries for their daughters and travel expenses for their sons—were all more of a noble than of a burgher way of life. Even young Thomas Shippen of republican Pennsylvania, since he was of a family that had held many public offices, was considered noble enough to be presented at Versailles in 1788. In Germany—that is, the Holy Roman Empire—the higher nobility were sovereigns in their own right, "immediate" to the emperor, while the general run of the *Adel* were more like the provincial nobility of France. In Eastern Europe, the lordly class comprised between 5 and 10 percent of the population and was therefore less select than the nobility of the West, to which it nevertheless freely compared itself. The Polish constitution of 1791 declared that all Polish nobles were equal not only to each other but also to the nobility of "all other countries." Catherine the Great, in her Charter of the Nobility of 1785, in effect guaranteed to all "well-born persons" in Russia a body of rights modeled on those of the Western nobility, such as exemption from certain taxes and the right to use the name of an estate as a personal title.

In its most general sense, "noble" meant simply "not common," not of the *roture*, to use the French expression. Much effort was spent on attempts to escape from the common class. In England anyone with the right appearance, deportment, and manner of speaking could be considered a gentleman, at least in casual social contacts. In the towns of Switzerland, where everyone's ancestry could be known, it was more difficult to "pass" as a true patrician. In Germany, burghers were inclined to accept their place and had little association with the territorial nobility anyway. The situation was most sensitive in France. Here, in a large country, where it was usual to mix with strangers, and educated commoners were both numerous and had much the same schooling as nobles, there were complaints at least since the time of Louis XIV against persons who falsely pretended to noble rank. Others simply tried to make their names seem more aristocratic. P. A. Caron, a clock-maker's son, moved in more elegant circles as Caron de Beau-marchais. Pierre Samuel Dupont, also the son of a Paris clock-maker, was known and is remembered as Pierre Samuel du Pont de Nemours, economist, moderate revolutionary, and founder of the American industrial family. Lazare Carnot, in his youth, tried to discover some noble line in his genealogy in order to marry a socially superior young lady. He could find none, nor did he marry the girl, but he became an ardent republican in 1792.

Outside England, noble status was defined by law and conveyed specific rights or privileges. Some of these were honorific, such as the right to carry a sword, put a coat of arms on one's carriage, or have a special pew in church. Others, while valued as marks of social standing, were of more practical usefulness. They varied from country to country, and distinctions were sometimes blurred in practice, or depended more on personal influence than on actual legal status. Typically, however, noble privileges included tax exemptions, or payment of other kinds of taxes than those paid by commoners; a prior if not exclusive right to positions of command in the army or navy, or to posts in the diplomatic service or other high government offices; more rights of jurisdiction over peasants in nobly owned manors than in manors belonging to commoners; the right to have a lawsuit initiated in higher tribunals, only commoners using the lowest courts; and rights of primogeniture, entail, or family trusts, by which estates were kept together and aristocratic families perpetuated, through inheritance by the eldest son only, the younger sons being provided for by allowances from their older brothers, or by offices in the government or the church, and the daughters being given dowries, or if unmarried sent into convents.

But the most important of all privileges, and the most honorific, was the right of special access to government. This took many forms. In the republics and city-states the hereditary patriciates occupied the various "councils"—the Ten, the Twenty-five, the Sixty, the Two Hundred, the number varying from city to city. In Poland, Bohemia, and Hungary there were bicameral assemblies, with an upper house for magnates and prelates, and a lower house composed of nobles elected only by nobles. In England, the peers sat in the Lords by personal and hereditary right; in the Commons, many families represented the boroughs and counties generation after generation, through more modern devices of property and political influence. In France the parlements, which claimed a kind of legislative power derived from their judicial functions, were almost entirely hereditary, through the institution of property in office; that is, the seats could be bought and sold but were in fact mainly inherited, so that the incumbents were neither elected nor appointed, and prided themselves on their independence. In two of the French provinces, Brittany and Languedoc, the old medieval estates continued to assemble throughout the eighteenth century. A few chartered towns (like English boroughs) represented the third estate; in Languedoc the bishops predominated, but they were all nobles in their social origin; in Brittany every nobleman of the province had the right to attend in person. For France as a whole this privilege of special access to government did not present itself acutely until 1789. No Estates General had met since 1615, and the country had willingly accepted government by the king and his ministers. The reactivation of the estates system, the expectation of the French noblesse in 1789 that, as the second estate of the realm, they should form a separate house of hereditary nobles elected only by nobles but carrying equal weight with the third estate, presumably for all future time, was what really precipitated the Revolution.

Estates, assemblies, *Stände*, councils, and parlements, together with the church in its corporate capacity acting through its bishops, and along with the local authorities in autonomous provinces and chartered towns, all composed what Montesquieu, in his *Spirit of the Laws*, called the "intermediate powers." They formed constituted bodies in their own right, largely hereditary, basing their legitimacy on tradition or on agreements made in the past. They were dependent neither on election from below nor on appointment from above. In the republics and city-states they were themselves the government. In the monarchies they were "intermediate" between the king and his subjects, and as such, in their own eyes, the very guardians of liberty against despotism. "Abolish in a monarchy," said Montesquieu (who was himself a nobleman and member of the parlement of Bordeaux), "the prerogatives of lords and clergy, nobility and towns, and you will soon have either a popular or a despotic state." This doctrine became the political creed of the aristocracy throughout Europe in the decades before the Revolution and remained essential to the thought of Alexis de Tocqueville a century later. It was a theory of political pluralism or internal decentralization of power, but it was also more than that, for it put exclusive value on inheritance of position, on special rights, and on "independent" forms of authority. It was a conservative doctrine also, for the intermediate powers resisted almost all reforms proposed by kings and their ministers, whether of taxation in France, the law courts at Milan, or serfdom in the Hapsburg empire.

For all this mass of intermediate, overlapping, and usually obstructive powers, with their emphasis on birth, rank, and inheritance, together with the manorial, or seigneurial, land system, in which lords retained a certain jurisdiction or at least influence over their peasants, reformers in the eighteenth century found a word, or term of reproach—"feudalism." It was well understood to be different from the feudalism of the Middle Ages. It meant the tissue of live and vigorous institutions that came between sovereign and subject, or stood in the way of modernization of the state and of legal equality for its citizens. It was of course "feudalism" in this somewhat abusive sense, in France and Europe, that the Revolution was to "abolish," by confining inheritance to private property only, and opening public life to the free play of "virtues and talents" and the possibilities of development through modern enlightenment.

Though it is hard to define the Enlightenment, it is certain that some kind of intellectual revolution occurred in the eighteenth century. It is associated with the names of various *philosophes*—Montesquieu, Voltaire, Diderot, Rousseau, Helvetius, and Holbach in France, Hume and Gibbon in England, Beccaria and Filangieri in Italy, Lessing and Kant in Germany, Lomonosov in Russia, Franklin and Jefferson in America. But the Enlightenment went much further than great names or their influence. Its net effect was to produce a generation of people who were very critical of the institutions just described. The feeling was not one of mere negative dissatisfaction, such as living with the institution might itself produce, but was heightened by a belief that an improved society was possible and even probable in the near future. Perhaps the idea of progress was most basic to the new mood.

In part the Enlightenment derived from the scientific revolution of the preceding century, the creative age of Galileo, Descartes, and Newton. There was a general expectation that science would have important practical consequences, and the name of Francis Bacon became famous in this connection, but in truth the direct impact of science upon invention was not yet very important. The unchanging character of military equipment has already been mentioned, and in such typical novelties as the steam engine, the chronometer, the balloon, and vaccination against smallpox the role of actual science was minimal.

What came from the great scientific discoveries, rather, was a new belief in the powers of the human mind, in unfettered intelligence, or "reason." It was a new critical approach, insisting on the need for evidence and observation. There was general agreement with what Locke had said in his *Human Understanding*, that all ideas came from sensation, or from the individual's perception of his environment. It followed, as one corollary, that much of what most people believed depended in fact—though it ought not to in reason—merely on what they were told by their elders in childhood or by authoritative persons in later life. This seemed an inadequate basis for either true or useful knowledge. The new view undermined all tradition and weakened the case, for persons who were dissatisfied anyway, for all institutions that justified themselves by appeals to the past, to inheritance, to social status, or custom, or the wisdom of ancestors.

The church, institutionally so important, lost much of its truly effective authority. Insisting as it did on a historic revelation, on a tradition of apostolic succession, on the need and inevitability of mystery, and on evidence from the Bible that seemed increasingly doubtful, it found itself speaking a language that was alien to modern ears. Memories were still alive of the religious wars and of the long tale of intolerance and persecution, to which was added the current spectacle of Jansenism and anti-Jansenism in France, or of "enthusiasm" in England and elsewhere. Even people who went to church and called themselves Christians, as most still did, thought that religion had caused a good deal of trouble and that some of its doctrines were very peculiar. The educated classes adopted a kind of deism, a generalized belief in a God whose only revelation was in nature. Religion was seen by its most vehement critics as only a human invention, or a social phenomenon based on fear, superstition, and imposture. The church used its power to suppress such ideas, but they circulated anyway, especially in France, first in manuscripts handed around secretly, and after the midcentury in printed books.

In this view, false and alleged knowledge was to be discarded, but correct knowledge was all-important. If error and evil were due in large part to bad environment and wrong education, and if the true way to reliable knowledge had been discovered, then everything depended on a correction of the environment, to be accomplished by improved education—education in the broadest sense, through all possible channels. Much writing of the Enlightenment was essentially educational, if not propagandistic—the publicizing of what was already known. Some was devoted to education specifically. Rousseau's *Émile*, in describing how a young man could be brought up according to "nature," really argued that he should be protected against the false ideas instilled by conventional education.

The educational system itself stood apart from the new Enlightenment. Common schools remained undeveloped. Secondary schooling, designed for the elite of the noble and middle classes, carried on the ideals of moral training and classical studies as developed in the Renaissance and was successful enough to exert its influence well into the twentieth century. With the dissolution of the Jesuit order, reforms were introduced into Jesuit schools, from France to Poland, with a view to a more civic, "patriotic," or socially minded education; the founding of the Collegium Nobilium at Warsaw, in the 1770s, marked a new step in the political education of Poland. At the university level, there were professors concerned with the sciences, modern philosophy, and public affairs in Germany, Italy, and Scotland, but the universities of England, France, and Spain were very traditional in their subjects of study and were organizationally involved with the church as privileged corporate bodies. On the whole, the movement of the Enlightenment went on outside the universities. Its most characteristic institution was the academy, such as the seventeenth-century Royal Society, the French Academy of Sciences, and the Italian Accademia dei Lincei.

Academies multiplied rapidly in the eighteenth century. They became numerous in the French provinces; the Academy of Dijon, in 1750, made Rousseau famous by awarding him its prize on a subject it had prescribed for a contest. His essay, a *Discourse on the Arts and Sciences*, was indeed a critique of the Enlightenment, arguing that mere reason, knowledge, and complex civilization were not enough to make a livable world; but that such views were regarded as "paradoxical" shows the strength of the beliefs that he attacked. Other academies sprang up in the borderlands of intellectual Europe, in Prussia and Russia, and in the American Philosophical Society, "held at Philadelphia," to use its full title, "for promoting useful knowledge." Members of such academies exchanged long letters on scientific subjects, elected foreign members and published their findings in journals that were widely distributed, forming a wide network of the new thinking like that of university professors in later times.

The press grew rapidly. More books were published than ever before; they were written in a more popular style; and Latin went out of use as a language of communication on weighty subjects. It is not clear how much actual literacy increased. The popular classes remained illiterate or nearly so virtually everywhere. But in the middle and upper classes, people who formerly would have been content to read works of piety or idle chivalrous romances, or used their knowledge of reading and writing mainly for household and business accounts, now increasingly read newspapers, or more especially the journals and magazines of all kinds that were aimed at a new audience, or books by authors, like Voltaire, who expressed important ideas with pungency and unmistakable point. Women joined the reading public. Some ladies held *salons*, in which conversation on various topical subjects was highly prized. Men joined the Masonic lodges which spread throughout Europe after 1700. Behind their veil of mystery, they offered forums for discussion of "enlightened" ideas in which clergy and laity, nobles and bourgeois, came together. And where the learned formed their academies, more ordinary persons formed reading clubs, which could be found in many European cities after about 1770. Typically a group of local citizens would rent one or two rooms, pay dues, subscribe collectively to journals and newspapers, and buy a few books, and then meet from time to time for a discussion of their contents.

The pamphlet became an increasingly popular means of expression. From the midcentury, the French parlements, in their conflicts with the king, published their official protests or "remonstrances" for all to read. In the 1770s, the debates in Parliament began to be published in England. In all dynamic countries there grew up a new force called "public opinion." It was a new term for a new phenomenon. It meant that literate people were taking a new interest in affairs of state, becoming critical of secrecy in government, whether on the part of kings, ministers, bureaucrats, or councils and assemblies meeting in private; developing a new desire for participation; conceiving the idea of a public welfare; discovering that there were many other people, like themselves, unknown and far away, who were reading the same publications and were concerned with the same questions.

In content, the new movement of thought was extremely varied. It was generally very critical of revealed and organized religion, but many good Christians were "enlightened"; the very pastors at Geneva thought that Calvin had been too extreme; the minority

religions might be either behind or ahead of their several establishments in their use of "reason"; some French bishops were
worldly philosophers, and some were conscientiously concerned
with purifying religion; in Italy, under the combined influence
of Jansenism and the Enlightenment, significant numbers of
churchmen favored reform in both church and state. In England,
Hume and Gibbon were radical in religion but very conservative
in politics. In France, Montesquieu must be classified as an enlightened aristocrat, favoring the privileged orders. Voltaire was
a monarchist in French affairs, because he wanted a strong royal
power against the church, the nobility, and the specious claims
of the Parlement of Paris; but when he wrote about Geneva he
became more of a republican, praising the advantages of equality,
civic virtue, and the unpretentious life. Rousseau was a democrat,
but in a sense that must be carefully understood. He cared nothing
about universal suffrage or representative institutions, but he
undertook to show, in the *Social Contract*, that in a free society
no man can be ruled by another, that each one is both subject
and citizen, that legitimate power must arise from the consent of
the governed, that sovereignty lies in a general will, an *unanimité*,
or consensus, and that all public officers act not by their own
right, or by inherited right, but by a delegated authority which
may be given or withdrawn. Such ideas were upsetting to all
eighteenth-century institutions, and were denounced as much in
Geneva as in Paris. Rousseau's *Discourse on the Origins of
Inequality* was likewise disapproved in established circles. Modern
socialists, delighted to find Rousseau criticizing private property
in this book, have tended to overlook its more central and highly
moral message: that man's desire to dominate, to possess, to be
admired, to show off, and to gratify his desires, all facilitated by
civilized living, are the main cause of his tribulations. As for the
famous *Encyclopédie*, launched by Diderot in 1751, it was a
repository of knowledge and opinion on all manner of questions,
almost all unfavorable to current institutions and beliefs; but most
of it was in fact concerned with very practical matters, such as
how best to operate a tannery or build a bridge. Its novelty lay
in considering such vulgar concerns as worthy of intellectual notice,
in taking the "mystery" out of ordinary trades, and in making

known, for all to use, the best methods already employed by the best practitioners, in the hope of advancing the wealth and welfare of mankind.

The same guiding purpose, to increase wealth and stimulate production, inspired most economic thinking, whether in Adam Smith, whose *Wealth of Nations* appeared in 1776, or in the French physiocrats, or in Turgot and other reform-minded administrators of the various monarchies. The means generally favored was to encourage economic freedom, since the existing forms of control, varying from one country to another—monopolistic or privileged overseas trading companies, the guild system, the self-protectionism of towns and provinces, local and internal tariffs, controls on the movement and price of grain, requirements as to processing or quality in various manufactures—in effect protected older, established, and less-efficient interests. The French physiocrats were the first to use the term *laissez-faire*, though it had no currency until almost a century later. The idea was to stimulate production by giving freer play to market forces, allowing the incentive of profit to producers, attracting new men into new kinds of economic enterprise, making it easier for employers to hire labor, and enlarging the trading area by reducing provincial tariffs, or getting rid of the river and road tolls which impeded the movement of goods, or raised their price, but which gave income to noblemen in some places, or to towns in others. To reformers everywhere, both in and out of government, it seemed necessary to reform and simplify the taxes, while increasing the yield, both through production of new wealth and abolition of privileges. This generally meant shifting the tax burden to the ownership of land, and the new idea was for the government to deal with its subjects not as members of status groups, noble or common, but as taxpayers and property owners, who would differ quantitatively in the amount of their wealth but not qualitatively according to social rank or estate. The famous Turgot, a nobleman of the tenth generation and a professional government servant, was in this sense a "bourgeois."

It would be leaving on a false note to conclude a survey of the Enlightenment with a word on its economics. The prevailing state of mind, for a generation before 1789, was one of altruism and generous expectation. If the Old Order was not really old, many of its practices now seemed benighted and old-fashioned. The words liberty and equality were in the air, enough so to arouse the derisive comments of skeptics. There was much concern for man and humanity, and the humanitarian current was very real; torture was discredited not only because it was a poor way to produce evidence but also because it now seemed a shocking cruelty to human beings. The pursuit of happiness, *bonheur*, the *bonheur commun*, seemed the true goal of life on earth. The Marquis de Chastellux, a French soldier who fought in the American War of Independence, published a book with the characteristic title *De la félicité publique*. After the American Revolution, with the publication in Europe of the constitutions of the new states, there was a new interest in the setting up of new government by a "constitution." There was disgust at the paternalism of bureaucrats, a dislike of irresponsible despotism, a general desire on the part of middle-class people—not merely of the aristocracy, as formerly—to have some part in the life of the community, to be the "patriot" and the "citizen." And there was a new sense of world history, carrying confidence in the future. Condorcet, a hunted fugitive in 1793, was to give it expression in his *Sketch of the Progress of the Human Mind*. Before 1789 the common word was perfectibility, *la perfectibilité du genre humain*. It meant not so much expectation of future perfection as belief in a continuing process of improvement.

[2]

The French Revolution, 1789–92

SINCE MUCH OF EUROPE HAD SIMILAR INSTITUTIONS, ideas, and social conditions, it is easy to understand why a revolution, once started, should spread. It makes it harder to explain why a revolution began in any one particular country. Why did the volcano erupt in France? Why must this turning point of all European history be permanently and correctly known as the French Revolution?

The question is the more pertinent since revolution, broadly conceived, did not really begin in France at all. In 1789, the American Revolution was almost fifteen years in the past. The Irish Volunteers and the Dutch Patriots, from the late 1770s, rose in armed and organized defiance of their governments. At Geneva, a minuscule revolution ran its course for a generation after 1763. A Belgian revolution broke out in 1789 independently of events in France. In Poland the Four Years' Diet set about revolutionary reforms in 1788. But except for the American Revolution, none of these enterprises was successful. The British preserved their hold in Ireland, the Austrians in Belgium; and the new elements in Geneva, in the United Provinces, and in Poland were suppressed by foreign intervention in alliance with native conservatives. Seen in this light, the peculiarity of the Revolution of 1789 in France was simply that it was able to sustain itself.

The leaders in Paris had a mass following throughout the country. With 25 million people, who at first were overwhelmingly united in favor of the New Order, France was simply too big to be intervened in. When the experiment was tried in 1792, it came near to succeeding—but it failed.

If not the first to attempt revolution, neither were the French, as a people, more violent or unruly than others. Sporadic popular tumults were frequent in many places. The Gordon Riots of 1780 did more physical damage to London in a week than Paris suffered in a decade of revolution. Poverty and unemployment produced everywhere a potentially turbulent populace. With the undeveloped state of transportation, famines and rising food prices could occur locally even in good years. Governments controlled the price of grain in the cities to prevent bread riots. In rural areas, the numerous day laborers and handicraft workers did not raise their own food. Even self-supporting farmers lived in fear of rough characters, vagabonds, beggars, smugglers, woodcutters, or passing strangers. Vast peasant rebellions, reflecting discontent with the whole social system, shook Russia in 1774, Bohemia in 1775, Hungary in 1790. That France in 1789 suffered from the worst bread shortage and highest prices since the death of Louis XIV, that the peasantry rose in rebellion and the Paris populace marched to Versailles demanding bread, were facts that added force to the Revolution but were not its primary cause or even its most distinctive feature.

The conditions generally described for Europe in the last chapter may have been more acute in France. Were measurement possible, one might find that the difference between France and other countries was more quantitative than qualitative—that the strain between social classes, between the intellectual revolution and customary ways of acting, between the needs of government and the privileges of subjects, and between the declining real incomes of laboring people and the mounting burden of rents, taxes, tithes, and seigneurial dues, though not peculiar to France, was at least after about 1770 more pronounced in that country. One sees also in France a process by which impersonal social conditions became suddenly politicized, turning into specific questions on which real flesh-and-blood individuals had to make decisions, take action, appeal for support, and engage in controversy. In particular, the immediate cause of the French Revolution was the failure of government. The monarchy simply ground to a halt.

The War of American Independence greatly increased the national debt of the two principal combatants, Britain and France. The French debt after the war stood at over 4 billion francs, the British, expressed in French money, at about 6 billion. Per capita indebtedness was much higher in Britain, which had less than half the population of France. Annual income of the two governments was roughly the same. In both countries half or more of it was required for debt service. Yet the British were successfully to triple their debt by the time of Waterloo. The smaller French debt overwhelmed the monarchy.

In France, to be sure, before the Revolution, there was no "national" debt at all. No representative body had ever accepted it as a public obligation. The debt was the king's affair, and its true dimensions only became known after the American War, when two successive controllers general, Necker and Calonne, found it impossible to increase either loans or tax revenues in sufficient amount. In former times the monarchy had lightened its burden by repudiation of debt or devaluation of the currency. Neither the ministers of Louis XVI nor the Revolutionary assemblies that followed (until 1796) considered such solutions. The financial interests were now too strong to be offended. In addition, various important persons among the king's subjects, far from wishing to relieve him, saw in the financial crisis an opportunity to press for political changes—to turn an absolute monarchy into a constitutional monarchy. To paraphrase Mirabeau, the national debt became the nation's treasure.

The difficulty in France was that while there was a good deal of wealth in the country, the tax revenues could not be increased, because the poor were already taxed to the utmost, while the rich and even middle classes largely escaped. Nobles were exempt from some taxes on principle and from others by influence. Wealthy commoners benefited from special arrangements. The Catholic church owned between 5 and 10 percent of the real property of the country; it presented the government with a periodic "free gift" in lieu of taxes, which was less than taxation would have produced. Whole provinces benefited from special concessions made as long ago as the fifteenth century. Subjects were protected against the tax collector by their special rights or privileges. The monarchy, if the greatest in Europe, was still a makeshift confederation of towns, provinces, regions, ecclesiastical establishments, and social classes, each trying to accept government on its own terms. A fiscal crisis automatically turned into a crisis of political structure.

Calonne, who became controller general in 1783, devised a program which seems to have been adequate to the immediate need. It included a new land tax to be paid in proportion to land values by all owners regardless of their class status or province of residence. It likewise envisaged the selling of some of the church's properties to private owners, the equalization of the salt and tobacco taxes throughout the kingdom, and the removal of certain excises and internal tariffs that stood in the way of economic development. Calonne proposed also, going to the heart of the matter, to involve the taxpayers in the work of government by creating provincial assemblies with the power to apportion the taxes in their own areas. These assemblies were to be elected by property owners simply as property owners, without regard to the three estates.

Any such plan to disregard the difference between noble and commoner was bound to run into difficulties, because for at least a generation there had been a trend to a greater aristocratic exclusiveness. Every bishop in the French church, every provincial intendant, and every minister of the royal government—except the wealthy foreigner, the Genevan Necker—was a noble in the generation before the Revolution. The parlements of the kingdom now commonly required four quarterings of nobility for their members. In resisting tax reforms as long ago as 1751, and in opposing the reforms of Turgot in 1776, the Parlement of Paris had appealed to the ideals of a hierarchic or aristocratic society. Nobles of all kinds, civilian and military, urban and rural, were consolidating as a distinctive upper class. In 1781, though the French army had long had nonnoble officers, it was ruled that only young men with four quarters of nobility should henceforth receive commissions. When the government proposed a new military school for noble and nonnoble youth alike, the Parlement of Paris objected. Though nobles and nonnobles had long gone to school together in France, the Parlement now deplored the practice. "Each estate," it announced, "has its own occupations, ideas, duties, genius and manner of life, which should not be adulterated or confused by education."

What made the situation in France explosive was not that a middle class was rising while an old feudal class declined, but that two legally distinct groups had conflicting purposes at the same time. The nobility, sensing a danger, became more self-conscious and insistent on its rank. The upper levels of the third estate might well have sensed an attempt to freeze them out.

Calonne, knowing that the Parlement would refuse the innovations he called for, sought to obtain public support in another way. He convoked an Assembly of Notables, chiefly composed of great lords and prelates. The Notables, after much disputation and criticism of government extravagance, accepted equal liability to taxation in principle but insisted on preserving the distinction between clergy, nobles, and commoners, and in any case declared that they had no powers to speak for or to bind the country. They thus threw the question back to the Parlement of Paris, which, after another year of disputes, announced that any new system of taxation would require a general assembly of the whole kingdom in the Estates General, which had not met since 1615.

It was from these well-publicized controversies among the existing authorities, as much as from the books of radical writers, that the French people learned the language of revolutionary accusation. Calonne denounced the rights defended by the Notables as unjustified "privileges." Louis XVI himself called the Parlement an "aristocracy" acting against the interests of the "nation." The Parlement, like the Notables, darkly hinted that the government was a "despotism." It insisted that France had or must have a "constitution" in which the rights of "citizens" would be protected. It defended the "rights of man," using these very words; it denounced arbitrary arrest and arbitrary taxation, and called for representative government.

At this point the Parlement enjoyed overwhelming support from

politically interested persons of all classes, both nobles and nonnobles. There was a high degree of national agreement against
the traditional absolutism, and in favor of some kind of constitutional and representative regime. In July, 1788, Louis XVI,
still financially desperate, announced the meeting of the Estates
General for the following year.

Now the really big question was presented. Granted that there
was to be a national representation, what form was it to take?
Were clergy and nobility to have the former historic right of
special representation, each in a body elected only by members of
its own order, and each equal to a third estate, in which 97 percent
of Frenchmen would be included? If so, and if such proved to
be the permanent future constitution that everyone demanded,
the organized clergy and nobility would wield more power than
ever before in the history of France. A new height in the rising
claims of the nobility for recognition would be reached. Such
seemed to be the trend when in September, 1788, the Parlement
of Paris ruled that the future estates should meet as in 1614–15—
that is, separately as the Three Orders. A second Assembly of
Notables took the same line, adding ominously that if the third
estate proved too obstinate the two upper orders might secede,
repudiate the assembly, urge nonpayment of taxes, and organize
resistance. Thus the counterrevolution already announced itself.

Leaders of the third estate—lawyers, government officers and
employees, writers, doctors, merchants, municipal notables, and
persons of indefinite occupation who lived on the income of
property—were made more acutely class-conscious by these developments. They turned violently antinoble. The Abbé Siéyès,
who enjoyed a good income from the church but was the son of a
postal employee, wrote his famous and truly revolutionary pamphlet, *Qu'est-ce que le Tiers Etat?* Its main message was that the
nation was sovereign, and that the third estate was in effect identical with the nation, the nobility being a tiny, presumptuous, and
useless minority that could be eliminated without loss. The government, in which Necker was now again the chief minister, hit
upon a compromise solution, which only postponed and aggravated the problem. It provided that in the coming estates, the
third should have as many deputies as the other two combined.

Whether they should sit and vote as three separate houses (in which case the number of persons in each house would be irrelevant) was left for decision after the assembly met.

The elections took place in March and April of 1789. Nobles met to elect nobles. The clergy, including ordinary parish priests, met in their own assemblies, choosing as deputies a number of bishops, especially the more liberally minded bishops, and a great many curés of modest social origin who had their own grievances against the church and their own ideas on the country's needs, so that, as it turned out, the first estate felt sympathetic to the third. The third estate met in some 40,000 assemblies, from the level of villages and guilds upward on a complex ladder, to choose some 600 national deputies. There was no isolated or individual voting, since in the absence of parties there were no known candidates or nominees. Each assembly debated the merits of persons proposed for election, and in addition, following the traditional practice in effect in 1614–15 and before, discussed and drew up a *cahier des doléances*, or statement of its grievances, opinions, and wishes both on local matters and for the whole country, which the deputies were to take to Versailles.

The effect was to produce not only the needed deputies but also an extraordinary heightening of political consciousness throughout the whole population. Every man on the tax rolls, and twenty-five years of age, had the right to attend the village assemblies. Never during the Revolution, nor after it for many decades, and nowhere else in Europe then or in former times, was there so "democratic" and universal a consultation of a whole people as that ordered by Louis XVI in 1789. It is a mystery how a country of 25 million inhabitants—given the great diversity between regions, in the conditions of literacy, transport, and communication that then obtained, and in the absence of any true guidance or agitation in prior years—could have suddenly become so alert, so politicized, so concerned with public questions. The explanation lies partly in the wave of pamphleteering that had risen since the first announcement of Calonne's program, but mainly in these thousands of electoral assemblies in the spring of 1789. Throughout the length and breadth of the land, at all social levels, including the most modest, men met to reflect upon their own and the country's troubles, and to choose deputies and send them off armed with a written statement of grievances. They then waited for the results. The machinery of the election allowed the really popular classes to be aroused and involved, but it also enabled, through elimination in a rising series of electoral assemblies, the most articulate, determined, and capable to emerge at the national level and to go to Versailles. Had actual peasants, shopkeepers, and workmen been elected, the third estate when it convened in May would have been more docile. As it was, its 648 deputies included 278 men holding some kind of position in government, 166 lawyers in private practice, 85 merchants, 67 who lived from their property, and 31 of various professions, among whom doctors were prominent. They were of the very type least likely, at such a moment, to yield to a second estate of some 300 nobles, most of whom, apart from prominent liberals like Lafayette, were country gentlemen not much in tune with modern developments.

The opening weeks of the Estates General, which met on May 4, were disappointing. By an absurd anachronism, protocol required that on the first day the nobles and prelates should appear in their respective finery, while the third estate wore the plain black costume of the historic "bourgeois." One may imagine the feelings of those required to obtain such court dress for use on this occasion. A stalemate then developed, in which the second estate insisted that meetings take place in three separate houses, with vote "by order," which the third estate refused, insisting that the three orders meet and deliberate together, as one house, with vote "by head." In that event the third, with its double number of members and with its sympathizers among the clergy, would have a consistent majority. This in turn the nobles rejected. The whole principle of their separate status and separate powers was at stake. The third estate, losing patience, voted on June 17 to repudiate its old name and declared itself the National Assembly, which priests and nobles were invited to join. Here was the moment of defiance, with a kind of arrogation of sovereignty, from which, if one wishes, the French Revolution can be dated. The king locked the self-styled assembly out. The former third estate held an unauthorized meeting in an indoor tennis court, where it swore its famous oath—that "wherever its members are gathered the National Assembly is in being," and that it would not disband "until the Constitution of the kingdom is laid and established in secure foundations."

Louis XVI now offered a compromise. He had played a weak role throughout. He had supported Calonne, but since 1787 he had repeatedly retreated in the face of noble and episcopal opposition. Soon after the Estates General opened, his young son died; he had no taste for public and controversial politics and could hardly side with either nobility or third estate without making one of them into an enemy against whom force would have to be used.

On June 23 the king met with the three orders. He promised to rule in the future through periodic estates that would have power to consent to taxation. He proposed certain reforms of detail and the guarantee of certain individual civil rights. In short, he offered to become a constitutional monarch. But with what kind of constitution? He refused recognition to the new National Assembly. He insisted on "the ancient distinction of the three orders . . . in its entirety as essential to the constitution of the realm." The new France would have a kind of representative and constitutional government, in which, however, the organized Catholic church and the organized nobility would each have a special role equal to that of everyone else. In effect, the incumbent of the throne of France, which in its way over the centuries had protected the common people against the privileged orders, was now forced to choose sides and chose to side with the privileged. The king also now began to summon troops to the neighborhood of Paris and Versailles, with a view to dispersing the contumacious assembly and perhaps starting afresh with a new one more carefully selected, since his financial problem was still unsolved.

It is important to bear in mind this royal offer of June 23. It expressed the greatest single issue in the Revolution. It had its liberal side, and a France ruled through estates might, it would seem, come to resemble an England ruled through Lords and Commons. The king's program entered into the general philosophy of the counterrevolution after 1789, and indeed the idea of a corporate society long had an appeal in conservative circles. The third estate, however, or its 648 deputies at Versailles, had no liking for the royal program. It is uncertain what they would or could have done, had not popular violence and real revolution soon intervened. They disliked the king's proposal because they distrusted, from experience, the nobility and the upper clergy, to whom it would give new powers. The Frenchman of a certain class, in the face of the nobles, felt a sense of discrimination, of exclusion, humiliation, irritation, and now in 1789 even hatred, which the commons in England did not feel for the lords. The first meaning of equality in the Revolution was that the difference between noble and nonnoble should be abolished.

At this point the rest of the country was heard from. The movement for national regeneration, up to now mainly an affair of words and legalistic maneuvers, authorized by the king himself until June 17, turned into a genuine mass revolt. Economic conditions were unfavorable to the maintenance of either patience or order. Long-term trends had for years been unfavorable to the laboring classes. The ratios between farm prices and rents had worsened for the peasants since 1770. Wage earners both in town and country suffered from the fact that, since 1740, wages had risen only about 22 percent as against a 65 percent rise in prices. The immediate short-run situation was very bad. The harvest of 1788 had been poor throughout Western Europe. The price of grain rose continually until by July of 1789 it took over half a worker's daily wage simply to buy bread for an average family, when it was obtainable at all. Here was one of the great ironies of history. The mass of the French people, through the action of impersonal forces, had enjoyed relatively favorable economic conditions under an inferior king, Louis XV. Under Louis XVI, his more admirable successor, they sank into privation.

Suffering alone, as already intimated, is no explanation for revolution. In 1789 the economic distress, like everything else, became politicized and explosive. Those who suffered from deteriorating economic conditions attributed them to political causes. They had heard echoes of the recriminations exchanged in high places. In the spring of 1789, by the king's own order, they had drawn up considered statements of their difficulties and had taken steps to send deputies to Versailles to do something about public problems. The Estates General had aroused enthusiastic expectations. Now the word spread that the great national conclave was blocked, and blocked by the nobles sitting in their own noble house—which for the lower classes in Paris and other cities meant the rich and for the peasants signified their own seigneurs or lords. It was not too much to believe that the nobles and their accomplices were the cause of the food shortages, that from sheer selfish obstinacy they were planning to starve the common people into submission. Hatred turned against "aristocrats" and evil counselors by whom a good king was presumably surrounded.

Paris became very restless at the news that troops were concentrating about the city. Actually, the troops had no definite orders. No one knew what to do, and Louis XVI was not the sort of man to shoot down his own subjects. From July 12 there were clashes between parties of soldiers and miscellaneous gatherings of civilians. Groups under improvised leadership began to search for arms at the Arsenal and the Invalides to defend themselves against nameless evils that the army might be ordered to enforce. Word spread that arms were stored at the Bastille. This ancient structure, whose historic relation to the city was like that of the Tower of London, was now used as a place of confinement for special prisoners, of whom at the moment there were only seven, all detained for legitimate reason if not by strict legal process. In any case, the crowd that swarmed about the Bastille on July 14 was not concerned with the prisoners but in general was protesting against dark and unknown forces arrayed against the people and in particular was asking for weapons—at a time when progressive thinkers, like the authors of the new Constitution of the United States, believed that an armed citizenry was a guarantee against militarism. The Bastille was held by only eighty retired soldiers and thirty Swiss, who at first refrained from firing on their besiegers. When the latter broke into the inner courtyard, the defenders fired and killed about a hundred of them. The assailants were now joined by a few trained soldiers from the *Garde française,* who brought five cannon. The mere threat produced surrender. The mob streamed in, enraged by the resistance and by the

casualties it had suffered, and massacred about six of its adversaries. In the following days, as disorder spread, a number of
officials believed to be responsible for the bread shortage, or in
collusion with aristocrats, were likewise murdered. Their heads
were cut off, put on pikes, and paraded about the city.

Soon after the event, it proved that the fall of the Bastille
was in fact a turning point, deservingly a symbol of the Revolution. It was clear that the king and the old government had lost
control. The troops had not been used. Probably they could not
have been; if ordered to undertake systematic repression, the
organized units would probably have fallen to pieces. As the old
authorities collapsed, the more substantial Parisians tried to restore
order in the city. The electoral assembly of a few months ago now
took over as a municipal government, chose the astronomer Bailly
as mayor, and organized a National Guard, of which the Marquis
de Lafayette consented to be commander. He devised a flag, using
the red and blue of Paris with the white of the royal family, and
so producing the tricolor in the hope of fusing the old and the
new.

Louis XVI, on the very day after the fall of the Bastille, appeared before the National Assembly at Versailles and, implicitly
disavowing his stand of June 23, professed his good intentions.
On July 17 he met with the new municipal authorities in Paris.
There was mutual embarrassment, but he accepted the tricolor
cockade. In the general rejoicing, it was possible to hope that
the Revolution was over.

It was, of course, only beginning. Upon hearing the news from
Paris, cities throughout France, with or without insurrection, staged
their own municipal revolution, in which local citizens' committees
took over from the former officials. They emphatically declared
their solidarity with the capital and with the new assembly. They
organized their own National Guards and tried to cope, with varying degrees of actual sympathy, with the problems of scarcity
and bread prices by which the poorer townspeople were afflicted.
Representatives of the old order, from the royal intendants on
down, receiving no instructions and overtaken by events, abandoned their posts. The result seemed like "spontaneous anarchy"

to Taine, the most famous of anti-Revolutionary historians, but it was an anarchy in which everyone looked forward to a new constitution and a fair and workable government.

Meanwhile the rural population also revolted. For farm laborers, for some small farm owners and tenants, for the weavers, iron workers, miners, carters, and draymen who also lived in the country, life had become more difficult for twenty years. Farm prices had fallen, yet taxes had increased, and the owners of manorial properties, in what is called the "feudal reaction," and to meet their own needs in a society that made luxury a rising goal for the upper classes, had attempted a more strict collection of the seigneurial dues. The long-run decline of farm prices was abruptly reversed, in 1788–89, by the purely short-run crisis of the poor harvest, extreme shortage, and hence soaring prices for foodstuffs. The more substantial peasants were dissatisfied, the poorer ones in destitution and misery. They too had met, talked, drafted lists of grievances, and sent off deputies in March of 1789. A profound hostility to the seigneurs had been expressed in the village assemblies. The peasants, like everyone else, waited for news from the Estates General. Nor were they isolated. As already explained, French peasants had frequent occasion for visits to town, which in the summer of 1789 meant that they easily picked up both news and rumors. The peasants, like the "bourgeois," or upper stratum of the third estate, saw the nobility as their enemy. This convergence of interests—which did not occur in the massive and almost contemporary peasant rebellions of Eastern Europe, and which was due in France both to basic elements of social structure and to the momentary political situation produced by the deadlock in the Estates General—is what made possible the French Revolution of 1789.

Agrarian revolt began in northern France as early as May. It spread as the food crisis deepened, as beggars and vagabonds increased on the roads, as news came of the fall of the Bastille, and as local towns set the example of thrusting aside the older authorities. Late in July the revolts merged with the Great Fear, a series of panics that spread over large portions of the country, carried by rumors and false news of the coming of brigands, of horrors in other places, and of plots by the aristocracy to impose its will. Gripped by such fears, the peasants armed themselves and thronged together. The revolt itself, however, was distinct from the fear, which in fact it preceded. Peasants trooped to the manor houses, broke in, demanded an end of seigneurial dues, and often committed the papers on which such dues were legally grounded to the flames. Many manor houses and châteaux were burned. Many seigneurs fled. Considering the scope of the uprising there were very few murders. But the socioeconomic system of rural France was in dissolution.

The National Assembly was now formally recognized by the king. It conceived its principal task to be the drafting of a written constitution—an emphasis on judicial priorities of which the great interest in France in the American Revolution was surely one of the principal causes. The assembly was henceforth called the Constituent Assembly. Conditions were highly unfavorable for the writing of a constitution. The country was in chaos. The peasants were out of control; the towns were in the hands of inexperienced citizens' groups. Emigration was beginning; the king's brother the Count of Antois (who in 1824 became Charles X) went abroad with various great lords and princes to solicit foreign intervention. In the assembly, now sitting as one over-sized house, the nobles and the clergy elected to the Estates General were still present as members. As time passed, most of them dropped out, but their presence added to the difficulty of agreement, and their departure added to the force of counter-revolution. While the assembly deliberated, the ordinary machinery of government fell into ruins. Yet Louis XVI still remained as the head of the state. He could neither govern nor lead. He was still popularly acclaimed, but his true views could be judged more from his stand on June 23 than on July 17. He did not really approve of the Constituent Assembly. Yet the assembly had no opportunity, and not even the desire, to make anyone else the chief executive under a new constitution. The differences from the Philadelphia Convention of 1787 are apparent.

It was impossible to pacify the country by force. To use the army against rebellious peasants and townspeople, if successful, would strengthen the king and undermine the assembly. The army was an uncertain quantity anyway. Even among the officers there

were a few nonnobles, and the bulk of lesser nobles or country
gentry had become embittered against the court nobility, for whom
the highest and most honorific military appointments were generally reserved. The enlisted men were the sons and brothers of the
popular insurrectionists. As France was already more of a nation,
so its army was already more of a citizen army than in the Prussian
or Austrian monarchies, where the use of polyglot and foreign
troops was very common. There were foreign units in the French
army, like the Swiss and the Royal German, but to employ them
at such a moment against Frenchmen would be folly.

It was necessary to make concessions and to set up a new symbolism. If the assembly was to preserve its prestige and initiative,
in conditions of incipient anarchy, in a country which was erupting
spontaneously from below, it must do something dramatic, spectacular, and inspiring. Three months before, on convening at
Versailles, the deputies had been strangers to each other. Now
acquaintances and affiliations had been formed. A group of like-
minded deputies formed a patriot party called the Breton Club.
Since many of the former third estate still felt a middle-class
timidity in public life, many of the leaders of the party of movement, at this time, were in fact nobles—*déclassé* nobles like Mirabeau, liberal nobles like Lafayette, Noailles, Condorcet, and La
Rochefoucauld-Liancourt, or nobles who were also bishops, like
Champion de Cicé, archbishop of Bordeaux, and Boisgelin, archbishop of Aix-en-Provence. Under such leadership, the assembly
decided on the morning of August 4 to appeal to the country
by issuing a Declaration of Rights. That same evening, by a kind
of parliamentary stratagem, it produced one of its most sensational
outbursts.

The night of August 4 has become the symbol of voluntary
renunciation of privileges. Actually, the peasants were refusing
payments of seigneurial dues and tithes in any case. The assembly
confirmed what it could not prevent. Liberal noblemen rose to
repudiate all privileges of taxation. Tithes payable to the church
were declared at an end. The whole seigneurial system was wiped
away, in a sense, for where peasant obligations deemed to arise
from personal servitude were abolished outright, those considered
as arising from a kind of property were to be abolished with

compensation. (The compensation was itself abolished three years later.) Manorial justice, hunting rights, property in office, and provincial privileges were done away with. The admissibility of all citizens to public functions, regardless of class, was declared. All this was popularly remembered as the "abolition of feudalism." Though subject to later difficulties in implementation, it represented a long step toward a society based on equality of legal rights.

On August 26 the assembly issued the Declaration of the Rights of Man and the Citizen. That "man" had such rights was widely agreed to, except by thinkers like Edmund Burke; even the Parlement of Paris had said so. The question was what the rights were. It is important to note that the declaration specified the "citizen" as well as the "man." Condensing much of the philosophy of the Enlightenment, it was essentially a moral affirmation, an ethical guideline for organized civil society, not for human beings in a supposed state of nature. Its purpose was to rally the country, to arouse confidence in the assembly during the long and difficult debates on the constitution. It was meant also to repudiate the legalized inequalities of the Old Order and to justify the revolts that had already occurred. Having only seventeen articles in about three hundred words, it could be printed on one sheet of paper. It was placarded all over France, translated into all European languages, endlessly discussed in cafés, and expounded in public speeches; it was designed to be and in fact became the main symbol of the New Order. It remains the chief document of the entire eighteenth-century revolution.

"Men are born and remain free and equal in rights. Social distinctions can be founded only on common utility." Such was the text of Article I. The basic rights were "liberty, property, security and resistance to oppression." Liberty meant the power to do what was not injurious to another, which in turn could be determined only by law. Law was the expression of the general will; it must be the same for all; and all citizens, "personally or by their representatives," had a right to take part in its formation. No one could be arrested except by law; but all citizens must obey the law instantly. Any man was to be presumed innocent until adjudged guilty. Only strictly necessary punishments were to be allowed. Opinion and the press were free, "even in religion," subject to the needs of public order and responsibility for abuses. Armed forces and taxes were said to be necessary, but only for the benefit and under the control of society as a whole. There must be a separation of powers under the constitution. Property was by inviolable right; one might lose it for reasons of public necessity but only with compensation. All agents of government could be held accountable for their actions. All persons should qualify for all appointments according only to their abilities. Lastly (actually, in Article II), "the principle of sovereignty resides essentially with the nation. No body [such as the self-perpetuating Parlement of Paris or any status group of any kind] and no individual [such as even a king] may exercise authority which does not emanate from the nation expressly."

The idea of such rights came from the intellectual revolution and from disgust with the unequal, arbitrary, secret, and sometimes brutal institutions with which the men of 1789 had actually lived. The idea of codifying them in a brief numbered list, attaching them to a written constitution, and so relating them to the origin, powers, and limits of government itself undoubtedly came from the American example, especially that of Virginia, which was often referred to in the French debates. The American declarations had been more concrete and empirical, full of echoes from the English past, and have often been praised for that reason. But at least as an ethical foundation for a new kind of state and society, the French declaration seems superior. Compact and lucid, addressing the citizen as well as the man, recognizing the necessity of law and government as well as the safeguards against them, related closely to practical questions yet abstract and universal in its formulations, it could be carried on a wave of revolutionary enthusiasm with powerful appeal to other countries. In France itself the declaration was reissued with significant amplifications. For example, in 1793, equality was more clearly stated to be a right in itself, as were the rights to education and to the means of subsistence.

Meanwhile, the assembly proceeded to lay down the main outlines of the new constitution. The first problem was the role of the king. Was the king an independent figure in himself, by historic or dynastic right, with whom the assembly must negotiate as an equal, so that the constitution would be a kind of contract between them? Or was the assembly, as a true constituent body exercising the national sovereignty, simply to create and define a royal office which it would then call upon Louis XVI to occupy? Could the assembly write into the constitution only what the king would allow, or must the king accept whatever the assembly decided to put in? In a word, was the king a sovereign or only the highest executive officer? Was the royal power intrinsic or delegated? The question was of the utmost theoretical import and was compounded by the fact that Louis XVI showed great unwillingness to accept either the Declaration of Rights or the decrees that followed upon the night of August 4. Hence, those whose position under the Old Order was damaged by these developments began to uphold an independent royal authority.

It was generally agreed that the royal office, once constituted, should carry with it, under the separation of powers, some kind of veto. Some thought the veto on actions of the legislature should be absolute; others preferred a veto that the legislature by appropriate actions could override. There was the question, also, of whether the legislature should be in two chambers, as in both the British and American examples. The Patriot party, as the revolutionary vanguard still called itself, strongly insisted on a single house; anything else, said Sieyès, would violate the principle of one man, one vote, be a relapse into the system of orders, and so favor the nobles. In fact, even the conservative nobles in the assembly, really preferring the old plan of a noble house elected by nobles, had no taste for an upper chamber of a more modern kind, to which they would have to be elected by the ordinary people. The single house was carried by a majority of 10 to 1. As for the king, the assembly decided on September 11 to give him a suspensive veto. That is, when the constitution went into effect, he would have the power to veto legislation, but if three successive legislatures, elected every two years, re-enacted the same measure, his veto would be overruled. The king thus received a delaying power that proved very dangerous when he used it under circumstances of public excitement in 1792. Fundamentally his position remained ambiguous. He had offered to be a constitutional monarch on his own terms, and the whole country had desired some kind of constitutional monarchy since the issue first arose; but neither Louis XVI nor the various conservative groups now forming in opposition to the Revolution accepted the role of constitutional monarch as the Constituent Assembly understood it.

The Patriot party in the assembly, which still sat at Versailles, grew more radical in the face of this resistance. In Paris there had now been time for a militant leadership to develop at the neighborhood level. A veritable revolution in journalism had taken place in the preceding months. Before 1789, France had no newspapers or magazines with any political content. By September, Paris resounded with the shrill cries of journalists of every stripe. (Over a thousand such papers were to appear during the next ten years.) Leaders in the assembly, sensing the hostility of the king and court, began to consider moving the assembly to Paris. For this purpose, the continuing turbulence of the city proved very useful. In Paris, all classes of the former third estate, from bankers to paupers, were at a high pitch of direct political involvement. All feared the countermoves of aristocrats. The poorer class lost employment as the rich fled the city. Though the harvest of 1789 was good, it was not yet available on the market; movement of foodstuffs was interrupted by fears and disorders in the provinces; bread was expensive and scarce in Paris.

On October 3 Paris heard of a banquet at Versailles, at which the queen and her aristocratic friends had insulted the new tricolor and had spoken scornfully of the common people and the Revolution. Crowds composed largely of women swarmed about the city. They demanded bread and cursed aristocrats. The National Guard took no action against them. Several thousand women then started on the twelve-mile walk to Versailles. They were accompanied or followed by various male activists, by some of the National Guard, and finally by the Marquis de Lafayette himself. It was a confused human upheaval, and highly placed persons in the new revolutionary municipality, while wanting to restrain a mob of angry women, meant also to use them to bring pressure against the king and the royalists.

On October 6, having spent the night waiting outdoors, the impatient, weary, and dirty crowd burst into the palace of Versailles, looking for the royal family, streaming through the state apartments, killing three or four guards, and crying "Bread!" The National Guard cleared the château but could not persuade the demonstrators to return to Paris. Cries arose for the king to come to Paris himself. A reverse procession formed that afternoon, heading back to the city, composed of the National Guard, some Swiss and other troops from the palace, a hundred members of the Constituent Assembly, a horde of jubilant and bedraggled women, singing and joking—and the king and queen and their son, the "baker and his wife and apprentice."

The age of Versailles in the long history of France was over. The royal family moved into the Tuileries, which Louis XIV had abandoned as old-fashioned a century before. The king was hailed as a benefactor of his people. He was, in fact, its hostage. He was the prisoner of the Revolution, and not unnaturally its secret foe. Within a few days the assembly also moved to Paris. For the second time, in October as in July, its position against a reluctant monarch had been strengthened by a mass uprising.

The Revolution had established itself and could now go on. At the same time the Counterrevolution gathered strength. Even patriots who had signed the Oath of the Tennis Court and who had voted for the great declaration were now alarmed at the descent into what seemed to be mob rule. Some left Paris, some left the country. France was divided. For years every government would face the same problem: to prevent restoration of the Old Order on the one hand, and on the other to try to satisfy, placate, guide, or evade the demands of an aroused, expectant, and militant population.

The Constituent Assembly sat for another two years, until September, 1791. It laid the foundations of modern France, at least in principle and in spirit. It devised a new system of taxation, mainly a direct tax to be paid by all persons alike, in proportion to their property. It reorganized the law courts, legal procedures, and judiciary, the old parlements being abolished, with financial compensation to those who lost their seats. It abolished all titles and ranks of nobility. It swept away the guilds and various economic regulations, favoring an economic freedom in which any person could enter any business or trade. Preferring to encourage small business and free artisans, and believing like Adam Smith that all occupational associations become a kind of conspiracy against the public, it made such associations illegal, and, like all governments of the time, it prohibited labor unions. It liquidated the seigneurial regime and the church tithes and introduced a more modern conception of property, in which the owner was freed of all vestiges of dependency and was liable to no irredeemable payments except taxes to the state.

The assembly abolished the old provinces, with their separate legal arrangements, and made the laws, rights, and obligations identical throughout the country. In place of the provinces, and of the judicial, fiscal, military, and administrative districts accumulated by the French monarchy since the twelfth century, it created eighty-three new *départements*, all presumably alike, each named after a river or natural feature so that old habits might be forgotten, and each of such a size that anyone could reach the *chef-lieu* in a day's journey. It set up busy institutions of local government. The ending of the manorial-seigneurial aristocratic order in the country, and of old-fashioned burgher rights in the towns, together with the actual facts of popular revolt and upheaval, made a thorough reorganization inevitable. A new uniform system for urban and rural municipalities was created. While legislation remained highly centralized, administration was decentralized to an extreme degree, with local election of public attorneys, tax collectors, and representative councils at the departmental and local levels. Thus the impetus of popular participation, gained in the 40,000 electoral assemblies of the spring of 1789, was carried on in 1790 and the following years. Plain people took part in continuing revolutionary activity at the bottom, while the Constituent Assembly and its successors governed at the top. A remarkable evidence of this spirit was given in the *fédérations* of 1790, culminating in the *fête de la fédération* in Paris on July 14 of that year, when delegates from local governing bodies, National Guards, and political clubs met with one another regionally, and finally in Paris, to pledge themselves to one another and to the new nation, enacting, as it were, the creation of a new community by the general will. It was the high point of unity in the Revolution, when it seemed that aristocrats might yet be rallied and the poor did not yet feel excluded.

The Declaration of Rights had announced that all citizens, "personally or by their representatives," had a right to take part in the formation of the law. That all Frenchmen were citizens, enjoying civil rights, there was no doubt; even free blacks in France and its colonies were made citizens in 1791. On political rights— that is, the vote, with the attendant question of the meaning of representation—there was more disagreement. A handful in the assembly, of whom Robespierre was one, argued for a universal suffrage of all adult males. Most argued against it, advancing a variety of reasons: that the poorest citizens were too illiterate to entrust with such power, that if they had it they would endanger order and property, or that in their ignorance and indifference they would merely sell their votes or follow the orders of their employers. What went on in England, in the few parliamentary boroughs that had a popular suffrage, was hardly an advertisement for democratic elections. In America, in those states having an almost universal male suffrage, it was rare for as many as 40 percent to cast a vote. The assembly adopted a series of compromises. It divided citizens into "active" and "passive." Active citizens were those men who paid a certain tax, were at least twenty-five years of age, were domiciled locally for a year, and were not in domestic service. There were about 4.3 million active citizens. These received the vote, but (except in local elections) they voted only for "electors." By meeting a slightly stiffer requirement, most active citizens (probably about 3 million) could qualify as electors. One elector was chosen for each hundred active citizens. In practice, it was generally the more well-to-do who were so chosen. Since there were no parties to propose slates of candidates to a mass electorate, the electors met in assemblies to discuss and choose departmental officials and members of the national legislature. In order to qualify as a member of the national legislature, one had to pay a tax of 54 livres, on property worth a few hundred livres of annual income. It was estimated that from 60,000 to 80,000 might qualify as national deputies. The number was barely larger than that of adult male nobles before the Revolution.

It was clearly the intent of the Constituent Assembly to confine politics at the national level to a substantial elite, recruited from the higher-income groups of the former noble and common orders. To the rest of Europe, at the time, these provisions seemed madly democratic. Few countries had any elections at all, and in England, to sit for a county, it was necessary, at least in law, to have a landed income equivalent to 15,000 French livres. It was also remarkable that over 4 million active citizens were admitted to even a limited vote. Yet a great many were excluded, not only the poorest, but men who paid no tax because they lived with their parents, those who had not lived in the same place for a year, and those of all classes not yet twenty-five years of age, but old enough to take an active part in politics especially in conditions of revolution and acute political consciousness. Probably about 3 million men, including many young men, were "passive" citizens. To exclude them, at such a time, was to create a grievance among a potentially dangerous element. In fact, many "passive" citizens slipped in among the "actives" anyway, and the whole distinction collapsed in 1792.

Given the role of the church before the Revolution, it is hardly surprising that the Constituent Assembly had trouble with religion. It was not that a majority were won over to Voltairian or aggressively rationalistic ideas. Many in the assembly reflected the Gallican and Jansenist traditions, believing that the French church should enjoy a certain independence from Rome, or that it was too aristocratic, with its wealth too unequally distributed among its own clergy, or too indifferent to the poor, and not earnest enough in religion. The movement for church reform was part of the revolutionary movement itself. The clergy, in May and June of 1789, had shown much sympathy for the third estate. Yet much happened that they could not approve. Churchmen, shortly before the Revolution, had opposed the extension of civil rights to Protestants and had defended the exemption of their property from taxation. In August, 1789, they lost their tithes, and had to accept, in the Declaration of Rights, the admissibility of non-Catholics to public office. In November came a greater blow. It so happened that the estimated value of the wealth of the church was about equal to the national debt. Governments had been confiscating church properties in bits and pieces since the Middle

Ages. Now all church property was confiscated at once. This was more than had happened even in England under the Tudors.

The transfer of church property was central to the financial and social policy of the Revolution. By it, perhaps as much as 10 percent of the real estate of the country, in land and buildings, passed to lay owners. The mechanism was as follows. The government issued paper, the *assignats*, first as a kind of bond, later as money for which the church lands provided the security. It thus financed itself in the general breakdown of tax receipts. Holders of this paper could use it to buy agricultural or urban properties formerly belonging to the church. Since the main purpose was financial, the properties were sold, not given away, but the prices and terms, which eventually included installment buying, were generally favorable, and gave a great advantage to persons who had any money. It was obviously not the poor or the agricultural wage laborers who most benefited from these transactions, which went on very actively for ten years. Thrifty and well-established peasants added to their holdings, former nobles were attracted by such bargains, and townspeople acquired either convent buildings in the towns or farm properties to add to their income. Under conditions of monetary inflation, from 1792 to 1795, it became easier even for some quite poor people to convert *assignats* into land. The result was to give a strong material interest in the success of the Revolution to a great many persons of diverse social origins.

Having deprived the church of both its property and its income, both its lands and its tithes, and yet believing religion to be socially necessary, the Constituent Assembly made itself responsible for reform of the church in France. Though strongly committed to religious freedom, or civil equality for non-Catholics, and believing that such matters as marriage, the family, and education should be put under civil auspices, the Constituents did not believe in the separation of church and state. They valued the church as the moral arm of society. Religion, they would have said, was too important to be left to the priests. In this they followed closely in the steps of Joseph II of Austria, not to mention Henry VIII of England, to go back no further.

The result was the Civil Constitution of the Clergy, adopted in 1790. Though various liberal bishops at first favored it, it was a radical document. It was not negotiated with the pope, but expressed the conviction that the French people, as sovereign, had a right to modify not indeed the faith but the "civil" or external features of their branch of the Catholic church. In place of the former dioceses, which had numbered about 130 (the number was unclear because some overlapped into Belgium and Germany), the assembly now put 83 bishoprics, each identical in area with one of the new departments, as if the bishops were a kind of civil official. All clergy now received salaries paid by the state. Where formerly the incomes of the bishops had varied from 500,000 to 5,000 or 6,000 livres, they were now put on a more rational though not illiberal scale. Parish priests, who had received about 750 livres a year under the Old Order, now received 1,200. The mode of election was equally revolutionary. Parish priests were to be elected by the active citizens in local assemblies, bishops by the electors of the department. Since a religious service was prescribed for these elections, it was expected that non-Catholic citizens would absent themselves. Only priests acceptable to the bishops could be elected. The bishops, when elected, were to notify the pope but not ask for his approval. No papal message could be circulated in France except with the permission of the government. Under the Old Order kings had claimed similar powers and had appointed the bishops; the appointment of many parish clergy had rested with lay patrons. The innovation, therefore, was not primarily in the encroachment of secular power. It was rather in the democratization in recruitment of the clergy.

The Civil Constitution referred only to the "secular" clergy, those having a pastoral function. The "regular" clergy, those in religious orders, were abolished outright, with pensions paid to the monks and nuns. They had long been declining in France and were the butt of anticlerical jokes; even before 1789, the agencies of education, poor relief, medical care, and social welfare had been passing increasingly to civil auspices. The process was now abruptly completed in principle. In fact, while the state assumed the responsibility and developed many modern ideas, the institutions of welfare and education long suffered from the confusion of revolution, war, and inflation.

The adoption of all these measures naturally produced disagreements, both in the assembly and throughout the country. Organized revolutionary formations, which it would be misleading to call parties, emerged in connection with events themselves. On the other side were those who spoke of the need for "another Revolution," or counterrevolution, by which the course of events might be reversed. (From their seats in the Constituent they were for a while called the Left and the Right, but these terms soon went out of use, to be revived by revolutionary ideology and reminiscence in the following century.) Both sides, until 1792 (and from 1795 to 1799), had their journalists and their clubs. The chief revolutionary club was the Jacobins, so called because it held its meetings, which were public, in a great hall formerly belonging to the Jacobin monks. Its real name until 1792 was the Friends of the Constitution, and from 1792 to its dissolution late in 1794 the Friends of Liberty and Equality. The Jacobins were predominantly drawn from the well-to-do and educated level of the former third estate. For less affluent citizens, or those who could have no influence in a large upper middle-class assembly, a great many clubs were organized in the various neighborhoods of Paris, of which the Cordeliers were the most famous. Thousands of similar clubs, the "popular societies," sprang up all over France. By 1793 they had about half a million members. They corresponded with the Paris Jacobins, which they regarded as the "mother society." In these revolutionary clubs there was nothing secret, underground, or conspiratorial. Their purpose was to exercise a visible leadership, keep in touch with the national deputies, explain the actions of the assembly to the local people, set an example of *civisme*, and block the moves of "aristocrats." On both sides the atmosphere became charged with suspicion, a fear of merely tepid, compromising, or moderate persons, a belief that only the most committed or the most "pure" could be relied upon. On the Left, the mere liberals of 1789 fell into disfavor. The Jacobins repeatedly "purified" or purged themselves. On the Right, both among the swelling numbers of émigrés and among conservatives remaining in France, mere liberalism seemed to be playing with the fire of revolution, and Louis XVI himself was thought to be a dupe of the Jacobins.

The king's position, and hence the whole attempt at constitutional monarchy, became increasingly difficult. It was made worse by the religious troubles. Somewhat tardily, Pius VI condemned the Civil Constitution of the Clergy, after about half the parish priests had accepted it (but almost none of the bishops) and after Louis XVI, under pressure, had given it his formal approval. Both the clergy and the faithful were now divided. Oaths to the new constitution were required of the clergy. They were taken, refused, or evaded. The church had its "juring" and "nonjuring," or constitutional and refractory, priests; the former believed themselves to be good Christians and patriots, while the latter considered themselves to be better Catholics and were increasingly allied with and exploited by the forces of counterrevolution. Louis XVI, by personally using the services of a refractory priest, fell more deeply under suspicion among partisans of the Revolution. He was urged by his more determined wife, Marie Antoinette, and the vestiges of the court party, to take a more positive stand. Marie Antoinette was a Hapsburg; her brother, Leopold II, was now emperor. One of the most enlightened of eighteenth-century princes, he had urged his sister and her royal husband to come to terms with the Revolution. Nevertheless, driven by the ever-mounting demands of the Revolutionaries, Louis XVI decided that his only course was to get out of the country, join the émigrés, and obtain help from abroad.

On June 20, 1791, the royal family, secretly and in disguise, set out for the eastern frontier. They were stopped at Varennes, near the border, and forced to return to Paris. The king's intentions were known; he had meant to re-enter the country with an Austrian army, dissolve the assembly and the clubs, and restore the situation to what it had been before 1789. He was now clearly both the enemy and the prisoner of the Revolution. Whether a constitutional monarchy could be made to work was very doubtful. A republican party now came into being; some of its popular adherents, gathering in the Champ de Mars to sign a republican petition, were shot down by the National Guard. Some fifty were killed in what the incipient republicans called a "massacre." The more upper-class Jacobin Club divided. Some of its members seceded and, believing that the symbols of monarchy must be preserved, however discredited, as a protection against anarchy and lower-class turbulence, formed a club of their own, the Feuillants. The more vehement revolutionaries were thus left in control of the Jacobins, where Robespierre became more prominent. Eager though the Jacobins were to make the constitution work, they could hardly be indifferent to the republican arguments.

The Constituent Assembly dissolved itself on September 30, 1791, pronouncing its work to be accomplished. A newly elected Legislative Assembly immediately convened. The king again seemed to accept the situation. But the constitutional monarchy in France, repudiated by its monarch beforehand, lasted only ten months from its official promulgation. It was the first victim of the wars of the French Revolution.

With Louis XVI clearly detained in France against his will, the clamor for intervention became more difficult to resist. The French émigrés issued threats of their early return. This only stirred up radicalism in Paris. The Emperor Leopold II was no admirer of the privileged classes of Europe, which he was trying to keep under control in his own dominions. He was beset, however, by the French émigrés, by the demands of his sister, and by various princes of the Holy Roman Empire who, thanks to the Constituent Assembly, had lost seigneurial rights in Alsace. He held a meeting with the king of Prussia at Pillnitz in Bohemia. The ensuing Declaration of Pillnitz, dated August 27, 1791, announced somewhat ambiguously that the two powers would intervene by armed force to restore the king of France to his proper rights *if* the other leading powers would also lend support. Leopold thus hoped at least to obtain a delay, since other governments, and notably the British, had at this time no intention of intervening. Leopold resisted the step; and in most of Europe, including the Hapsburg dominions, the middle and lower classes were strongly opposed to interference in the French Revolution. Among the upper classes, on the other hand—those who frequented royal courts, nobles, aristocrats, gentlefolk, and prelates—it seemed outrageous that a king had been arrested by some of the most vulgar of his subjects at Varennes. In France there was the same feeling in reverse: it seemed outrageous that the French people, as a sovereign nation rearranging its own affairs, should be stopped by the threats of the crowned heads of Europe. The Declaration of Pillnitz, boasted of by the French émigrés, was taken as an outright threat.

Many factors converged to make for war. In France the true royalists hoped that in a war Louis XVI might be able to crush the revolutionaries. The Feuillants, or constitutional monarchist group, expected that the king's position would be clarified and strengthened. The radicals—the emerging popular democrats in the lesser clubs, and the Jacobins, for whom Brissot de Warville was now a leading spokesman—believed that a war would be short and easy, that the European peoples would refuse to support it, and that they might even rise in a universal revolution against all the monarchies of Europe. In addition, for the radical party in France, the emergence of war would make it possible to identify and get rid of "traitors" and so press forward with the Revolution. Only a small group warned against war, among them Robespierre. He thought it absurd to believe, like Brissot, that the French would liberate the world. "No one loves armed missionaries," he said at the Jacobin Club in January, 1792; but he was not heeded. Meanwhile Leopold II died and was succeeded by his son Francis II, who was more sympathetic to the privileged classes in his own empire than his father had been and more ready to join in a crusade to uphold Louis XVI and save Europe from the Revolution.

It was the French who declared war, on April 20, 1792, in a wild session of the Legislative Assembly, with only seven negative votes. For the first six months the French suffered a series of defeats. The army was in no condition to fight. It was mostly the army of the Old Order in a state of dissolution. Of its largely noble officers corps, many had emigrated, and many of those who remained had no liking for the new government. The men were overwhelmingly patriotic, enthusiastically devoted to the Revolution, but some were untrained volunteers, and even in the older regiments the spirit of liberty made the discipline very relaxed. At the first encounters, somewhat as for the North in the American Civil War, the troops broke and fled. Louis XVI, expecting an

Austrian victory, vetoed certain measures of defense passed by
the assembly in this crisis. The country was at war under a king
which it quite rightly did not trust. The Austrians and Prussians
approached the French frontier. Working with emissaries from
Marie Antoinette, they issued a manifesto to the city of Paris.
Published on August 3 in Paris, a city now thoroughly aroused
and indeed fanaticized against all monarchs and aristocrats, this
incongruous document ordered the city "to submit at once and
without delay to the king," failing which, upon the arrival of the
Allies, the most fearful punishments would be inflicted.

The city rose on August 10 against Louis XVI, against the
aristocrats, who up to now had been able to print their opinions
freely, against all "traitors" who really hoped that the Allies would
come, against the constitutionalist Feuillants, and against the
hapless Legislative Assembly, believed to be verbose, incompetent,
and inadequate, if not actually treacherous at a moment of military
disaster. This uprising of August 10, sometimes called the Second
French Revolution, was a concerted but far from secret action.
The "sections" in the municipal government, reinforced by the
popular clubs, openly prepared for insurrection. Tradesmen, shopkeepers, and small manufacturers rallied their own employees
in a general mixture of "active" and "passive" citizens, known to
history as the *sans-culottes*, who were to play a dominant role for
the next two years. These popular democrats in Paris, in default
of everyone else, now took it into their own hands to save the
country from invasion and the Revolution from extinction. They
were assisted by volunteers from Marseilles, who brought with
them a new song, destined for fame, composed for the Army of
the Rhine. At the Jacobin Club, Robespierre called for the dethronement of Louis XVI and the election, by universal male
suffrage, of a new governing body, to be called the National Convention. The sans-culottes attacked the Tuileries Palace, which
was defended only by the Swiss Guard, and captured it in a few
hours with over a thousand casualties on both sides.

The result was the dethronement of Louis XVI and the end of
the French monarchy. The Prussians crossed the frontier on the
way to Paris. The city was wild with excitement. Early in September, mobs broke into the prisons, mistakenly believed to be full of

conspirators, and put to death over a thousand in the streets. In this atmosphere of horror and terror, the elections for the convention, technically democratic—and indeed quite democratic in some parts of the country—went ahead.

Three years had passed since the fall of the Bastille. State and church, law and society, had been redesigned. But the work of the Constituent Assembly might yet have been wiped away. Or—and this is what happened—the incursion of the actual common people might push the Revolution forward and, while frustrating the Counterrevolution, attempt a more democratic organization of society.

[3]

A World Aroused

It is not easy to recapture even the most general features of the European world upon which the wars of the Revolution broke. The French, with their population of 25 million, were by far the most numerous people under a single government. Even distant Russia had hardly more. The German-speaking peoples were equally numerous, but divided into principalities of which there were a hundred in the Rhineland alone. The 20 million subjects of the Hapsburgs were ethnically diverse and geographically disconnected. Three million Belgians lived in their autonomous provinces under a remote Hapsburg rule, except for those who lived in the large separate bishopric of Liège. There were only about 2 million Dutch. Hardly more than 10 million lived in England and Scotland. Italy was a mosaic of small states, and there were 10 million somewhat disunited Spaniards. The United States, by the first census of 1790, had about as many people, slaves included, as the Dutch and Belgians combined.

France was a colossus which, if only its manpower could be effectively utilized, was a match for even a strong alliance against it. It had also held a leading place in European civilization since the days of the Gothic cathedrals. In the eighteenth century the French language was well known and indeed currently used by the upper classes in many parts of the Continent. Journals were published in French from Holland to Warsaw. Except in England, the various nationalities were still undeveloped as politicocultural units, and the fact that ideas came from France, or were believed to be French, was before the Revolution no reason to oppose them. The outpourings of the new Paris press after 1789 or the debates of the Constituent Assembly as published in the *Moniteur* were perfectly understandable all over Europe. No such barrier of linguistic difficulty or relative backwardness screened Europe against the Revolution in France as it did in the twentieth century against revolution in Russia or in China.

News of the fall of the Bastille was hailed everywhere— briefly—with satisfaction. The Bourbon monarchy was widely disliked, and no civilized European was opposed to liberty or to law on principle. The English were gratified to think that the French might now follow them in the ways of free government. To the Prussians it seemed that the French were passing from despotism to the *Rechtstaat*, as in Prussia. But as early as August, 1789, it became clear that the French assembly had in mind something different from the institutions of English liberty or Prussian law. The idea of "equality" proved distasteful to the established groups in these and other countries.

In many places, as already mentioned, attempts at far-reaching change, if not actual revolution, had been in progress long before the Revolution in France. It is difficult to offer a general characterization. Nowhere had the true mass of the people been involved. Disputes were within perhaps the upper quarter of the population, the lower classes remaining generally faithful to customary superiors. Quarrels were not essentially between rich and poor, nor even the not-so-rich and the very wealthy; and the pattern of a conflict between bourgeois and feudal elements is singularly inappropriate to Holland and Switzerland, and for different reasons to Britain, Ireland, and Poland. Given the prevalence, as described in Chapter 1, of official churches and ruling elites recruited largely by inheritance or co-optation—which is to say by birth, though not necessarily noble birth—the conflict may be thought of as a stress between insiders and outsiders under the existing forms of society. In a sense, it was between privileged and unprivileged classes, as in France. Disaffected persons might be members of

religious minorities, or men whose fortunes and social position
were new, or those interested in new forms of business, investment,
production, or technology for which the guild system and the
older economic regulations were an obstacle, or lawyers and law
graduates who did not work for the older interests, or men active
in science and medicine, or journalists and writers interested in
the intellectual revolution, or career civil servants in the Continental monarchies who found their rural and town oligarchies
an impediment to modernization, or young men of diverse parent-
age who sensed the promise of a new age. There was a widespread
feeling among such people against what a later age would call
the establishment.

In 1792 those partisans of a New Order, from Ireland to Poland,
had been effectively silenced. But they had not vanished, and
they were highly receptive to events such as the French Revolution of 1789 and the war of 1792, by which their several movements might be reactivated.

Ireland was a separate kingdom, about half as populous as
England, with its own parliament and its own established (Anglican) church. The English conquest, accompanied by a mass
settlement of middle-class Scots, had been finally accomplished
in the preceding century. Two-thirds of the people were Roman
Catholics, about two-ninths were Presbyterian, and the remaining
one-ninth, the Anglicans, owned five-sixths of the land and
manned the parliament, the church, and the government. All had
reason to object to the Parliament of Great Britain, by which
trade controls very unfavorable to Ireland were imposed. The
American Revolution made a great impression, especially among
the Presbyterians. To express political sentiment, and in preparation
against a possible French invasion, free companies of Volunteers
began to form, who numbered 80,000 by 1782. Armed and uni-
formed, they engaged in drills and exchanged delegations. Mainly
Presbyterian, the Volunteers were at first favored by the Anglicans,
but when the British government, in 1782, granted further autonomy to the Irish Parliament, many of the Anglicans were
satisfied, and the Volunteers turned to the reform of the parliament, whose powers were thus extended. The Irish House of

Commons, like the British, was characterized by a variety of decayed, uninhabited, rotten, and pocket boroughs by means of which, it was estimated, about a hundred persons controlled it. In 1783 the Volunteers held a Grand National Convention (the first "Convention" of the eighteenth-century revolution), and staged a march through the streets of Dublin, culminating in the presentation of a reform bill. They were weakened, however, by seeming to impose a military threat in a civilian society, by representing mainly a rather modest clientele of linen weavers, small traders, etc., and by internal differences on the matter of equal rights for the Catholics. Although a few of the landed elite voted for the reform bill, including the father of Viscount Castlereagh, it was overwhelmingly defeated. There was an outburst of conservative oratory, in which Sir Hercules Langrishe, the correspondent of Edmund Burke, called the bill "subversive of the constitution," which he declared to be "the admiration and envy of all nations and all ages." The Volunteers gave up in discouragement. Meanwhile a few concessions were made to the Catholics, who were granted the right to buy land in 1782. But in 1792 no Catholic could open a Catholic college or vote for a member of the Irish House of Commons.

In England dissatisfaction was evident even before the American Revolution. It was indeed one of the complaints of reformers that a more truly representative British government would never have quarreled with, or lost, the American colonies. Followers of John Wilkes founded the Society of Supporters of the Bill of Rights, the first English society for parliamentary reform, as early as 1769. It was in response to these pressures, for example, that the debates in Parliament first came to be published. The first of some fifty reform bills (culminating at last in the Act of 1832) was defeated in 1776. Wilkes's movement was confined to London, where it found favor even with wealthy merchants. In the following years a similar agitation spread among gentry and landowners in the counties, especially Yorkshire. There was talk of another Magna Carta, a second Runnymede, a General Association, and even a National Assembly by which pressure might be brought to bear upon a reluctant Parliament. County "associations" corresponded with one another as a kind of civilian counterpart to the Irish Volunteers. Then the movement subsided, partly because the Gordon Riots aroused fears of the populace, partly because the more conservative reformers, led by Burke, to prevent any real reallocation of political power, deflected attention by a reform of jobs, pensions, and sinecures. When the young William Pitt, however, who was no friend of the great Whig aristocracy, became prime minister in 1784, he believed that the country would be actually strengthened by a more adequate representation. He was handicapped by lack of support among the rising factory owners of the Midlands, who were not yet seriously concerned that Manchester and Leeds had no members in Parliament and were in fact alarmed by the tariff concessions that Pitt contemplated for Ireland. Pitt's reform bill failed to pass, and he dropped the matter.

It was in opposition to these attempts at the reconstruction of the House of Commons, even when proposed by a prime minister, that Burke developed his principles of conservatism. Like Langrishe in Ireland, he believed such attempts to be subversive. The object of the reformers, he said in 1784, was "the destruction of the Constitution by disgracing and discrediting the House of Commons." From 1787 to 1789 three attempts were made in Parliament to give equal rights to Protestant Dissenters—that is, to relieve them from the provisions of the Test and Corporation Acts, passed over a century before, at the time of the Restoration, as a protection against the aftereffects of the Puritan revolution. The Anglican gentry who ruled in Parliament had no affection for the mainly middle-class and urban Dissenters. The bills all failed. Burke fumed against abstract ideas, and even Pitt remarked, when the Dissenters cited the example of religious freedom in America, that "the American Constitution resembles ours in neither church nor state." This was in 1789; he could soon say the same of the French.

The Dutch Patriot movement also began in connection with the War of American Independence. Dutch interests were closely allied to the British; indeed, Dutch investors in 1777 owned 40 percent of the British national debt. The House of Orange was much intermarried with the British royal family and generally followed the British lead. The powers of the Prince of Orange, however, were strictly limited by the complex of autonomous towns, boards, colleges, councils, and estates which constituted the Union of Utrecht. These bodies were in the hands of a small group of self-perpetuating regent families. When the Americans threw off the British connection, they sought to enter into direct trade with Continental Europe. The regents of Amsterdam made their own treaty with the United States, to which the Prince of Orange, William V, objected. A struggle developed between a pro-British Orange party and a large mixed pro-American group called the Patriots. The Patriots were composed in part of certain regents, who had long resisted the royal pretensions and English orientation of the House of Orange, and in part of a wide variety of persons, from bankers and wholesalers to master shoemakers, journalists, and students, whose common tie was that they stood outside the regent and Dutch Reformed oligarchy. A Dutchman wrote in 1786 that his country was troubled by a "cabal" of "aristocrats and democrats." The democrats organized into the Free Corps, which armed and drilled as in Ireland. The Free Corps demanded that the various estates and councils be recruited by election, not co-optation. They opened their ranks to Catholics and Protestant sectaries, and they convoked a National Assembly of Free Corps, in what was probably the strongest revolutionary movement in Europe before the French Revolution of 1789. The estates of Holland deposed the Prince of Orange, but then took fright at the demands of the Free Corps, so that the Patriots were divided. In the fighting that followed, the French secretly aided the Free Corps, and the British worked to restore the Prince. When the Princess of Orange, a sister to the King of Prussia, was stopped on the road by a party of the Free Corps, like Marie Antoinette at Varennes four years later, her royal brother, more chivalrous than Leopold II, loudly denounced the outrage and sent 20,000 troops into the Netherlands. The Free Corps dissolved before these regular soldiers. A confrontation had occurred between royalist Europe supported by British diplomacy and a democratic-republican movement aimed against its reigning dynasty and aristocracy. The British and Prussians restored William V and the former order in the United Provinces, which they guaranteed by treaty. Thousands of Patriots fled to France. In 1792 there were perhaps 10,000 Dutch political exiles in France, and the towns of Holland were full of angry former Patriots who had hoped for assistance from the French army in 1787, and would do so again in 1793.

As revolution faded among the Dutch, in 1787, it began in the Austrian Netherlands. These were ten provinces embalmed, as it were, since the close of the Middle Ages. The sixteenth-century struggle against Calvinism had left an exaggerated Catholicism, in which piety was common and half the land belonged to the church. The river Scheldt had been closed to international trade at the insistence of the Dutch and English; Antwerp had declined; there was a minimum of modern or long-range commerce and a maximum local activity in guilds and towns. Guildsmen, burgo-masters, abbots, and nobles defended their ancestral rights. The ten provinces had no union (the last Estates General having met in 1634) except what the Austrian authorities provided. After 1780 the energetic Joseph II began to try to modernize his Belgian provinces along with the rest of the Hapsburg empire. He ordered the toleration of Protestants, the abolition of torture, the opening of the Scheldt, the reduction of town and guild barriers, the control of seigneurial courts, the closing of a few monasteries, and the reform of the University of Louvain. The Belgians rebelled in 1788–89 in a conservative revolution to defend ancient liberties against such encroachment. The party of the Old Order, called the Estates party, sought British or Prussian intervention. A group more interested in internal change, who called themselves "Democrats" and were called Vonckists by their enemies, after their leader J. F. Vonck, hoped to organize native Belgian resist-ance to Joseph II and at the same time to obtain representation in the estates for persons and towns hitherto excluded and to have elected councils and officers. A few thousand men, hastily organized in free companies and supported by insurrections, proved sufficient to drive out the Austrians in 1789. The revolutionaries then clashed with each other, since the Estates party, in ridding itself of the Austrians, would entertain no proposals from Vonck, who was in fact extraordinarily compromising and moderate. The Estates party, forestalling the Democrats, declared itself sovereign, set up a United States of Belgium, and in the name of the Three Orders and of the Catholic church began a systematic repression of the Democrats, whom it could now discredit, early in 1790, as partisans of the French Revolution. Thousands of Belgian Democrats, like Dutch Patriots before them, fled to France. The momentarily victorious estates, afflicted by the disorders into which the country had fallen, were then in turn overthrown by the returning Austrians, who—to the satisfaction of some of the Democrats—restored their authority at the end of 1790. The Belgian Democrats were made more radical, more anticlerical and antiaristocratic, by the duplicity and violence used against them. Many were ready to support the French for the liberation of Belgium in 1792.

Switzerland had scarcely more political identity than Belgium. It consisted of thirteen German-speaking cantons, associated in a loose, defensive league. The main ones were Zurich, Bern, and Basel. All the regions of French or Italian language, and many of German, were without cantonal organization but belonged as subject districts to one or another of the ruling cantons. Geneva was a tiny independent city-state. It had a long series of upheavals, in which the theoretical question was whether sovereignty lay with the whole citizenry or with the governing Small Council of some twenty-five members. After another flare-up in 1781, the patricians of the Small Council called in the outside "guarantors"—France, Zurich, and Bern. By the Pacification of 1782, all concessions made since 1768 were revoked. The reformers at Geneva were denounced as "sectaries of J. J. Rousseau and other false philosophers of the day." Among the democrats who fled to France in 1782 was the banker Etienne Clavière, who ten years later was French financial minister and political colleague of Brissot. Meanwhile restlessness developed in other parts of Switzerland. The famous educator, Pestalozzi, in his youth, was arrested at Zurich for opposing the use of Zurich troops against the revolutionary party at Geneva. At Bern, the most aristocratic of the cantons and the one with the most extensive dependent territories, the governing families were becoming more exclusive; there were only 230 of them qualified to hold office in 1780, whereas there had been 500 a century before. One of the dependencies of Bern was the French-speaking Vaud, with Lausanne as its capital. Here a banquet was held in July, 1791, to celebrate the anniversary of the fall of the Bastille. To speeches made in favor of the liberation of mankind, the Bern authorities responded by removing several Protestant pastors from their churches and imprisoning or exiling various laymen. The sentiments of the Vaud aristocracy may be seen in the two La Harpes. One became a general in the French Revolutionary army in 1792. The other, after acting as tutor to the future Tsar Alexander I, to whom he taught "republican" principles, and after being driven from Russia in 1796, was one of the leading Swiss revolutionaries of 1798. At Basel, after 1780, the young patrician Peter Ochs turned his mind to the need for a general reorganization of all Switzerland. He was aroused by the Revolution across the river in France, where he owned property and where his sister was married to the man who became the first Revolutionary mayor of Strasbourg. It was in fact in her drawing room in that city that Rouget de Lisle composed the *Marseillaise*. It is evident that Switzerland, in 1792, was full of both warm friends and determined enemies of the French Revolution.

Among other features of the eighteenth century that are hard to recapture is the fact that the Hapsburg monarchy, under Maria Theresa, Joseph II, and Leopold II, was one of the most enlightened, modern-minded, and reform-oriented governments in Europe. The impact of Joseph II on Belgium has been mentioned, as has the attitude of Leopold II to his frivolous sister, Marie Antoinette. In Western Europe, or what was called the second zone in Chapter 1, the Hapsburgs possessed the duchy of Milan and the grand duchy of Tuscany in addition to Belgium. In Tuscany, where Leopold was for many years grand duke before inheriting the throne at Vienna, he had introduced so many successful innovations in taxation, tariffs, the guild system, town government, and church affairs as to make the population relatively impervious to any French example. At Milan, similar attempts at reform were less successful. Milan was an active center of the European Enlightenment. One of its citizens, Beccaria, in his famous book *Crimes and Punishments*, had strongly condemned the use of judicial torture. Yet it was precisely in Milan, as in Belgium, because of the attachment of local magistracies to local liberties and ancestral customs, that Maria Theresa was unable to have torture abolished. Liberals at Milan became disgusted both with their own oligarchy and with the Hapsburgs. The economist Verri observed sardonically, shortly after the fall of the Bastille, that at Milan the French were denounced as "metaphysical" as soon as they began to question the Three Orders. Others looked on the French with more favor.

The main body of the Hapsburg dominions—Austria, Bohemia, and Hungary—was still shaking in 1792 from the "revolution" attempted by Joseph II. Joseph's reign had been a magnificent failure. He had attempted a kind of one-man or at most bureaucratic transformation of the empire, seeking the usual reforms in church and state, abolishing tax privileges, suppressing monasteries, confiscating church property, instituting civil marriage, putting the clergy on salaries paid by the state, extending the rights of Jews and Protestants, and insisting on a new legal equality between nobility and bourgeoisie, including equal access to public office. He had even begun to do away with serfdom, hoping to turn the peasant into a subject of the emperor rather than of his manorial lord and into a kind of property owner from whom the lord would only receive a money income. Among the peasantry and the town middle classes Joseph had a good deal of inarticulate support. But when he died, early in 1790, all the organized bodies of the empire were in revolt against him. The Belgian provinces had declared their independence. The diets, or estate assemblies, of Hungary, Bohemia, Styria, Carinthia, and the rest, representing only the landowners and Catholic prelates, were angrily defending their position, and especially their powers over their peasants, in the name of their historic constitutional liberties.

Leopold, succeeding Joseph, was obliged to compromise. The diet of Hungary was in rebellion against him, with a minority in it even sounding like the Constituent Assembly in France. The peasants, in a massive upheaval of their own, more ferocious than the French peasant rebellion of 1789, were rising against the lords and gentry who sat in the diet. To placate the diet, Leopold in

effect reconfirmed the charter of 1740, thus disavowing the reforms
of half a century. He restored order in Hungary, as in Belgium, by
use of the army. He died in 1792, and was succeeded by his son
Francis II a few weeks before the outbreak of war with France.
Francis II, a young man of twenty-four, was socially more conservative than his father and more inclined to agree with the aristocratic estates, and in any case he needed their support in the war
against France, for which only the privileged orders felt any
enthusiasm. Among the peasants memories lingered of what
Joseph II had tried to do, and news trickled in of the rebellion and
liberation of the peasants in France. Middle-class persons, especially
government servants, also remembered Joseph with favor. It was
evident that the same forces that had blocked Joseph now opposed
the French Revolution. Outside the various kinds of privileged
classes there was little sentiment, in the Hapsburg empire, either
for the Declaration of Pillnitz or for the war of 1792.

Poland, to conclude this survey of disturbed areas in Europe,
was, like France, the object of actual military invasion in 1792.
After the First Partition, effected in 1773, a party dedicated to
strengthening the country had arisen in Poland and beginning in
1788 had developed its program in the Four Years' Diet. It had
produced the constitution of May 3, 1791. This document, conservative in its way, did nothing to relieve the peasants from
serfdom. It was designed to correct the weaknesses which had laid
Poland open to exploitation by its neighbors: the periodic election
of the king, in which foreigners had commonly interfered, the
"free veto" enjoyed by individual members of the diet, the
exclusion of towns from political life, and the domination of
Polish affairs by a few great magnates, who owned enormous
estates and who enjoyed huge followings of very poor, landless,
and dependent "nobles." The constitution of May 3, with its
accompanying Statute of Cities, therefore provided for a hereditary
monarchy in Poland, abolished the free veto, strengthened the
middle ranks of the nobility by measures aimed against both the
magnates and the landless nobles, and took steps toward incor-
porating the burghers (excluded since 1505) into the political
life of the country. Nothing like the new French idea of citizen-

ship was to be found in the Polish constitution of 1791, which
therefore seemed to the French Revolutionaries to be a kind of
aristocratic fraud, but enough rights were given to burghers to
create an unsettling and even revolutionary example in Eastern
Europe, and indeed elsewhere. Thus the national diet, while
remaining in principle a meeting of gentry, was to have burgher
spokesmen with a vote on certain subjects. Town residents, if
neither serfs nor Jews, were to be enrolled as burghers, with
rights to govern the towns by actual elections, to purchase noble
rural estates, to qualify for higher appointments in state and
church, and to hold commissions in the army, except in the more
aristocratic cavalry. Nobility was far from abolished; it remained
highly prized, but elevation of burghers to the noble estate was
made quite easy. Toleration was promised to non-Catholics, along
with freedom from arbitrary imprisonment for burghers as well
as nobles.

The Polish constitution of 1791, moderate in comparison with
the French constitution of the same date, yet radical in its way,
represented a compromise between contending factions, and its
promulgation was followed by continuing conflict among the
Poles themselves. On the one hand was the aristocratic party of
the great magnates, with their horde of displaced noble retainers,
who violently resented the new arrangements and looked to Russia
for their social salvation. On the other hand were the Patriots, who
had wanted a less grudging recognition of the towns. They pointed
to the French and American Revolutions with approval, and
some were considering the abolition of serfdom. A middle party
was led by the king himself. In 1791, after the constitution was
proclaimed, political clubs began to multiply in Warsaw and
other cities. The press developed, and there was much free discussion and lively argument on political questions.

The governments of the three powers by which Poland was
surrounded—Russia, Prussia, and Austria—saw in these developments a dangerous example to their own peoples. Neither burghers
nor even middling nobles enjoyed such rights in the three neighboring monarchies. Poland was a more alarming center of infection
than the other center in France, if only because it was closer geographically and socially. The Polish revolutionaries were de-

nounced as pernicious and fanatical Jacobins. In addition, the
three powers had no desire to see Poland successfully consolidated.
Each had territorial ambitions that could best be satisfied by a
further partition. In 1791–92, as the Austrian and Prussian governments moved toward intervention in France, Catherine II of
Russia moved toward intervention in Poland. In April, 1792, under
her protection, the disaffected Polish magnates, counterrevolutionaries, and émigrés who flocked to St. Petersburg issued the
Act of Targowica. This document arraigned the various revolutionary ideas of the day, attributed the Polish Revolution to a
"plot," equated the Poles with the French, and promised to
restore the Old Order in Poland.

The Russians invaded Poland in May. They met with little
resistance. No aroused and regenerated nation opposed them.
On July 24 King Stanislas surrendered as the Russian armies
drew near to Warsaw. On the next day the rulers of Austria and
Prussia issued their Brunswick Manifesto against the city of
Paris. It met with a different reception; the French monarchy fell,
along with the French Constitution of 1791; but the Allies pressed
on across the French frontiers. The same allies, Austria and
Prussia, signed an agreement with Russia to restore the situation
in Poland as it had existed in 1773.

The war of 1792, in short—that is, the hostilities between
France, Prussia, and Austria—was only part of a much larger
operation, in which the three Eastern monarchies, supported by
French and Polish émigrés and miscellaneous aristocracies, led a
counterrevolutionary movement against both France and Poland,
and in which the French Revolutionary armies, disorganized and
temporarily unsuccessful though they were, enjoyed the excited
moral support of dissatisfied persons, mainly of the middle social
ranks, who had tried and failed to obtain changes in their own
countries—Irish, British, Dutch, Belgian, Swiss, Austrian, Polish,
and others.

The war revolutionized the Revolution in France and became
the vehicle for its spread to other countries in a series of reverberations that repeated themselves, in different ways, until the fall of
Napoleon twenty-two years later. The effect of the war, at moments

when it seemed that the allies and the Counterrevolution might win, was to radicalize the situation in France, throwing power into the hands of those willing to appeal for mass support by offering a democratic program. This happened most notably in the summer of 1792, as already described. It happened again in the spring and summer of 1793; it almost happened in 1799; and a faint echo was heard even in 1815, when many old republicans, repelled by the Bourbon restoration, rallied to the emperor upon his return from Elba. When the tables were turned, when the French were winning, as proved to be generally the case after the middle of 1794, the force of internal democratization in France was slackened. A French government strong enough to hold off the enemy, beginning with the Committee of Public Safety in 1794, was strong enough also to hold down popular turbulence and to do without "demagogic" appeals. But as the French won, the Revolution spread—temporarily to Belgium at the end of 1792, to an array of "sister" or satellite republics after 1795, and in less revolutionary fashion, though in a way still upsetting to the Old Order, to the various states of the Grand Empire, which Napoleon reorganized in conjunction with native reformers.

Each combatant naturally sought support among persons most likely to give it, both within its own borders and beyond them. The result was to produce a truly ideological struggle that overflowed all political frontiers. The French Jacobins in 1792 made common cause with their own social subordinates, the sans-culottes. They developed a psychology of world revolution to enlist the sympathy of the disaffected and frustrated elements that already existed in other countries. The Revolution, threatened by aristocrats, became more democratic. The allied powers, which in 1793 became the First Coalition, professed their concern for the French royal family, the church, and émigrés, appealed for support of their own upper classes and established churches, and in the hope of immunizing their middle and lower classes against the French contagion, developed a philosophy of conservatism, in which respect for tradition, avoidance of change, and a kind of organic or hierarchic society were held to be natural for the lower as well as the higher strata.

This conservative philosophy antedated 1789. It was as much a reaction against the whole drift of the Enlightenment as against the Revolution, which merely accentuated it. It carried on the philosophy of the French aristocratic resurgence, of a Parlement of Paris which had said in 1776 that education should preserve the distinction of orders, and of a French nobility which in the Estates General had expected to receive perpetual special treatment. It reaffirmed the views of those who had said that the Irish reformers were "system mongers" and the Geneva democrats "sectaries of J. J. Rousseau." Germany was much divided, and many Germans shared in the rationalist, universalist, and emancipating ideals of the European Enlightenment, but Germany long before 1789 was also the home of a conservative counterphilosophy, which valued the old, the ancestral, the medieval, the local, the peculiar, and even the irrational, looked upon authority with deep veneration, and favored duty at the expense of freedom. In the 1780s, as an offshoot of Freemasonry, or as an erratic manifestation of the Enlightenment, there was formed in Germany a secret society called the Illuminati, the "enlightened ones," which recruited a few hundred members. The Illuminati had vague ideas of world renewal by infiltration of the existing authorities. They were suppressed as an undesirable secret group by the Elector of Bavaria without difficulty. Their importance lies in the philosophy developed against them. It became the fashion to believe, in some conservative circles, first in Germany and then elsewhere, that revolution wherever found was caused by "philosophers," Freemasons, and Illuminati.

The great work in the new vein was Edmund Burke's *Reflections on the French Revolution*, which he wrote in 1790. It was translated into German immediately by Friedrich Gentz and was vehemently answered by many counterpamphlets in England, where Burke's favorable repute was greater in later times than in his own. On the whole, the French Revolution prompted in him the same "reflections" as had the British reform bills of 1782–84. It was in 1784, against his own countrymen, that Burke first denounced the false theory of "the supposed rights of man." It was in 1784, as well as in 1790, that he warned against the delusion that men could, after all, freely choose their rulers or forms of government, instead of receiving them gratefully by inheritance. At both times he expressed his distrust of reason in politics, rejected the modern ideas of political representation, declared that criticism of the form of government would invite anarchy, dilated upon the wisdom of ancestors, and set forth his theory of pre-scription. Magnified by the Revolution against which they were directed, the *Reflections* of 1790 became a classic statement of counterrevolutionary conservatism, or rather reaction, since there were many practical conservatives who preferred to deal with problems on a less ideological basis.

For Burke, the Revolution was to be explained by the foolish-ness and mistaken ideas of inexperienced and insignificant persons of the middle classes. Other extreme antirevolutionaries, unable to see that the French Revolution had any serious causes, were easily persuaded that it was the work of conspirators. They attributed its appeal in other countries to similar causes. Actually, there was no organized or official French propaganda and no inter-national revolutionary organization whatsoever. Sympathy for the Revolution in other countries arose from the facts themselves, from the actual conditions and recent history of those countries, from promulgation of the Declaration of Rights, from the reading of the new French newspapers, and from hearing of various acts of defiance or rebellion. After July, 1789, with the revolutionaries in power, it was, in fact, the opponents of the Revolution, includ-ing the émigrés, who were reduced to conspiratorial methods and who therefore more readily attributed the same to their enemies. They saw Jacobin plotters everywhere. The king of Sweden, Gustavus III, preached a monarchist crusade against France. In March, 1792, he was assassinated by a Swedish nobleman. The "Jacobins" were blamed for his death. As early as 1790, in French émigré circles at Turin and Coblenz, it was said that "a democratic party" in Paris had set up a secret *club de propagande* to carry revolution to other countries. The idea spread in both Europe and America among persons hostile to the French Revolution. Actually, there was no such thing. The word itself was new, taken from the *De propaganda fide* of the Catholic church. Revolutionaries of the 1790s never spoke of "propaganda." It was the Counterrevolution that gave the word to the modern European languages and to some extent even invented the idea.

But if no government of the French Revolution ever sponsored an organization, secret or open, for the overthrow of neighboring governments, or even conducted any official campaign to advertise the merits of revolution for other countries, it is nevertheless true that the French Revolutionaries, especially in 1792 (with a few notable exceptions, such as Robespierre), believed and hoped that other peoples would soon rise up in revolutions of their own. They believed that such risings would be spontaneous. Nor were they altogether wrong. If the ideology of the Counterrevolution carried on that of the aristocratic resurgence and the anti-Enlightenment, the ideology of the Revolution, on its international level, carried on certain themes of the European Enlightenment itself. The French had a ready-made audience in all countries. When governments tried by censorship to keep out news of the French Revolution, they only added to the grievances against themselves.

"The moment has come for a new crusade, a crusade of universal liberty." So said Brissot on December 31, 1791. It was in vain that Robespierre resisted the drift toward war. "Begin by turning your attention back to your internal position," he advised at the Jacobin Club on January 2, 1792; "re-establish order among yourselves before carrying liberty elsewhere." Or again: "To want to give liberty to others before conquering it ourselves is to assure the enslavement of ourselves and the world." Robespierre never believed in the existence of any real revolutionary movement except in France. He feared that the antidemocratic elements in France would be strengthened by war. But most of the Jacobins, the popular revolutionaries of 1791–92, agreed with Brissot. They expected, in the event of war, a kind of universal upheaval in support of France.

The war, declared on April 20, soon took on a kind of international coloring. Brissot had been in America in 1788 and at Geneva during the troubles of 1782. The finance minister, Clavière, was a Genevan exile. The foreign minister, Lebrun, had spent years as a journalist at Liège and had contact with the Belgian Democrats. The commanding general, Dumouriez, was a ·

much-traveled adventurer of the eighteenth-century type. His second in command, the South American Miranda, dreamed of a revolution in Venezuela. Other generals were the Swiss La Harpe, several Irish, and an American named John Eustace.

Refugees from the unsuccessful Dutch and Belgian revolutions urged the French assembly to allow them to form fighting units of their own. A Belgian Legion was organized soon after the declaration of war against the Hapsburgs. For the Dutch exiles, eager to return in triumph to their own country, the problem was more difficult, since the United Provinces did not enter the war until 1793, and the Jacobins of 1792, for all the talk of world revolution, hesitated to add to their enemies. In July, 1792, however, at the demand of the Dutch exiles, and in the crisis of the Brunswick Manifesto, the assembly authorized a Free Foreign Legion, soon called the Batavian Legion. It was followed by an Allobrogian Legion for Swiss and Savoyards, a Germanic Legion, and an English Legion, which never took on much reality. From distant Kentucky, George Rogers Clark wrote to France asking for help in forming a "legion" to liberate the regions west of the Mississippi from Spain; he received it in 1793 when Genêt went as minister to the United States.

An "American Legion" was actually formed in September, 1792, and it illustrates especially well the prevailing mood of humanitarian liberation. It was not indeed organized for Americans from the United States, nor even for refugees of any kind, but at the request of free blacks living in France, who had mostly been born in the West Indies. The Constituent had granted full citizenship to free blacks in 1791; the Legislative Assembly had reaffirmed it against objections from the French *colons* in March, 1792. In their petition of September the French blacks, noting those facts, declared themselves to be eager like all Frenchmen "to fly to the frontiers." "If Nature," they said, "inexhaustible in its combinations, has made us different from Frenchmen in external signs, it has given us, like them, a heart that burns to fight enemies of the State." (It was rare during the French Revolution to speak thus of the "State," but at the moment there was no longer a monarchy and not yet a republic.) The president of the assembly, accepting with thanks, hailed this new evidence that

France would "soon become the capital of the free world and the grave of all thrones in the universe." A *Légion des Américains* was authorized, with a grant of a million livres. Its colonel was a certain Chevalier Saint-George, its lieutenant colonel Alexander Dumas, later a general in the French army and father of the novelist. Both Saint-George and Dumas had been born in the West Indies of French fathers and black mothers, then brought to France for their education and careers. This legion, which recruited several hundred officers and men, was later converted into a regular cavalry regiment.

But in this atmosphere of a universal struggle for liberty, for and against the Revolution, it was, of course, the French themselves who rushed to the colors to repel the invaders.

The Prussians crossed the frontier at the end of August and took Verdun. They were met by the French at Valmy on September 20 and retreated after a prolonged and inconclusive cannonade. They had expected no serious resistance, perhaps recalling the collapse of the Dutch Free Corps before Brunswick's Prussian army five years earlier. This time the citizen-soldiers held their ground. They made an impression on Goethe, who was there as an observer: "Here and on this day begins a new era of world history." They made a different kind of impression on the Prussian and Austrian governments, which were preoccupied by Russian successes in Poland and had no taste for a really difficult operation against France. The French passed to the offensive and crossed into the Austrian Netherlands. On November 6 Dumouriez, accompanied by the Belgian Legion, defeated the Austrians at Jemappes. All Belgium now lay open to the enthusiastic hordes of the French Republic.

For the Republic had been, in effect, proclaimed on September 22, 1792, simultaneously with the news from Valmy, in the opening sessions of the National Convention. This body, elected in principle by a universal male suffrage, was to govern for three years. More is said of it in the next chapter. In its early months it was preoccupied by three main developments. First, the Jacobins were again splitting. A new and determined group, led by Robespierre and called the Mountain (so called because they sat in the top seats of the hall in which they met), worked to get rid of Brissot, Condorcet, and other Jacobin luminaries of the preceding year who became known as the Gironde. So far as there was a difference between them, the Girondins were men who, while radical and democratic in their ideas, now tended to deplore the recent popular violence and to warn against anarchy, while the Mountain were more willing to raise no question about such outbreaks as the September massacres and welcomed cooperation with the aroused sans-culottes against the foreign enemy and the Counterrevolution.

The second question was what to do with Louis XVI, deposed and imprisoned since August 10. Of his "treason," or in objective language his nonacceptance of the Revolution, there was no doubt, and additional evidence was soon produced by discovery of an iron chest, in which letters written by the king to the Austrians were found. Some in the Convention favored bringing the king to trial, or after the verdict insisted on his execution; others demurred or sought delays or alternatives. Louis XVI was, in fact, tried by the Convention and put to death on January 21, 1793. His execution now entered into the orthodoxy of the Revolution. Those who had voted for it, the regicides, could not go back. Any compromise would be dangerous to them. Those who had opposed it, and who might therefore survive in some future negotiated arrangement, could not be trusted by those involved in the king's death. The latter reinforced the Mountain. The former, whose leaders were finally expelled from the Convention in June, 1793, fell into the limbo called the Gironde.

The third question was created by the French victories. What was to be done in foreign countries occupied by the forces of the Revolution? The Convention was not exactly a free agent. The Belgian exiles were returning to Belgium, and the suppressed Belgian Statists and Democrats were coming back to life. Dumouriez, the French commander, also developed a policy of his own.

It is well to look carefully at what happened in Belgium in the months following Jemappes, for it illustrates the mechanics by which the Revolution was to spread in the following years. On the one hand, the French Convention wished Belgium to be liberated or at least taken away from the Austrian empire, but it did not wish this liberation to be at French expense. On the other hand, Belgian revolutionaries came forward to greet the invaders, from whom they expected support for the independence that they had attempted in 1789. Like Bonaparte at Milan in 1796, Dumouriez found himself solicited by these advocates of revolution in their own countries; and not only by the Belgians, but also by the Dutch, who urged him to press on into the United Provinces, whose government was still technically neutral. Dumouriez, again like Bonaparte later, did not regard himself simply as the agent of a new, uncertain, and probably temporary regime in Paris. His very success was indeed a threat to that regime. He planned to build strength for himself among the Belgian Statists and Democrats, that is, among all anti-Austrian elements, and emerge as the prince or stadtholder of an independent Belgian republic. As such, he might even (again like Bonaparte later) have an influence on events in France. The Convention, however, reacted more violently against Dumouriez than the Directory ever did against Bonaparte. It did so because it had a popular enthusiasm on its side which the Directory never enjoyed.

The French at first favored the idea of an independent Belgian republic. Local elections were held in which the Belgian Democrats took most of the initiative. They had been inflamed by their previous failures and by the sojourn of many of them in France. To win mass support, they promised the abolition of tithes and seigneurial dues, proposed to shift the tax burden to the well-to-do, and in some cases promoted anticlerical outbursts. Dumouriez tried to hold the Democrats in check and to make himself agreeable to the Statists as well, since he hoped for support of the Belgian clergy against Austria and of Belgian businessmen for the provisioning of his army. For the same reason, he paid his Belgian contractors with hard money, not with assignats. His efforts to please the Statists were unavailing. From their leaders, some of whom had been in refuge in England since the Austrian restoration of 1790, came a troublesome message. While thanking the French for expelling the Austrians, it proposed a loosely confederated republic, with each province retaining its old constitution (as in 1790), but with a president or stadtholder to be elected from the ruling family of England, Holland, or Prussia. Neither the Convention nor Dumouriez nor the Belgian Democrats could entertain any such prospect.

The French replied in November by "opening" the river Scheldt. That is, they repudiated all the treaties by which the Dutch and British, for over a century, had held back the economic development of Belgium. The Convention thus appealed to the modern-minded Belgian businessmen, at Antwerp and Ghent, who tended to be Democrats on the Belgian scene and to be interested in maritime commerce.

Meanwhile the French armies had had other successes. They entered Frankfurt and Mainz in the Rhineland. They flowed into Savoy and Nice, two provinces of the king of Sardinia, who had come into the war on the side of the Prussians and Austrians. Local patriots flocked to meet the French generals. They sent delegations to Paris. They requested French aid against counter-revolutionary reprisals. The Convention, agitated by other questions, and not yet decided on a policy toward occupied areas, enacted as a temporary measure its famous decree of November 19, "according aid and fraternity to all peoples wishing to recover their liberty." Though officially explained as having no application to neutral countries, the decree aroused the fears of conservatives everywhere and was seized upon as a promise of support by revolutionary sympathizers of all nationalities. These were numerous, indeed; for example, on the very day before the decree, the Convention had received a letter of congratulation from the London Society for Constitutional Information, and an English-speaking group in Paris presented a similar statement; and a few weeks later Kosciuszko arrived to seek aid for Poland.

The French could do nothing for Poland, but the question of the occupied areas demanded action. As for Savoy, where the population was closely akin to the French, it was decided late in December to incorporate it as an eighty-fourth department. The northeastern regions presented more difficulty. Brissot and Danton spoke of pushing the French border to the Rhine. Condorcet wrote a pamphlet calling on the Dutch to revolt. The Dutch in Paris formed a Batavian Revolutionary Committee, but its spokesmen were received with skepticism when they appeared at the Jacobin Club. It was thought at the Jacobin Club that the Dutch patriots were rich enough to make their own revolution without depending on France. Nor was there much sentiment in France in favor of assisting the Belgians, still less of annexing them; the French thought the Belgians rather backward. It became clear also that because of internal disputes between Statists and Democrats no independent Belgian republic was feasible.

The war was costing the French about 100 million livres a month, much of which had to be paid out in gold and silver beyond the French frontiers. "There is everlasting talk that we are carrying liberty to our neighbors," said Cambon in the Convention. "What we are carrying to them is our hard currency and our food supplies." It was possible neither to abandon Belgium to the Austrians in time of war, nor to produce there a viable republic that would be of use to the French. Cambon, who was certainly not one of the wilder revolutionaries in the Convention, therefore proposed that the enemy governments and privileged classes should pay for the costs of war. *"Guerre aux châteaux, paix aux chaumières,"* he said in a seeming slogan of class struggle —war on the palaces and manor houses, peace for the huts of the poor.

The result was a second famous decree on December 15. French generals in occupied areas were instructed to proclaim "the abolition of existing taxes and revenues, of the tithe, of feudal dues both fixed and occasional, of servitude both of property and person, of exclusive hunting rights, nobility and all privileges in general. They will declare to the people that they bring peace, aid, fraternity, liberty and equality." They were also, in the name of the sovereignty of the people, to suppress all the old Belgian authorities, conduct new elections, and set up a provisional administration. The French, in short, while making no commitments of future independence to the local revolutionaries, would make use of the resources of the occupied areas, and especially the wealth of the former privileged classes, to support their own war effort.

The decree ended Dumouriez's plans for an independent Belgium of which he might be the head. He rushed to Paris to obtain its repeal, but only added to the suspicion which his

previous actions had aroused. The Convention had no desire to
use French men and money to obtain a principality for Dumouriez.
The Statists gave up all hope; they represented the very privileged
classes against which the decree was aimed. The Democrats were
discouraged also. They had wanted a republic in which they might
be in control, not a situation of wartime emergency with no
guarantees for the future, with French generals and civil commissioners exploiting the wealth of the country, and with little
protection against reprisals by fellow Belgians. For many Democrats, it would be better to be annexed to France. The Convention also, in these hectic weeks, during which Louis XVI was
put to death, and Dumouriez seemed increasingly disobedient,
came increasingly to favor annexation.

The first request for annexation came from Liège. The bishopric
of Liège, though it occupied about a fifth of the modern territory
of Belgium, which it in fact bisected, was not one of the ten
Austrian provinces. It was more industrialized than the Austrian
provinces, with more of both a business and a wage-earning industrial class. It had had a serious revolution of its own in 1789.
The Liège democrats had no desire to be incorporated with the
old-fashioned Austrian provinces in any such new invention as a
Belgian state. They preferred France. In the Austrian provinces
elections were held once again in the towns and villages. Dominated both by the French military and the Belgian Democrats,
who again promised abolition of tithes and seigneurial dues, which
an Austrian or Statist restoration would preserve, many of these
assemblies declared for incorporation with France.

The Convention annexed Belgium in February, 1793. Both the
Austrian provinces and Liège were to be recast as French departments, their citizens receiving the same rights as the French—and
the same obligations to accept paper money and to support the
war.

The Dutch revolutionaries viewed these events with consternation. And revolution in the Dutch Netherlands seemed increasingly
possible. Since the opening of the Scheldt, in November, the
British and Dutch governments had believed war with France
to be imminent. The execution of Louis XVI made the regicide
republic even less palatable in governing circles. The French,

seizing the initiative, declared war on the Dutch and British, who joined with Austria, Prussia, Sardinia, Naples, and Spain to form the First Coalition. The Convention instructed Dumouriez to invade the United Provinces. The Batavian revolutionaries went with him. A Dutch nobleman, Capellen van der Marsch, and a Dutch banker, Abbema, prepared a new constitution defining Liberty and Equality for their own country.

The Batavians wanted no such fate as had struck the Belgians, neither annexation nor application of the decree of December 15. They wanted their country to be not an occupied area but a separate republic in which a Dutch regime, while allied to France, would itself deal directly with the Dutch population in waging war against the Counterrevolution. The French resisted these demands. As Cambon dryly remarked to a Batavian delegation, the Dutch had had their revolution two centuries before, so that neither their Reformed church nor their Orange dynasty possessed much of the kind of wealth qualifying for confiscation under the December decree. Cambon proposed, therefore, to maintain the existing public revenues of Holland, subject to French control during the occupation. The French government, in short, did not in 1793 favor the revolutionizing of Holland. It was more stormy spirits, like Marat, who never held any office, that demanded a complete liquidation of the old Dutch institutions. In any case, a reversal in the military situation put an end to the problem for two years.

The Rhineland was simultaneously aroused. In these hundred-odd tiny German states, as in Belgium, there was as yet no defined sense of political nationality. It was easy to see the Revolution as a universal movement in which all could take part. "The spirit in these countries could not be worse," as Freiherr von Stein, the future reformer of Prussia, wrote to Berlin at this time. There were grievances everywhere. Peasants hoped to throw off seigneurial dues and dependency. At Catholic Aachen, the Protestants were irritated by the refusal of toleration. In the territories of Trier and Cologne the third estate demanded equality of taxation. The sight of French émigrés gathered at Coblenz turned many people against aristocratic pretensions. At Mainz Georg Forster, librarian of the University, organized a club of

French sympathizers in the summer of 1792. At first it was secret, but when the French occupied Mainz in October the club came into the open. In March, 1793, the members of similar clubs throughout the Rhineland assembled at Mainz. They called themselves the "Rhenish-German National Convention," and asserted the sovereignty of the people, for which purpose it was necessary to abjure the sovereignty of no fewer than twenty-three rulers within a space of merely fifty miles. The Convention, having really no base of its own, then voted for annexation to France. These Germans expected more liberty and equality, and more protection against Counterrevolution, inside the French Republic than in a political Germany that did not exist.

At Geneva also, though it was neutral and not occupied by the French, the thirty-year-old Genevan revolution renewed itself. The reaction imposed in 1782 had left many persons disaffected. With the French border only five miles away, and with French peasants forming their own municipalities and refusing to pay dues and taxes, the peasant "subjects" of the city of Geneva became restless. They joined with the "natives," or the judicially lowest class in the city, to form a new party of *égalisateurs*. In December, 1792, with adjoining Savoy becoming part of France, and with agitation spreading in the Rhineland and Belgium, the *égalisateurs* effected a small revolution at Geneva. They proclaimed a National Assembly for the minuscule population of about 30,000, developed their own political clubs, and two years later produced both a small indigenous Terror against the "traitors" of 1782 and a formally democratic constitution. But Geneva, now actually an enclave within France, never having been part of the Swiss Confederation, and unable to maintain its separate identity, was annexed to France in 1798.

All these revolutionary reverberations were abruptly terminated by a sharp change in the political weather. After Valmy, the Prussians shifted their counterrevolutionary effort from France to Poland, lest the Russians should have exclusive control in that country. To combat "the spirit of French democratism," and to undo the alleged "maneuvers of Jacobin emissaries" in both Poland and Prussia, Frederick William II sent his troops into Poland in January, 1793. Prussia and Russia signed agreements that led to the Second Partition, while recognizing a reduced and safely counterrevolutionary Polish state under the Targowica Poles. The Polish revolution was suppressed. Kosciuszko, unable to get French assistance in Paris, returned to Poland to lead another effort.

Meanwhile the Austrians resumed the offensive in the West, where they reoccupied Aachen and Liège. Dumouriez returned hastily from Holland to Belgium. Blocked in his plans for Belgium by the Convention, unable to dominate the conflicting Belgian parties, under suspicion in Paris for his dealings with army contractors, his independent behavior and his connections with Brissot and others who lacked enthusiasm for the king's death, Dumouriez was in need of another spectacular military victory, as at Jemappes. He gambled and lost, defeated by the Austrians at Neerwinden on March 18. He made his own armistice with the Austrians, turned "moderate," denounced the radicalism in Paris, and arrested five members of the Convention sent to inquire into his behavior. He tried to persuade his troops to follow him to Paris in a move to dissolve the Convention. The troops refused; the common man still believed in the Revolution. With a handful of followers, including the future king, Louis-Philippe, Dumouriez gave himself up to the Austrians.

The defection of Dumouriez was one of the many turning points of the Revolution. The French were driven from the Rhineland and Belgium. The Austrians re-entered France. The Revolutionaries were thrown into a frenzy. If the famous Dumouriez was a traitor, who could be trusted? The Brissot group, having long boasted of his merits, was hopelessly compromised. Thousands of Belgian, Dutch, and German revolutionaries fled back into France. Their recriminations added to a nightmare of fear and confusion in Paris that was compounded by food riots, by the denunciations of radical journalists, the beginning of insurrection in western France, and the cries of sans-culottes that the Convention was too timid and must be purged.

On the other hand, the forces of the Counterrevolution believed, in the spring of 1793, that the disturbance in France would soon be extinguished, as it apparently had been in Poland. They began to make plans for a restoration of order.

[4]

France: The Revolution Invincible

In the three years of the National Convention much of the later history of Europe was prefigured. A distinction between a more liberal Western and a more autocratic Eastern Europe began to form. The Counterrevolution was victorious in the East. Poland was crushed and partitioned. The Hapsburg monarchy turned conservative. The three Eastern monarchies after 1795 spent much of their energy, for generations, with spasmodic interruptions, in holding on to their respective shares of Poland, in nervous apprehension over continuing democratization in the West, and in protecting their noble, landowning, military, and courtly classes against a rising tide of popular disapproval, until all three monarchies were washed away in the First World War.

In France, and hence in the parts of Western Europe influenced by France, the course of events was different. Here the Counterrevolution had no such successes. It was defeated by the Convention, or rather by the French people as aroused, mobilized, equipped, and directed by the men who took that name. The word itself—Convention—new in French in this sense, was derived from the constitutional conventions in the United States.

The French Convention was surely one of the most remarkable bodies in the history of the world. "It created the politics of the impossible," said Alexis de Tocqueville, who did not admire it. "Stranger set of cloud-compellers the earth never saw," said Thomas Carlyle of its leading committee, the Committee of Public Safety, which Napoleon once called the only serious government of France during the Revolution. It was a "miracle," according to the archconservative Joseph de Maistre.

The Convention was composed of some 780 members, elected by universal suffrage at a time when there were no political parties to recommend candidates and under circumstances of war, invasion, suspicion, chaos, and popular tumult in September, 1792. Though including about twenty former nobles and forty clergy, the *Conventionnels* were overwhelmingly of the French middle classes. Almost half had been lawyers or in other professional careers before the Revolution; another quarter had been government officeholders; a tenth, in business. Hardly more than twenty were natives of Paris. They were men who had made themselves known in Paris or in their own districts during the preceding three years, but with few exceptions, such as Condorcet and the painter David, they had enjoyed no prominence before 1789. Apart from handfuls of political allies, for some had sat in the Constituent or Legislative Assemblies, they were largely unacquainted when they first came together. Yet this assemblage of nobodies, as they seemed to the elites of Europe, constructed a government, raised an army of almost a million men, and defeated the First Coalition. The Coalition, which in 1793 included every European power except Russia, was reduced at the end of 1795 to hardly more than Austria and Great Britain—and the British withdrew their small army from the Continent.

The Convention first followed Robespierre and then repudiated him. It first worked with the popular Revolutionaries and then brushed them aside. It conducted the Terror, then it stopped it. It instituted a system of price controls and managed economy, which it then abolished. It first produced the highly democratic constitution of 1793, then the constitution of 1795, which was more suited to the taste of the educated, property-owning, profit-seeking, energetic, and nonnoble elements of the French people, the "bourgeoisie," and which was soon copied in the Batavian, Helvetic, Cisalpine, and other sister republics as an example of democracy and indeed had admirers among the Irish and the Greeks. Thus situated in the mainstream of modern constitutional doctrine, this same extraordinary Convention, in its Robespierrist period, also expressed for the first time the modern theory of revolutionary dictatorship, endowing special courts and committees with special powers, which it then withdrew.

It is true that different men took the lead in these different phases, that about 120 members of the Convention were put under arrest for varying lengths of time, and that another 74 were executed; but it is equally true that many members simply changed their minds according to the shifting dangers of the moment as they saw them, and that the Convention as a whole can be blamed or credited for the actions taken in its name.

The Convention, to be sure, was no more a free agent in the politics of France than in its policies toward Belgium as described in the previous chapter. During its first year it was hard pressed by the militants of Paris, the popular democrats, or sans-culottes. These were the true activists among the common people. They were not of the lowest class, not recruited from the destitute, vagrant, unemployable, or most beaten-down members of society, yet in position and income they stood below the men who filled the Jacobin Club and the Convention. They were retail shopkeepers, small manufacturers, traders, artisans, barbers, and owners of cafés. Some lived by a daily wage, some by the profits of trade, some by the sale of articles produced by themselves and their employees. What they had in common was not the nature of their income or their role in production, so that Marxist historians refuse to call them a "class," and point to internal contradictions within their ranks. Being of the respectable and laboring poor, they shared in a simple manner of life and in a hostility toward the upper classes, including at times the Convention itself. They were inflamed by the excited expectations which the Revolution had aroused. They busily attended meetings at the neighborhood level in the "sections" of Paris or other cities. They belonged to popular clubs, and read or had read to them the inflammatory journals written by Marat and Hébert. As members of section committees, they served on patrols, conducted house searches, and administered a system of identity papers and ration cards. Occasionally they swarmed in a grand *journée révolutionnaire*.

The sans-culottes, like others, expected the Revolution to produce advantages for themselves. In their economic ideas they were traditional. Attached to the world of the small shop and of handicraft production, they were suspicious of wholesale trade, had an aversion to bankers, and looked upon large-scale or novel business enterprises as self-seeking devices of the rich. City dwellers, and poor at that, they were in no position to benefit by the purchase of former church or émigré properties. Nor would their problems have been relieved if farm plots or townhouses had been given to them free. They wanted a decent and familiar minimum livelihood, a wage they could live on in their existing jobs, and prices for bread and other necessities that they could afford to pay. They were the hardest hit of all social classes by inflation. Soaring prices and empty shelves at the bakers' or grocers' shops made them desperate—or it was their wives in such conditions that drove them on. They favored a strict control of prices for the goods they had to buy. The failure of goods to appear in the market they attributed to greed and conspiracy. They had in truth no economic theories. Their interest in constitutional liberties was minimal. The idea of the sovereignty of the people meant for them that they should take action themselves. They distrusted merely delegated authority and remote representative bodies. They favored a kind of direct democracy which expressed itself in section assemblies and demonstrations in the streets.

With a fierce belief in equality, they resented the scorn and condescension of their social superiors. Too close to practical life to expect an actual equality of wealth, they nevertheless wanted a real as well as a merely legal equality, and as small-scale economic conservatives of the eighteenth century they thought in terms of a fairly low level of material comfort, which they believed conducive to virtue. They assumed that equality would be served more by a prevention of great fortunes than by an increase of production or general rise in the standard of living. On matters of education and opportunity their ideas were unformed; if they had a popular suspicion of book learning and acquired refinements, they wanted more education, more literacy, more schools, and more vocational training for their children. They scoffed at the dress and manners of persons who did not work with their hands. Against the foppish frivolity, knee breeches, and lace cuffs of the upper classes they asserted the dignity of the long-trousered and rough-handed patriot, the good citizen and the common man. Anyone who seemed to waver in support of the Revolution they denounced as an aristocrat. They hoped eagerly for a new world, yet lived in fear of betrayal. Nor can their fears be dismissed as paranoid. They had once trusted Louis XVI, and he had turned against them. They had even trusted Lafayette and he had decamped. The émigrés of the aristocracy and church threatened to return. And it was simply a fact in 1793 that Europe was in arms against the French Revolution.

These were the people who had overthrown the monarchy on August 10 and to whom, in an important sense, the Convention therefore owed its very existence. The defection of Dumouriez reawakened the fear of betrayal. At the same time, the value of the assignat was rapidly falling, as huge amounts of paper money were issued to cover war costs by a government whose future was open to question. Price inflation and actual scarcity added to the popular anger. News also came of rebellion in the provinces against Paris. In the Vendée, near the mouth of the Loire, the rural population revolted against their neighboring towns and against the orders of the Convention. Priests, gentry, and secret agents of the émigrés and of the British government exploited their discontent. An altogether different kind of revolt also began, the "federalist rebellion," in which many of the great provincial cities turned against Paris. Their local leaders, often men of wealth, hitherto in the forefront of the Revolution, believed that the Convention that was supposed to represent them had fallen victim to the ignorant masses in the capital. France was sinking into civil war, while Austrian, Prussian, Dutch, Spanish, and Sardinian troops, together with elements of the British fleet off the Breton coast, threatened at least five sides of the hexagon.

A majority in the Convention shared the alarm of the sans-culottes while hoping to escape their domination. A few days after the defection of Dumouriez the Convention created a special executive committee which, re-elected every month, became the famous Committee of Public Safety. It also set up a Revolutionary Tribunal to satisfy the clamor against suspects, and to avoid outbreaks of the kind of lynch law of which the September Massacres, not to mention the murders of July, 1789, had given such gruesome examples. It imposed a maximum on the price of bread. Still the sans-culottes were not satisfied. They were supported by the Commune of Paris and by Robespierre and certain others in the Convention, who either agreed with the popular militants, or believed that such people must not be spurned in time of war and emergency, or welcomed their aid in the overthrow of the "faction" —that is, Brissot and other rivals or obstructionists in the Convention. A three-day insurrection, from May 31 to June 2, culminated in the besieging of the Convention by tens of thousands of armed patriots from the city. Finding resistance impossible, the Convention yielded, promised further extraordinary measures, and decreed the arrest of twenty-nine of its own members, known historically as the Gironde. Early in September another monster demonstration against the Convention reaffirmed the popular pressure.

The Mountain, as the surviving active Jacobins were called, were now in power in alliance with the sans-culottes. It is impossible to give a figure for the number of *Conventionnels* who belonged to the Mountain. It is enough to say that a small group, without determinate membership, but including Robespierre, Saint-Just, and Danton, was able for a year after June, 1793, by exclusion, intimidation, persuasion, and arguments of public emergency, to carry a majority in the Convention, including some who became more moderate, or even reactionary, after the crisis had passed, and after the execution of Robespierre.

Since the Convention was in principle primarily a constituent body, the Mountain produced a constitution within a few days, later known as the constitution of the Year I, replete with much apparatus of democracy, including an elaborate declaration of rights, universal suffrage for men, and machinery for popular initiative and referendum. Submitted for popular ratification (as neither the preceding constitution nor the American federal constitution had ever been), it was credited with 1,801,918 affirmative against 11,610 negative votes. The Convention decided, however, reasonably enough, that the moment was unfavorable for the inauguration of constitutional government, and so put the new document in a state of suspension for the duration of the war. It never went into effect. Most of the genuine sans-culottes and popular democrats accepted this action. They had faith in the Convention now that the "soft" element of the Gironde was eliminated. But some of the more vociferous types, men like Hébert, who were not members of the Convention, and who less and less spoke for the real sentiments of the popular classes, began immediately to ask that the constitution be made operative. They were not constitutionalists; they simply wanted to dissolve the Convention and get rid of its Committee of Public Safety. They were revolutionaries even against the Revolutionary government, whom Robespierre soon branded as "ultras."

For the Convention, in suspending the constitution, created the *gouvernement révolutionnaire*, the Revolutionary government known as such, in the sense of extraconstitutional, which lasted until after the death of Robespierre a year later. Its most vital organ was the Committee of Public Safety, created in April, then strengthened after the expulsion of the Girondins by the addition of Robespierre, Saint-Just, Couthon, Carnot, and others. A Committee of General Security, never fully subordinated to the Committee of Public Safety, coordinated the surveillance of suspicious persons that had sprung up spontaneously throughout the country and so came to act as a supreme political police. Its work was organized under a draconian and omnivorous Law of Suspects. The Revolutionary Tribunal was enlarged, and its procedures were expedited. To assure the execution of its orders throughout the country, and to check deviations of every kind, the Convention dispatched its own members to the departments and to the armies, known as *représentants en mission*, who reported directly to the Committee of Public Safety. A law of December, 1793, in effect gave the same committee control over all local government, which had been left in chaos by the lack of time for the constitution of 1789–91 to establish itself, and by civil war and rebellion in some parts of the country. Alongside all this official machinery were the thousands of political clubs, which looked for guidance to the

Jacobin Club of Paris, without being controlled by it, and whose members lent aid on the local scene in carrying out directives from Paris.

For a year the best-known member of the Revolutionary government was Robespierre. He was not known, however, in the sense that leaders of twentieth-century revolutions have been known. The simplifications of memory, legend, and history in later times magnified his position. In his own day he was one among many. No cult of personality or aura of infallibility surrounded him in his lifetime. He owed his influence to his persistent faith in the Revolution, to his willingness to speak up at critical moments, to an eloquence which then found favor, and to the reputation for disinterested honesty for which he was called the Incorruptible. He held no office except membership in the Convention and its ruling committee, which had no chairman. Having written no books nor ideological tracts, he was known only by his speeches. The most important of these speeches, printed at the moment of delivery, and collected and reprinted beginning in the 1830s, offered a philosophy of the French Revolution at its most radical and democratic phase. Robespierre never used the word "dictatorship" in a favorable sense. Indeed, he repeatedly warned against the kind of military dictatorship with which Bonaparte "ended" the Revolution. There is no evidence that he regarded himself as any kind of personal ruler. He did express, however, in December, 1793, in justifying the Revolutionary government, a theory of a collective, civilian, revolutionary dictatorship such as later revolutionaries were to develop. He saw it as a powerful, supposedly temporary, and preconstitutional regime, acting by the authority of the people and designed to overcome opposition until a new form of government and society could be instituted.

The Year II of the Republic may be thought of with some abuse of exactitude as the year from July, 1793, when Robespierre was elected to the Committee of Public Safety, until July 24, 1794 (9 Thermidor), when he was outlawed by the Convention and put to death. It was the climactic year of the Revolution, a year, in Robespierre's phrase, of Virtue and Terror.

The Terror was an official and publicly acknowledged program of repression. Neither its courts, its prisons, nor its scaffolds were secret. It used neither torture, nor brainwashing, nor ostentatious self-abasing confessions. It was not the sporadic violence of individual daredevils and idealists in protest against an overwhelming power. It was not the act of a desperate government to extirpate its adversaries in one concerted slaughter, like the Massacre of St. Bartholomew of 1572. It was a policy of state of a more rational eighteenth-century kind, designed both to assure victory in the war and to consolidate the revolutionary Republic. Properly speaking (that is, ruling out the unauthorized terrorism of the preceding September Massacres, or the execution of Louis XVI by vote of the Convention), the Terror began in the spring of 1793, in the atmosphere produced by the defection of Dumouriez, the internal rebellions and the Austrian invasion. Its first justification was to ferret out friends of the enemy in time of war. The category of suspects and subversives, at first realistic enough, in that the Counterrevolution really existed and the Convention by no means enjoyed the support of the whole population, rapidly expanded to include those who were merely moderate, doubtful, or insufficiently enthusiastic for the new regime or the new rulers. Enemies of the state came to mean opponents or rivals to the men in power. Denunciation and use of the death penalty became a fatally easy habit. Anyone who had played any part in the Revolution, since 1789, in remote villages as much as in Paris, lived in fear that somebody might "return." But there was a note of special ferocity in the phrase of Barère, spoken in the Convention for the Committee of Public Safety: "Only the dead never come back."

Quantitatively, and in terms of persons actually condemned to death by the various revolutionary tribunals, the scope of the Terror was surprisingly limited. About 17,000 were convicted and executed. Two-thirds of these, including those who perished in the famous drownings at Nantes and fusillades at Lyons, were punished in consequence of armed rebellion. Three-fifths of those executed were peasants or workingmen. Only 8 percent were nobles; for nobles who accepted the abolition of their former status, and who neither emigrated nor had close relatives in the emigration, faced no official accusations. It is true that another

20,000 may have died "unofficially" in 1793–94 and that over 100,000 were detained as suspects. Quantitatively, however, the Terror by which the First Republic sought to establish itself took hardly more lives than the repression by which the Third Republic established itself against the revolutionary Commune of 1871.

But the Terror was not merely a quantitative phenomenon. For one thing, apart from the mass executions in punishment for rebellion, it tended to be very selective, falling on personalities and political groups whose memory was not forgotten in later times. Thus Marie Antoinette followed Louis XVI to the guillotine. The Girondins expelled on June 2 were executed in October. Next, under Robespierre's lead, came the turn of various "ultras," *enragés*, and persons called Hébertists; then came the "indulgents," or Dantonists, members of the Convention who wished to relax the program of repression before victory was assured. In the so-called Great Terror of June-July, 1794, many died for no more than guilt by association. On July 24 the end came for Robespierre himself and four colleagues in the Convention, some of whose members at the moment thought Robespierre too moderate, and some too strict, but all of whom were now afraid that he might strike them next. All these "martyrdoms" left their legends. The Girondin and Dantonist legends gradually faded out; but the French Right long remembered the king and queen as victims of the Republic, while the Left considered Robespierre a victim of the bourgeoisie until, after about 1950, a kind of New Left regarded Robespierre as a bourgeois himself and looked back with sympathy on those that Robespierre had denounced as ultras.

But the real peculiarity of the Terror was its association with Virtue, that is, with a dream of democracy. As Robespierre said, the mainspring of popular government in peacetime was virtue, but in time of revolution both virtue and terror—"Virtue without which Terror is evil, Terror without which Virtue is helpless." That virtue was essential to democracy was an eighteenth-century commonplace. It meant that democracy would not work without civic spirit, a degree of self-effacement, an acceptance of equality and contentment with simple things. But Robespierre went beyond former theorists of democracy such as Rousseau and Montesquieu, not to mention Jefferson and John Adams. For one thing, he was working to establish it in time of war against violent opposition. Hence the Terror, meaning the program of repression, followed from "the principle of democracy applied to the pressing needs of the country." For another, he had in mind a representative democracy in a populous, complex, and civilized country, not the direct democracy of a small and simple people to which political theory had hitherto confined it.

Robespierre's purpose, to make France a democracy, was by no means shared by the Convention as a whole, even at the height of excitement in the Year II. But it was clear enough, especially as expressed in his speech of February 5, 1794, in the Convention. Formerly, until the exclusion of the Girondins, he had favored the direct democracy and spontaneous local initiatives of the Commune and the sans-culottes in their "primary" section assemblies. He had even at times favored popular insurrection. Now he stressed the need of representative and centralized government. "Democracy," he said, "is not a state in which the people, continually assembled, itself directs public affairs." It would only fail if "a hundred thousand fragments of the people" acted in contrary directions. "Democracy" therefore (he often used the word in this speech) was a state in which the people, while sovereign, "does for itself what it can do well, and by its delegates what it cannot." He expressed, in short, now that he was in power himself, an idea quite foreign to Rousseau, of democracy as a form of representative government. Against ultras like Hébert (and the still obscure Babeuf of 1794), who demanded the constitution of 1793 and so in effect the dissolution of the Convention, Robespierre urged that the Convention be trusted as a true representative body. It would, he thought, assure the true and full equality of rights which was the aim of the Revolution. Democracy, rightly understood, would strengthen France in the war, because it gave each citizen and each soldier something to fight for. "That, in my opinion, is the real reason why the tyrants allied against the Republic will be defeated."

To reinforce this political or legal democracy, Robespierre, Saint-Just, and those who agreed with them favored a society of small private property, of family farms and family shops, in which great inequalities of wealth would disappear. The Convention, therefore, during the Year II, required the equal division of property by inheritance, and eased the terms on which the property of émigrés might be sold, allowing sale in small parcels and payment over ten years. At the end of February, 1794, by the two "laws of Ventôse," as they moved to liquidate the ultras, and to win over the sans-culottes, Robespierre and Saint-Just took a further step toward a redistribution of wealth. The new laws prescribed, somewhat ambiguously, that poor persons should be "indemnified" from the property of suspects. The innovation was that mere suspects, and not merely convicted émigrés and the church, should have their wealth subjected to confiscation, and that the proceeds should be given gratis to the poor as such, and not resold to those who had sufficient money or credit. The Ventôse program never went into effect. It seems neither to have impressed the sans-culottes at the time nor to have been remembered by Babeuf's Conspiracy of Equals only two years later. It was not even well suited to the actual needs of the sans-culottes, who would have preferred higher wages, lower prices, better housing, and controlled rents. It illustrated, however, the almost Jeffersonian ideal of the Robespierrists, a preindustrial world of nearly equal property owners, each independent in his own livelihood, as a foundation for an equal and democratic society.

It seems likely that the Terror, at least until its final two months, as a form of discipline imposed on a country in turmoil, and a means of repressing rebellious and subversive activities which really existed, contributed to the victory of the Republic in the war. Such was its main aim for most members of the Convention. It did not, and probably could not, serve the more specifically Robespierrist purpose of introducing democracy. That any free government could emerge from so much fear and suspicion was more than doubtful. Two more empirical facts made impossible the kind of democracy envisaged by Robespierre. The most eager democrats were not yet ready to settle for merely representative government. And the middle-class membership of the Convention, if willing to go along with Robespierre while the crisis lasted, were not ready to act as mere spokesmen of the lower classes, or passively reflect popular ideas at variance with the reconstruction of France, or those principles of the Enlightenment which remained even in 1794 the real essence of the Revolution.

But if the Convention in the Year II did not make France a democracy, it did a good deal else. Only one who has read its debates can appreciate the range of this extraordinary body, which, at the height of the Terror, carried on rational discussions from which the metric system, the *grandes écoles*, and the Napoleonic legal codes were in part derived. More urgently, the Convention organized the country for both foreign and civil war. Responding to the popular clamor for a maximum effort, it decreed the *levée en masse*, by which all young men were made subject to military service and women and older men were drawn into the production of supplies and munitions. Controls were extended to both prices and wages, and a Subsistence Commission, subordinated to the Committee of Public Safety, developed a program of priorities for production and distribution. Using these controls, the government was able both to buy what it needed with its paper money and to satisfy in some measure the complaints against shortages and high prices. The value of the assignat as against gold, which fell both before and after, was held steady while the Revolutionary government was in power. Never in the past, and not again until 1914, had the economy, resources, and manpower of a large country been so centrally managed for a single overriding purpose. It was not until the First World War that historians, instead of deploring its economic unorthodoxy, realized what the Revolutionary government had accomplished.

Thanks mainly to Lazare Carnot, the paroxysm of the *levée en masse* was converted into the discipline of an organized army. It was an army of a new kind, whose significance was soon seen by many enlightened military experts, especially in Germany. The Old Order, with its frequent but limited wars, had depended on small forces of professional, highly drilled, and more or less automatized soldiers. Now in 1793 for the first time a very large army was fired by a political idea. The officers, including the generals, were promoted from below at very young ages. They made up in dash what they lacked in experience, and given the simple military technology of the time they soon proved as competent as the more highborn officers of the Coalition. The common soldier prized his liberty but accepted command; he retained his dignity under a discipline which did not degrade him. Since he believed in what he was doing, he could be trusted to fight alone. Many fought as individual skirmishers, deploying in pairs, taking cover, and selecting targets at will, while preparing the way for the main body of troops which they rejoined when the order was given. "The physical agility and high intelligence of the common man," wrote the German professional Scharnhorst, "enables the French *tirailleurs* to profit from all advantages offered by the terrain and the general situation, while the phlegmatic Germans, Bohemians, and Dutch form on open ground and do nothing but what their officer orders them to do." Against the French *tirailleurs* the old tactics of infantry, consisting in essentially unaimed volleys fired by troops drawn up stiffly in line, was almost useless. The Republican armies benefited also from improvements in French artillery made before the Revolution. The development of the division as a combat unit between the regiment and the field army offered new room for generalship and made for speedier tactics on a large terrain. With new units of citizen soldiers combined with what was left of the Bourbon army, a force of a million men was created, the first truly national army, reflecting in both its officer and enlisted ranks all classes and kinds of people. Within a few months the internal rebellions were put down. In June, 1794, the new army defeated the Austrians at Fleurus, reoccupied Belgium, and initiated the French preponderance that was to last for twenty years.

Meanwhile the tide of spontaneous popular revolution from below reached its high point in the last months of 1793, and then began to recede. The Revolutionary government, once in power, proposed to govern. In organizing for victory, it turned against the popular forces that had brought it into being. A new kind of order replaced an anarchic enthusiasm. For example, the activists who had demanded a *levée en masse* also formed what was called an *armée révolutionnaire*, a straggling formation of armed civilians, recruited mainly in Paris, who went about the country arousing patriotism, exposing the moderate and the unreliable, and searching for food in peasants' barns. The Committee of Public Safety first accepted it but managed in a few months to get it disbanded. But the climax of revolutionary excitement was marked also by a movement to exterminate Christianity.

In October, 1793, the Convention adopted a new calendar. The first day of the Republic, September 22, 1792, was designated retrospectively as the initial day of Year I, and the names of the months were replaced by new ones. Each month had thirty days, with the twelfth month followed by five special supplementary days, or six in leap year. Each month was divided into three weeks of ten days each. The ten-day week (a reminder that decimal coinage and the metric system originated at this time) was known as the *décade*, and the tenth day as the *décadi*. Every *décadi* was set aside for rest and the celebration of various natural objects. Thus the Revolutionary calendar did away with the whole cycle of Sundays (the Sabbath), of church holy days, and saints' days, and was obviously designed to blot out traditions and customs of the past, especially those of Roman Catholicism.

Even the constitutional clergy now came under suspicion. Some unfrocked themselves and some took wives as if to prove themselves wedded to the Revolution. Throughout the country, and by no means only in Paris, crowds invaded the churches, smashed images, and dragged religious vestments through the streets, partly from hatred of priests and disgust at superstition and partly in a genuine belief that if Christianity was opposed to the rights of man, it could not be much of a religion. A cult of the Revolution sprang up, which used cathedrals and churches for improvised civil ceremonies. In Paris, the procurator of the Commune, Chaumette, brought it about that the Paris churches were reconsecrated to Reason. The most famous incident in this movement of dechristianization was the great festival of Liberty on November 10 at Notre Dame, now called the Temple of Reason. It is less well remembered that the same Chaumette, on the *décadi* of 30 Pluviose of the Year II (February 18, 1794), at another ceremony at the Temple of Reason, made a speech in praise of the equality between races and the abolition of slavery in the French colonies, decreed by the Convention a few days before. A group of *citoyens de couleur* presented laurel crowns to delegates from the Convention who were present.

The Revolutionary government, however, in the persons of Robespierre and the Committee of Public Safety, withheld its approval from the more extreme anti-Catholic manifestations, which it believed to be "exaggerated" and politically unwise. Not very successfully, it ordered that law-abiding priests should not be molested. "Atheism is aristocratic," said Robespierre, and in May he prevailed upon the Convention to announce, in a formal decree, that the French people recognized the existence of God and the immortality of the soul. In June, on Robespierre's initiative, the Convention instituted the cult of the Supreme Being, which, less aggressive than the preceding cult of Reason, was supposed both to be acceptable to religious believers and to offer an outlet for the new feelings generated by the Enlightenment and the Republic.

Throughout the Year II the same struggle between the Revolutionary government and the forces of popular revolution proceeded on other fronts. The independent pursuit of suspects by local militants was coordinated by the Committee of General Security. The committeemen of the section assemblies, hitherto self-starting instigators of local action, received a small wage and were turned into minor government functionaries. The sans-culottes insisted on control of prices, but the government attempted to control wages also, and to allow enough profit for the merchants on whom it depended to remain in business. Since the Paris Commune generally took the workingman's point of view, it was filled with Robespierrist appointees and ceased to be independent of the Convention. Persons who continued to storm against "the aristocracy of merchants," or those who continued to clamor for direct action in the Paris sections, and who accused the Revolutionary government of moderatism—persons like Hébert and the *enragés* Varlet, Leclerc, and Roux—were branded as ultras by Robespierre. (Probably Marat would have been included, had he not been assassinated in July, 1793.) Hébert reciprocated by denouncing a new faction of *endormeurs*, by which he meant that Robespierre and the Committee of Public Safety, like Brissot before them, were putting the Revolution to sleep. In March, 1794, the Cordeliers Club made plans for a new mass demonstration to purge the Convention, like the one of the preceding May, 1793, that had forced the arrest of the Girondins. Some of the foreign revolutionaries in Paris likewise believed that the Revolutionary government was becoming too moderate. On March 9 the Batavian Revolutionary Committee petitioned the Committee of Public Safety to invade and revolutionize Holland. One of the signers was the Dutch financier, Kock, a friend of Hébert's. The group included also the eccentric Anacharsis Cloots, a rich radical from the Rhineland who had close connections in Holland, but who had become a French citizen and member of the Convention. The only foreign-born member except Thomas Paine (who had been arrested because of his English birth and association with the Brissot group), Cloots was a devotee of world revolution who announced that his constituency was "the human race." Extremists of the international and the popular revolution had basically little in common, but they were both demonstratively anti-Christian, inclined to see all tyrants of the universe as their enemies, and to think that the Revolutionary government might betray the Revolution if it continued to oppose them.

Robespierre, or rather the Committee of Public Safety, sent a group of leading ultras to the guillotine in March, 1794, grouping them together in an imaginary foreign conspiracy. To preserve some kind of middle way, it decreed the same fate for Danton and the emerging "moderate" wing of the Mountain. Against moderates, it reaffirmed the policy of repression, producing the spasms of the Great Terror of June and July, when "the heads fell like slates," 1,376 of them in Paris alone. Against ultras of all kinds, it proceeded with the program of control over the Commune and the Paris sections, tried to enforce the wage controls, dissolved the Batavian, Belgian, and Germanic legions, crushed the Batavian Revolutionary Committee, recalled certain members of the Convention who had committed excesses as *représentants en mission* (like Carrier at Nantes, and Fouché at Lyons), and adopted the worship of the Supreme Being in the hope of peaceful celebration of the New Era.

But the Revolutionary government, while thus consolidating

its position, lost support. The popular militants, brushed aside, sank into apathy and frustration. The Convention, to which Robespierre had always looked for legality, became alarmed when so many of its members, whether moderate or extremist, came under suspicion. In July the Convention rebelled against Robespierre, whom the sans-culottes did not now seriously defend. By a kind of palace revolution, or conspiracy within the Convention, with little mass demonstration either for or against him, Robespierre was apprehended at the Paris Hôtel de Ville, and died on 10 Thermidor of the Year II, or July 25, 1794.

Since the forces against Robespierre were a mixed lot, it was not immediately clear whether the regime following his fall would be more vehemently revolutionary or less so. Within a few weeks, however, since the sources of popular revolution had been dried up by the Revolutionary government itself, those who had always opposed the Terror and the whole system of the Year II, or who believed that they had served their purpose and were no longer needed, asserted themselves. In June the French had defeated the Austrians at Fleurus, the armies of the Coalition were in headlong retreat, and emergency measures could no longer be accepted as a military necessity. Within a few months, the Convention cut down the powers of the Committee of Public Safety, abolished the Revolutionary Tribunal, closed the Jacobin Club, and discouraged the "popular societies" throughout the country. It was now the "terrorists," or those who had been most conspicuous in the repression and denunciation of the Year II, who found themselves pursued as anarchists and disorganizers. The Convention likewise abandoned the system of regulated economy and controlled prices. The system had made possible the mobilization of the country and the rallying of mass support, but it had not worked very well, and in the general state of economic science, statistical reporting, and administrative machinery, such procedures of planned production and distribution could hardly become permanent. But the abruptness with which the controls were removed caused great distress. The assignat fell to new lows. Food prices soared, while scarcities remained, and the common people of Paris suffered more from starvation, cold, and exposure in the winter of 1794–95 than at any time during the Revolution. Many began to look back on the days of Robespierre with regret.

In a kind of revival of sans-culottism, in May, 1795, an angry mass of men and women, shouting for food and the Constitution of the Year I, invaded the hall of the Convention. The event is known by its date, Prairial of the Year III. The reaction of the Convention was very different from that on a similar occasion, two years before, when invasion by the populace had caused the expulsion of the Girondins. Troops were called to the city. Assisted by young men from more comfortable homes, the "gilded youth," they pressed into the working-class quarters and stamped out the popular agitation. In the repression that followed, a great many militants were sent to prison, including "Gracchus" Babeuf. These episodes of 1795 have been better remembered in socialist than in bourgeois history, being seen as early manifestations of a new revolutionary movement against the bourgeoisie.

The Convention, composed of middle-class Frenchmen, and alarmed and annoyed by the continuing popular threats and provocation, proceeded to write a new constitution, by which the regime commonly known as the Directory was established. While granting an almost universal suffrage, this constitution of the Year III, like the one of 1789–91, provided a series of electoral colleges to assure that stable and substantial citizens would be elected. The new legislature was in two chambers (the Five Hundred and the "Ancients" or Senators), which in turn chose the Executive Directory, or five-man governing board. It was hoped that both democracy and dictatorship might thus be avoided.

The greatest fear of the Convention, however, as always, and despite the great military victories of 1794–95, was the Counter-revolution by which the monarchy might be restored. The new king, or rather pretender, who called himself Louis XVIII, made clear in his Declaration of Verona of 1795 what a royal restoration would entail: punishment for persons involved in the Revolution, re-establishment of the church, restoration of the Three Orders and return of the old parlements, in short a reversal of everything that had happened since 1789. And passing beyond mere declarations, a force of émigrés, supported by the British fleet, attempted to land at Quiberon Bay on the Breton coast, hoping to rally the disaffected peasantry of the west and then march on Paris. They were cut to pieces by a republican army under General Hoche.

To protect the incoming constitutional republic from such royalist reaction, as well as to assure their personal safety, compromised as they were by the Terror, the *Conventionnels* added a kind of rider to the new constitution before dissolving. They provided that, in the first elections for the two chambers under the Directory, two-thirds of those elected must be former members of the Convention. Places in the new government were thus created for about five hundred members of the outgoing Convention, safe at least until the elections of 1797. A cry of protest arose against this obvious move for self-perpetuation. It was especially sharp among those enemies of the Convention who now contemplated some kind of royalist restoration with increasing favor. The result, in October, 1795, or Vendémiaire of the Year IV, was a phenomenon new to the Revolution, a royalist or conservative uprising of almost mass dimensions in Paris, with demonstrators very different from those of the preceding Prairial swarming through the city and besieging the Convention. The Convention, as in Prairial, called on the army. General Bonaparte with his whiff of grapeshot dispersed the insurgents of Vendémiaire.

The Convention disbanded, and the Directory took over, at the end of October, 1795. The Directory lasted exactly four years. Throughout, it depended on the army, the republican army created in the Year II, and which the Convention had called upon in the Year III to protect itself from the violence of both Left and Right. Caught between extremes, seeking a middle course, despised by the idealistic of all camps, representing no crusade for either king or people, and later disparaged by the admirers of Napoleon, the Directory never enjoyed a reputation equal to its actual merits. Essentially, it meant to preserve the Revolution of 1789. It opposed, with equal anathemas, both a restoration of the Old Order and a revival of the turbulent democratic pressures of the year of the Terror. Detesting both the old aristocracy and the new popular militants, it was a regime of the upper middle classes, at a time when the "middle" had a clear social significance, and when the middle classes, including persons who were wealthy and well established, still felt and indeed gloried in their commitment to the Revolution.

In the oscillations between Left and Right from which the Directory was never free, the first disturbance came from the famous conspiracy of Babeuf. More of an actual conspiracy than any earlier action to push the Revolution forward, it posed no serious threat to the Directory, since, unlike the sans-culotte pressures of 1792 and 1793, it had no mass support, and, being secret, was in fact almost unknown until publicized by the Directory itself. It has been seen retrospectively, however, as an early stage, or indeed as the first practical effort, in the rise of a working-class or communist revolutionary movement. It represented a revival, not of the true sans-culottism or spontaneous popular democracy of 1792–93, but of those ultras whom Robespierre himself had refused to accept.

When the Directory came into office, the most recent threat had been from the Right, as shown in the Vendémiaire uprising and the attempted Anglo-royalist landing at Quiberon Bay. The Directory, therefore, began by seeking support on the Left. It hoped to favor reliable patriots. It released those whom the Convention had imprisoned after the Prairial affair. These included Babeuf and the Italian-born Filippo Buonarroti. Babeuf, who had been anti-Robespierrist before Thermidor, was mainly interested in a real equality of wealth in place of a merely formal equality of rights. Buonarroti, who had been a strong Robespierrist in the Year II, and had in fact faithfully served the Revolutionary government, was mainly interested in the revolutionizing of Italy, by which he meant less an equalization of wealth than a democratic upheaval against kings, clergy, and aristocrats. Buonarroti believed that a French government more radical than that of the Directory would support such a revolution in Italy.

Emerging from prison, in which they had the leisure for mutually instructive conversation, Babeuf, Buonarroti, and others began to frequent the Pantheon Club, and Babeuf edited a paper called the *Tribun du Peuple*. In its pages, at the end of 1795, Babeuf published and discussed a proposed *Manifeste des plébéiens*. The true revolution would not be over, he said, until everyone had a genuinely equal share of the world's goods. To obtain this real equality private property must be abolished outright, since a mere equal redistribution would not last. Each person, therefore, while working according to his interests and talents, would place the product of his labor in a common store, from which each would receive an exactly equal share of what he needed for his own use. It would suffice to have only a "simple administration," to provide "a sufficiency for all but no more than a sufficiency." He also pointed to the army, numbering "twelve hundred thousand men," to show that the idea was feasible. This uncomplicated community of goods, with equalization at a modest level—as much an abolition of the rich as of the poor—had formerly been described in books, notably in Morelly's *Code de la Nature*, which was then believed to have been written by Diderot. The novelty was that Babeuf, after living for six years in an actual revolution, proposed a line of action by which he believed the idea might be realized.

Reflecting on the past, early in 1796, Babeuf announced his conversion to Robespierrism. In 1794 Babeuf had favored Hébert, in 1795 he joined in the excoriation of the deceased Robespierre, in 1796 he adopted him as his predecessor. We must remember, he said, thinking of Robespierre and Saint-Just, that "we are only the second Gracchi of the French Revolution." His expressed reason was that Robespierre had stood for democracy, which Babeuf felt that he himself represented. In addition, Robespierre offered far more than Hébert for one seeking a sense of ongoing revolution. Robespierre had actually been in power, it might be thought that he had almost succeeded, his name carried prestige among revolutionaries unreconciled to the Directory. In fact, Babeuf differed widely from Robespierre in both ideas and methods, anticipating the socialist program and the more professional revolutionary activities of the nineteenth and twentieth centuries. To lend credibility to the new movement as a revolution, it was all the more necessary to establish its continuity with the Revolutionary government of the Year II. As Babeuf's associate, Sylvain Maréchal, put it: "The French Revolution is only the forerunner of another revolution far greater, far more solemn, which will be the last."

Babeuf developed a secret organization which in a few months probably involved several thousand people, most of whom knew only that an insurrection against the Directory was intended, after which political democracy in a Robespierrist sense was to be re-established. Only a handful in the inner circle shared in Babeuf's proto-communist program. These organizers expected to reveal their true purposes, even to their own followers, only after the Directory had been overthrown. Had they made the abolition of property an explicit objective, their followers would have been few indeed. Primarily, therefore, the conspiracy as a whole was another attempt at insurrection or renewed revolution, as in the past, only more secret; as such, it gathered a relatively large number of old-time political democrats and former sans-culottes around a small nucleus which intended a more thoroughly social reorganization. It incorporated an elitist principle by which a small and determined group, having no confidence in majority votes, prepared a revolutionary dictatorship beforehand in secret and undertook as an enlightened and vigorous vanguard to lead the true people in the necessary revolutionary direction. The idea anticipated Blanqui and Lenin more than Marx.

On March 30, 1796, the inner group set up an insurrectionary committee with a view to overturning the Directory in the near future. On May 10, through an informer, the committee was arrested by the police. The Directory might have consigned the conspirators simply to terms in prison, as it was habitually doing with the some two or three hundred other unregenerate activists of the Year II. It decided, instead, in order to inspire the confidence of conservative republicans, to publicize the supposed menace and subject the conspirators to a dramatic trial. Babeuf used the occasion to make speeches on democracy, saying little of communism, insisting that his views were no different from those of Diderot and the *philosophes* and hence denying the very originality for which he was later admired. Babeuf and one other were condemned to death as subversives; Buonarroti and others were imprisoned. Probably the whole affair would have passed unnoticed except for the trial, and except for the fact that Buonarroti, thirty years later, wrote an influential book, *La Conjuration de l'Egalité dite de Babeuf*, in which memories of 1796 were adjusted to the interests of a more socialistically-minded later generation.

The real danger to the Directory, to repeat, came from the Right, as became abundantly evident in 1797. The continuing war, though successful, inclined many people to royalism, since a restored king could readily surrender the conquests of the Republic, or repudiate the new revolutionary states which, by 1797, had been set up in Holland and Italy. Most such new royalists, to be sure, opposed a mere restoration of the Old Order with its absolutism and its privileges; they favored a constitutional monarchy which Louis XVIII had as yet shown no sign of accepting. Their royalism expressed mainly a dissatisfaction with the Directory. On the other hand, even conservative republicans, such as Carnot had now become, men who would settle for any form of government that preserved the principles of 1789, could feel no confidence in a monarchist restoration, knowing what Louis XVIII had himself said, not to mention his more extreme followers, *les purs*. If nothing else, they had their own security to think about. Many, like Carnot, had voted for the death of Louis XVI. The army also, still the republican and democratic army created in the Year II, was generally opposed to any thought of a royalist restoration. For Bonaparte and other generals, who were now finding wealth and glory in Italy, along with Italian revolutionary sympathizers, a Bourbon king would be the worst of all possibilities.

The spring of 1797 brought the first free elections under the constitution of the Year III, or indeed the freest since the spring of 1789. The "two-thirds" rule of 1795 no longer applied; the former *Conventionnels* had to face an open contest. The Directory did surprisingly little to prepare the elections in its favor. The opposition was active. Royalists of various stripes created a secret network that went beyond anything achieved by Babeuf, in which "philanthropic institutes" were a disguise for political formations, with the absolute monarchists secretly intending first to use, and then to dupe, the constitutional monarchists who were really more numerous—like the communists vis-à-vis the democrats in Babeuf's arrangements. The elections proved catastrophic for the ex-members of the Convention, only eleven of whom were re-elected. By law, a third of both legislative chambers was renewed. The newly elected third, heavily royalist, when added to the "free third" of 1795, produced a majority in the chambers which was opposed to the five Directors, and indeed looked on the republican regime itself with something less than enthusiasm. The chambers, in the summer of 1797, took steps to repress the republican political clubs, and passed measures that seemed to favor the émigrés and the clergy. Some were in contact with the royal pretender, some with the British government. Some considered a coup d'état against the Directors, but absolutist and constitutionalist monarchists were sufficiently at odds to delay any action.

It was the Directory itself that acted, in the coup d'état of Fructidor of the Year V. Constitutionally, there was a stalemate between legislative and executive; politically, a confrontation between republicans and neomonarchists. Three of the five Directors combined with Bonaparte, who sent Augereau from Italy. While soldiers stood by, they excluded the other two Directors and expelled about two hundred members of the legislative chambers. Many elections of the preceding spring were annulled. Over sixty political figures were exiled to Guiana, "the dry guillotine." Carnot fled to Switzerland. The majority in the chambers shifted back to the republican side. The Republic again oscillated to the Left, with the new Directory stiffening its attitude to royalists, émigrés, and Catholic clergy, favoring the reviving neorevolutionary and democratic political clubs, dropping the faltering efforts to make peace with England, and sponsoring revolutionary changes in Holland, Switzerland, and Italy.

The coup d'état of Fructidor (September 4, 1797) stopped the drift toward a restoration, which would probably have proved more intolerant and reactionary in 1797 than it did in 1814. It could not preserve the Directory itself, which lasted only two more years. Violating the constitution (and the elections of 1798, returning more democratic majorities, were violated again) it could not preserve constitutional government in republican form. It could not give stability, for the oscillation continued. It could not even assure civilian rule. Dependent on military intervention since 1795, the Republic became more clearly dependent on its own soldiery in 1797. It was to yield to Bonaparte in 1799.

But the Fructidor coup d'état, in checkmating the monarchists, preserved the Revolution in its main essence. It blocked the return of the Old Order. It kept alive the new form of society as outlined in 1789, most especially favored by the educated middle classes, the former unprivileged and nonaristocratic upper strata, both in France and in much of Europe. In this sense, the Revolution had proved invincible. The dismay and terror felt by European conservatives after Fructidor were enough to show that the Revolution —if not Robespierre's or Babeuf's revolution—was very much alive.

Fructidor was a European as well as a French event. It was from his strength gained in Italy, and partly for reasons of the revolution in Italy, that Bonaparte intervened to support the republicans in Paris. Democrats in Holland and Italy, as well as in France, had been disturbed by the monarchist revival and were relieved when that revival was blocked.

In the present chapter the events in France from 1793 to 1797 have been telescoped with almost ridiculous brevity. Let the reader remember that the present book is not meant only as another history of the French Revolution. It is time to return to the main theme, the waves and counterwaves of revolution beyond France itself—first to the victories of antirevolutionism in Eastern Europe and then to the revolutionary and democratic agitations in the West.

[5]

Poland and the East:
The Revolution Overwhelmed

IF THE FRENCH DEFEATED THE FIRST COALITION, it was mainly because of the unforeseen strength developed in France itself. But it is also true that neither Prussia nor Austria directed its maximum military power against the French revolutionaries because they were preoccupied by another revolution closer at hand, the revolution in Poland. The three Eastern monarchies were opposed to any successful reorganization of their weaker neighbor. A Poland that was consolidated and genuinely independent, especially if it gained strength by concessions to burghers and peasants, would have an unsettling effect on burghers and peasants under Prussian, Russian, and Austrian rule, and would make more difficult the acquisition of territory by the three monarchies at Polish expense. The Russians and Prussians, therefore, as described in Chapter 3, had intervened to suppress "Jacobinism" in Poland—that is, the Polish constitution of 1791. The attempt was more successful than the simultaneous effort against France. It led in 1793 to the Second Partition. This in turn left a rump of Poland supposedly independent, though occupied by the Russian army. This Poland of 1793, under Russian auspices, was the Poland of the Polish conservatives, the Targowica party, which destroyed the constitution of 1791.

In Poland, as generally in Eastern Europe, virtually everyone of any public importance was a "noble." Struggles among nobles did not seem very significant to the French after 1789. Nor for many historians have such conflicts seemed enough to be called a revolution. Yet the Polish nobles, who were very numerous, were heterogeneous and divided. They responded differently to the European Enlightenment, to the rise of the press and political interest, to the needs of the country when menaced from outside. The party of the Polish Revolution, forming at first around the constitution of 1791, while it included King Stanislas himself, appealed mainly to the middling nobles or gentry, who resented the magnates, and hoped to strengthen the country by giving an interest in it to citizens in the Polish towns. The counterrevolutionary, or Targowica, group was the more purely agrarian party of the great magnates and their huge personal followings of landless retainers, who, as a species of poor whites among nobles, believed all townspeople to be beneath them. The peasants in this view were lower still.

Targowica Poland did not prove to be viable. Within a few months even many of the Targowicans turned against the Russians, from whom they had expected more independence. A strong resistance movement soon developed against the Russian occupation. It was organized by the Revolutionaries of 1791, including those who had become émigrés, but many of the Targowicans joined it. Since this resistance was secret, the Russian authorities attributed it to a Jacobin conspiracy and French machinations. Actually the French, who had their own troubles in 1793, had nothing to do with it and scarcely listened to Kosciuszko when he appeared in Paris to appeal for aid. The Polish Revolution remained entirely distinct from the French. The Counterrevolution represented more international collaboration.

Facing rising resistance, the Russians ordered a reduction of the Polish army, which they had at first allowed the Targowica regime to maintain. Plans for an uprising included the use of this army. The leaders were obliged to issue the call to insurrection before the dissolution of the army went too far, which is to say before they were fully ready. Kosciuszko, arriving from exile early in 1794, took command of a movement which began with a revolt in

Cracow and soon spread throughout the country. In April he defeated a Russian force at the battle of Raclawice. At Warsaw, thousands of civilians joined with soldiers in a revolt that forced the Russian troops to leave the city. The Russians naturally reacted by sending more troops into Poland. The Prussians, not to be out-maneuvered, also again invaded the country.

The insurrection grew into a significant though abortive revolution, or rather a continuation of the revolution of which the constitution of 1791 had marked an earlier stage. Like all revolutions, it developed its Right and its Left. The Right now meant those, like King Stanislas himself, who in ejecting the Russians hoped only to restore the constitution of 1791. For the Left, the "Polish Jacobins," the constitution of 1791 was no longer sufficient. They believed that more must be offered to the mass of the population if a strong national movement was to be developed. Their leader was Hugo Kollontay, born in the lesser landed nobility, trained for the church, and known in former years as a university reformer and more recently as one of King Stanislas' associates in producing the constitution of 1791. Most Polish Jacobins were actually noble in the Polish sense, but most of the merchants and lawyers in the cities, who had lost their recent gains when the constitution of 1791 was abolished, if active in the Revolution at all, were Jacobins in 1794. The working classes and small shopkeepers fought in the streets on a few occasions, at Warsaw and elsewhere, but there was no sustained Polish sans-culottism. The rural mass, long confined in serfdom, exerted no influence of its own.

Kosciuszko, a professional soldier who had served in the American Revolution, was no Jacobin by conviction. It is the more significant that, as the responsible leader of the insurrection, he sided with the Polish Jacobins in 1794. For example, after the Warsaw uprising a club was formed in the city with the somewhat cumbersome name Citizens Offering Aid and Service to the National Magistrates for the Welfare of the Country. Modeling itself on the Paris Jacobin Club, which was then at its height, the Warsaw club sought to stimulate patriotism, expose the un-trustworthy, and keep a watchful eye on the public officials. Moderates feared it, and the king asked Kosciuszko to disband it, but he refused. He felt that at the moment, against the Russians, it was precisely the efforts of these most fervid activists that were needed. The main problem was presented by serfdom. Kollontay and the Left argued that the peasants must be freed if they were to fight against the Russians, and that if serfdom were not abolished now the moment for its abolition might never come. The Right argued, with equal force, that abolition of serfdom would give offense to the serf-owning nobles on whose military skill and leadership the insurrection depended; that some nobles would lose interest in expelling the Russians if, as a result, they lost control over their subjects on their own estates. The dilemma was real; it pointed up the most profound difference between Eastern and Western Europe; it revealed the Achilles' heel of the Revolution in Poland.

Kosciuszko nevertheless chose for the Left. On May 7 he issued the Polaniec Proclamation by which serfdom was abolished. He reasoned as the French Jacobins did. The people must be given an interest to fight for. "That," as Robespierre had said, "is the real reason why the tyrants allied against the Republic will be defeated." Or as Kosciuszko expressed it, "Victory will go to those who fight in their own cause." The Proclamation, therefore, declared the peasants to be personally free, and put them for the first time under the direct protection of the laws and of the new national government. This went much further than the constitution of 1791. It was a radical move, which, if successful, might undermine the patrimonial social order of Eastern Europe. Yet it was also cushioned with compromises, designed to assure agricultural production and hold the loyalty of the squires. The peasant was free but had to report his movements. His unpaid labor services were reduced, but some remained. He was urged to join in a *levée en masse* and to be a soldier but told that labor service would await him on his return home from the war. The peasants were not electrified. No *levée en masse* really followed. Perhaps the proclamation was not revolutionary enough. Perhaps no such declaration could have had the desired effect. After many generations in serfdom, which in Poland was not very different from American slavery, the sluggish rural laborer could hardly emerge instantaneously as an inspired patriot or defender of a new political order.

Since the attempted Polish Revolution was simultaneous with the Revolutionary Government in France, preceding the fall of Robespierre, the Polish Jacobins looked upon the Terror and upon Robespierre with favor and produced expressions of civic excitement like those of the Year II in France. In this they differed from the Dutch or Italian revolutionaries, in the Batavian and Cisalpine republics after 1795, who were usually careful to avoid the accusation of extremism. The Poles, it must also be noted, were the only people in Europe, in this revolutionary decade, who undertook a revolution without French military assistance, and even without the promise of it that the United Irish had.

The revolutionary impulse lasted long enough, having begun in 1788, and was often enough threatened or actually blocked to give rise to violent hostilities and fears of betrayal. Though the king joined the uprising of 1794, he had in fact surrendered to the Russians once already in 1792; the Jacobins distrusted him and developed strong republican tendencies. They naturally viewed with suspicion the old Targowicans, who were now in the insurrection against the Russians but who had conspired with the Russian empress to destroy the constitution of 1791. All "aristocrats" and "rich people" came under suspicion. The vindictive fury against traitors showed itself when a mob broke into a Warsaw prison and hanged eight of the inmates, six of whom had in fact collaborated with the Russians, including the bishop of Vilna. Courts were set up to handle such cases, and they were popularly called revolutionary tribunals, but in fact nothing so organized or so lethal as the French Terror quite appeared.

Sentiment expressed itself, as in France, in a proliferation of popular clubs, the wearing of Phrygian caps, the building of altars to the fatherland, in a great outpouring volume of prints and political caricatures, and in revolutionary marching songs. From this same spirit came the present Polish national anthem, though not until two years later, after the failure of the revolution, when refugees in the Polish Legion attached to the French army in Italy created it in 1796. Civic hymns and catechisms expressed a kind of revolutionary religion. Old religious beliefs, along with prejudices and superstitions, fell into disrepute. Polish intellectuals shared in the "natural religion" of the Enlightenment. Since the pope and Polish bishops had condoned the Second Partition, the Left in 1794 was intensely anticlerical. But there were many, as in France, who thought that the true religion of Jesus favored equality, and there were priests who took part in the revolution.

The new feeling even transformed the language. The Old Polish word for "citizen" had formerly meant nobles only. It now referred to all inhabitants, even the serfs—a shocking neologism to the old-fashioned gentry. The old word for "nation" had meant only the nobility as convened in historic political assemblies. It now meant the whole Polish people, not especially as a linguistic-cultural unit, but as a community in which all classes were merged in a common polity which gave them rights. For most Jacobins, even the numerous Jews in Poland, though they spoke Yiddish, should have belonged to this nation; and in fact a Jewish battalion helped to defend Warsaw against Russian reoccupation. A good deal of "Jacobin" poetry was also written. Ephemeral, repressed, concealed and then forgotten, it has been rediscovered in recent years and made known by Professor B. Lesnodorski. A *Catechism of Man* looked to France:

> France is our example,
> France will lend aid;
> Let Liberty and Equality resound . . .
> Let lords and nobles disappear
> Who refuse to fraternize with the people.

Others looked to the American Revolution and saw a vast intercontinental rising for liberty:

> May our two continents,
> In immaculate strength,
> Like children of the same lineage,
> Join in ties of fraternity.

And others found encouragement in neighboring Königsberg, in the "profound" German philosopher Kant, with his dream of universal fraternity and peace.

The Poles naturally hoped that revolution would break out in the neighboring states which threatened Poland with extinction. Kosciuszko himself believed, though he was no extremist, that revolution in Russia might be a prerequisite to a free Polish state. He sent emissaries to seek aid in Hungary, where a revolt against the Hapsburgs was being secretly prepared. Journalists in Warsaw used the language of universal revolution. Leaflets and broadsides were printed in Russian and German, and attempts were made to circulate them to the common soldiers of the Russian and Prussian armies. In these sheets the revolutionary Poles appealed to the enemy troops as fellow members of the common people who should dissociate themselves from their governments. They expressed sympathy for the Russians, "who aspire to liberty but cannot taste it under a barbarous government." To the Prussians, "our brothers," they appealed to shake off the yoke of the Margrave of Brandenburg, and cried, "Dare for once to be free." To revolutionaries of all other countries the Poles offered fraternity. But the great danger to the neighboring monarchies lay not in such verbal outpourings so much as in the possible success of the Polish Revolution itself, by which something like the constitution of 1791, reinforced now by emancipation of the serfs, might be installed in the very heart of the great agrarian-servile area of Eastern Europe, the "third zone" as described in Chapter 1.

Neighbors saw this genuine revolutionary menace as part of the French Revolution. The insurgent Poles, said Catherine II, were "the wanton Warsaw horde established by the French tyrants." The Polish revolt, according to Frederick William II, showed "the diabolical activity deployed by the Jacobins to light the fire of sedition in every corner of Europe." And he added that the war in Poland was part of "the great struggle of the old governments against revolution and anarchy." Such judgments were mistaken in attributing the Polish upheaval to French intrigue. They were right enough in sensing a common danger which existing governments had an interest in suppressing.

The superior power of the Russian and Prussian armies soon prevailed. Last-minute efforts by the Poles, in which Kollontay tried to give the peasant property in land as well as personal freedom, proved to be useless. Even if unified, Poland was too small to defeat such overwhelming opponents; in fact, its deep social and ethnic divisions made resistance very short. The peasants took little part. Brief and courageous efforts by the small people in the cities were of no avail. Mainly it was the Polish nobles who fought in the insurrection and who were defeated. Kosciuszko lost the battle of Maciejowice in October, 1794. He was captured but managed to flee to America. Kollontay spent years in an Austrian prison.

Russia and Prussia, joined this time by Austria, thereupon effected the Third and "final" Partition. Poland disappeared from the list of European states. Each of the successor powers proceeded to assimilate its segment of Poland to its own political system, in which, it need hardly be said, nothing like the Polish constitution of 1791 was retained, and the peasants remained in serfdom, while members of the Polish aristocracy began to mix, with varying degrees of good grace, with the corresponding classes of the conquering empires. Revolutionary Poles fled to France, to Italy, and to Turkey. More than a century of the Polish revolution-in-exile was initiated. But in Poland the revolution was over.

At the same time, late in 1794, the authorities at Vienna put down the disturbances in the Hapsburg empire. These were trivial enough in a sense, though they reflected deep and chronic discontents. Peasant rebellion had shaken Hungary as recently as 1790, and Bohemia as recently as 1775. News of the French Revolution, and then of the war in 1792, had seeped into the villages. The peasants remembered the efforts of Joseph II to do away with serfdom. They knew that he had failed, and they perceived that the new government, in which landlord influence was stronger, had both abandoned Joseph's program and gone to war against the French Revolution. A strong antiwar and even pro-French feeling pervaded the Hapsburg empire. Books were written to combat it. Burke's *Reflections on the French Revolution* circulated in German. Bohemian publicists, including the founders of the Czech revival, denounced the French as barbarians, published atrocity stories, told the peasants that they were very fortunate to live under existing conditions, and justified the *robot*, or forced agricultural labor. Such labor, they said, though uncompensated, was perfectly natural; it allowed the peasant to live on the estate and was only a legitimate return on the property of the owner. The real issue at the time, of course, in France and elsewhere, was not whether private property should exist but the kinds of collateral rights and legal powers that landed property should entail.

The Hapsburg empire (except for Belgium and the Milanese) was only slightly urbanized, but its capital, Vienna, was one of the great cities of Europe. Although its social life was dominated by aristocratic visitors from the provinces, Vienna had a middle class of intellectuals, journalists, lawyers, and government servants who had favored the program of Joseph II and were increasingly critical of the privileges of the nobility. These included the usual immunities to taxation and special rights of consultation by government. Over the centuries, the towns had been excluded from the accepted political life of the empire. The agrarian nobility had taken over. In the diet of Bohemia no city was any longer represented except Prague. In the Hungarian parliament only one person represented all the towns of Hungary. In the estates of Styria only one person spoke for all the towns of that duchy. Under such conditions, once the town notables began to think of such things, even the Polish constitution of 1791, not to mention the French, might seem attractive. For the urban middle classes of the empire, as for the peasants, the war against Revolutionary France seemed rather pointless, an aristocratic crusade in which they had no concern.

Leopold II, during his two years as emperor, was inclined to sympathize with the middle-class ambitions, if only because he correctly diagnosed the agrarian nobility as the chief rivals to his own position. A man of good will, an enlightened despot or a kind of political technocrat, he had no more desire to share power with the commoners than with the nobles. He resorted to secret methods. Through the Viennese journalist L. A. Hoffmann, who declared that the French Revolution was caused by a conspiracy of the Illuminati, Leopold built up a curious secret association which, in conjunction with the police, would report on the activities of both "democrats" and "aristocrats" in the imperial dominions. Some persons involved in these mysterious operations were genuinely reformers and modernizers, former co-workers of Joseph II, who saw the churchmen and the nobility as the main obstacle in their path. This meant that when Leopold died and was succeeded by Francis II, and after the war with France began, and ideas of reform began to be put aside, some of the men in Leopold's clandestine organization began to look with favor on revolution. In 1794, as the outlook for revolution seemed more hopeful in both France and Poland, the Austrian and Hungarian "Jacobins" came to life. The term is incongruous in this connection. Mere plotters, the Austrian and Hungarian Jacobins hardly resembled the actual Jacobins of France, nor even the Polish "Jacobins," whose public and open activities have just been described.

The Vienna conspiracy was of slight importance. It began when one of Kosciuszko's followers came to Austria to seek support for the Poles. He met with a small circle of Viennese intellectuals, one of whom offered the Poles the use of a new device he had just invented, designed to strengthen infantry against cavalry charges. The Austrians persuaded the visiting Pole to provide funds to enable one of their number to go to France to offer the same invention to the armies of the French Revolution. The Austrian emissary, a Protestant pastor named Held, successfully made the trip to Paris. The Committee of Public Safety, whose armies were just winning the battle of Fleurus and streaming into the Austrian Netherlands, felt no need of the proposed invention and no interest whatsoever in a handful of unknown so-called revolutionaries in Vienna. It put Held under arrest as an enemy alien. Meanwhile in Vienna the conspirators drew up projects for the government of the empire and circulated Paine's *Rights of Man* in French and a didactic poem of the same tenor in modern Latin. The Austrian police heard of Held's mission and arrested the conspirators. One of their number, Martinovics, assisted the police after his arrest by revealing a far more significant revolutionary conspiracy in Hungary, of which he had made himself the leader.

Hungary had an old tradition of opposition to Vienna. It had rebelled more than once. In general, it was the upper Catholic clergy and the wealthy magnates, some of whom had enormous holdings in land and serfs, who were most integrated into the multinational aristocracy and high culture of the Hapsburg empire. The small Magyar nobles or gentry were less cosmopolitan and more nationalistic. They were easily persuaded that their great magnates and prelates had sacrificed Hungary to the German dynasty of the Hapsburgs, to its pretensions, its needs, and its recurrent wars. They objected to the war against Revolutionary France, for which, indeed, the Hungarian diet refused any support until 1797. They were hardly, of course, revolutionaries on the French model; it was one of their grievances against the Germanizing Hapsburgs that Joseph II had tried to abolish serfdom. In their social level, and their strong national feeling, those lesser Magyar nobles resembled the revolutionary lesser nobility of Poland.

At the same time, even in Hungary, where the towns were small and many of them mainly German, small circles had developed composed of men of more modern views. They were largely government employees, lawyers, or free intellectuals; some of them were Protestants, for Calvinism had been strong in Hungary since the sixteenth century. A few were burghers, like Joseph Hajnoczy, the son of a Calvinist minister, who in Joseph's time had become the first nonnoble to hold office as vice-sheriff of a Hungarian county. He lost it in the aristocratic reaction after 1790. After Joseph's death both nonnobles and Protestants found themselves facing the old discriminations.

There were thus two distinct groups of potential revolutionaries in Hungary. One was essentially agrarian and conservative, the other more eagerly receptive to modern developments. Both were pro-French in the war. They read the Paris *Moniteur* and translated the *Marseillaise* into Latin (still the political language of Hungary) as well as into Hungarian and Slovakian. Ferenc Szentmarjay, one of the codifiers of the Hungarian written language, translated Rousseau's *Social Contract*, devising the modern Hungarian terms for "citizen," "people," "equality," "sovereignty," and so forth. Men of this kind fraternized with French prisoners of war brought to Hungary for internment. Szentmarjay traveled fifty miles to see some of those soldiers of the Republic. After fervent embraces he obtained from them a small tricolor, which he is said to have shown to friends only if they would respectfully kneel before it.

The Vienna government infiltrated these enthusiasts with police agents. One of the latter, in 1793, was the very Martinovics who was to reveal the conspiracy of 1794. Martinovics was a wandering intellectual, a Hungarian of Serbian background, educated for the church but now an atheist in the manner of Holbach, who in his travels had formed Polish connections and had been a professor at Lemberg in Galicia, the Polish territory acquired by Austria in the First Partition. The University of Budapest, however, when he applied to it, had pronounced him unfit to be on its faculty. In 1791, Martinovics had worked for the secret organization of Leopold II already described. An admirer of Leopold, and favorable to the program of reforming or enlightened "despotism" under Joseph, he detested the clergy and nobility, in Hungary and elsewhere, by which the reforming program had been obstructed. He appears to have worked willingly for the police so long as the police itself was reformist. But the new Emperor Francis was disinclined both to the reforms and to the police methods of his predecessors. Martinovics found his services less in demand. By May, 1794, both the French and the Poles seemed to be pressing the Revolution forward with success. Martinovics became interested in the revolution in Hungary. It was aimed, after all, against much of what Leopold had formerly opposed.

Martinovics therefore began to draw together the revolutionary elements that already existed. A latecomer to these Hungarian movements, active in them only a few weeks, he gave his name to the discontents which he organized into a conspiracy in which he was not otherwise of much importance. He impressed these fairly unsophisticated Hungarians with his apparent knowledge of the world and with boasts of having contacts with the Revolutionary government in Paris for which there was no foundation whatsoever. He organized two secret societies. One, the Reformers of Hungary, was for the disaffected but socially conservative Magyar nobles. To this group Martinovics promised an aristocratic independent future republic, in which serfdom and the "feudal system," as he called it, would be maintained. The

Reformers were told nothing of the other organization, the Society of Liberty and Equality. It was Martinovics' intention that once the Hapsburgs were overthrown, the second society should simply liquidate the first. To the second society, that of Liberty and Equality, he denounced the "feudal system" and nobility as vicious and intolerable institutions, proposed the abolition both of the nobility and of serfdom, and pointed to France as the great example. He wrote two political "catechisms," one for each society, and each issuing a call to revolution. For the noble Reformers he wrote in Latin, concluding his appeal with an echo of the *Marseillaise* which the French would have found ridiculous had they known anything about it: *Ad arma, cives patriae nobiles et ignobiles!* To the other society, addressed in Hungarian, the call was as in France: "To arms, citizens! Let us swear liberty or death!"

Martinovics and his followers may have recruited two or three hundred members for the two societies within the few weeks at their disposal. Had the time been longer, they might have attracted many more, since the discontents in Hungary were considerable. As it happened, Held's mission to Paris alerted the police. Martinovics, who happened to be in Vienna at the time, was arrested along with the Vienna conspirators. Whether because he believed the secret was already known, or because he hoped to re-enter the service of the police, he revealed the identity of the principal conspirators in Hungary. They too were arrested. Two Austrians and eighteen Hungarians, after trial, were executed for attempted subversion in time of war and others sent to prison.

The main effect of the Martinovics conspiracy was in the reaction to which it contributed. On the one hand, the general discontent and the antiwar feeling continued. The chancellor, Thugut, remarked in 1796, when the French invaded the Austrian provinces in Italy, that he feared Bonaparte less than the peace sentiment in Vienna. As late as 1800 the Archduke Karl, sojourning on his estates in Bohemia, found the peasants very ill disposed and declared that nine-tenths of them hoped that the French would penetrate into Bohemia. On the other hand, alarmed by the Martinovics conspiracy and by the Polish Revolution of 1794, which were followed by upheavals in north Italy in 1796, and by

the discovery of the Greek conspirator Rhigas Velestinlis in Vienna
in 1797 (who hoped to raise up all the Greeks in the Ottoman
Empire, which then adjoined the Hapsburg domains), the Austrian
authorities became increasingly fearful of modern ideas. Police
surveillance continued. The censorship clamped down. Writers
issued books dwelling on the horrors of the French Revolution.
Bishops were given new powers over the schools. Experiments in
rural education were discontinued, lest a more literate peasantry
become more discontented. Measures were taken to check economic expansion and prevent the growth of cities, in which movements critical of the Old Order seemed to be mainly nourished.
The reforming age of Maria Theresa and Joseph II was closed.
Austria was set on the course to be marked by the era of Metternich
and the revolutions of 1848, from whose effects the Hapsburg
empire never fully recovered.

Of the remainder of Eastern Europe not much need be said.
In the southeast, it was a time when various peoples, composed
largely of peasants, were beginning to renew their contacts with
Europe, and to develop their own literary languages, after centuries
of overlordship by the Turks. For some of these movements
Vienna was an important center. Thus the first Greek newspaper
was published in Vienna in 1790, and Francis II in 1792 consented
to the appearance of a new paper in Serbo-Croatian on condition
that it be printed in the Cyrillic alphabet (which Croats and
Slovenes could not read) and point out the evils of both the
French and the Belgian revolutions. The first Romanian newspaper, published in French and Romanian in 1790, carried news
of the French Revolution. A group of Vlachs—or Romanians
living in eastern Hungary—petitioned in 1791 for changes of the
kind publicized in France by the Revolution. Their request was
disregarded. For the Greeks dispersed throughout the Ottoman
Empire, Rhigas Velestinlis, already mentioned, organized a conspiracy in Vienna and drew up a proposed constitution for a
Hellenic Republic, modeled on the French constitution of 1795.
The Austrian police turned him over to the Turkish authorities,
who executed him at Belgrade in 1798. Yet the Balkan countries,
closed as they were, continued to receive influences from both

France and Poland. The Serbian revolution of 1804 initiated the modern history of Southeast Europe.

The greatest power of Eastern Europe was, of course, Russia. Here, in the long reign of Catherine II, a process went on by which the serfdom of the peasants was intensified, while the upper classes, the owners of lands and peasants, became increasingly Westernized and transformed into a privileged aristocracy on a Western model. The vast servile uprising of Pugachev's rebellion, which had spread through much of Russia in 1773, was vividly remembered. It was from groups of nobles, however, that Russian rulers had faced the most serious danger of overthrow or assassination. To please the nobles and to control the peasants better, Catherine issued a Charter of Nobility in 1785. It defined an area of liberty, status, personal security, power, and privilege for the *blagorodnyi* or "highborn," granting them the rights to bear titles, buy and sell serfs, enjoy tax exemptions, and meet in provincial assemblies. The Russian landowners were becoming a kind of legal estate, and Russia was moving toward a system like the Old Order in Europe at the very time when the direction in Western Europe was against it.

On the other hand, the new ideas also came into Russia. Catherine herself befriended Diderot and took an interest in "philosophy." She brought La Harpe from Switzerland to tutor her two grandsons—but expelled him in 1796. One of the greatest landowners of the empire, Count Stroganov, as a young man belonged to the Paris Jacobin Club in 1790 and had as his tutor Gilbert Romme, who was later a prominent member of the National Convention. By 1789 about thirty newspapers and magazines were published in Russia, which, though heavily censored, conveyed some knowledge of events in France and elsewhere. N. I. Novikov edited a journal aimed at subaristocratic readers, conducted a school for translators of foreign books, and helped to organize a public library in Moscow. Increasingly felt to be dangerous, he was sentenced in 1792 to fifteen years in prison. Alexander Radishchev wrote an ode to American liberty and in 1790 published his *Voyage from Petersburg to Moscow.* Its portrayal of serfdom and of other Russian institutions was so unfavorable that he was exiled to Siberia. He is sometimes called

the first Russian revolutionary. "Radishchev is worse than Puga-
chev," said Catherine; "he reads Benjamin Franklin." But the
French and Polish revolutions undoubtedly had more impact in
Russia than the American.

Even the "lower" classes, which in Russia meant anyone not
noble, were beginning to produce social critics. There were even
a few cases of intellectual serfs, usually belonging to enlightened
families like the Stroganovs. Professor M. M. Shtrange, of the
University of Moscow, has recently shown that discontent, or
sympathy for the French Revolution, was by no means confined
to a few members of the cosmopolitan upper strata. He finds the
evidence in obscure provincial periodicals, in surviving booksellers'
catalogues, pamphlets, prints and engravings, and police records on
the circulation of forbidden materials. In 1793 a surreptitious
pamphlet circulated in manuscript copies, the *Gospel to the Russian Israel*, which favored the rights of man, questioned the rights
of property and nobility, and called on the Russians and on all
the Slavs to abolish serfdom and do away with lords and princes.

Against such unrest it was the antirevolutionary mentality that
prevailed. The French embassy after 1789 was a source of
unsettling ideas. The ambassador, the Count de Ségur, favored
the Revolution, which he praised to various Russian noblemen,
but he returned to France in 1790. His *chargé d'affaires*, Genêt
(who later went to the United States), combated the claims of
the French émigrés and even reported signs of revolutionary
disaffection in Russia. He was ordered out of the country in 1792.
Catherine II abominated the French Revolution but took more
positive steps against the nearer menace on her own borders.
As she said, she "would fight Jacobinism and beat it in Poland."
In April, 1792, she combined with the counterrevolutionary Poles
who sought her aid and who issued the Act of Targowica, which
was actually drawn up and signed in St. Petersburg. She then
invaded the country and stamped out the Polish constitution of
1791. As already explained, her next step was to support and
occupy the satellite Poland of the Targowicans, and then, joined
by the Prussians, to crush the rebellion led by Kosciuszko.

Meanwhile, in Russia as elsewhere, a flood of writing began to
flow against the French and all other revolutions. It was an

"agrarian" literature in which cities were called parasitic and city people dangerous to society because they were inclined to delusions of equality. Revolution was attributed to the envy of a half-educated rabble of cobblers and lawyers, who looked somewhat alike to the scions of genuine aristocracy—what Burke called the "Jews and jobbers," the "tradesmen, bankers and voluntary clubs of presuming young persons" that cities brought together. The idea that revolution was caused by the mysterious plotting of mystics or Masons found especial favor in Russia. Secret societies, which in fact existed, were relentlessly pursued. A book published in St. Petersburg in 1793, while mainly directed against the French Revolution, noted with alarm the emergence of a lower-class intelligentsia in Russia itself, which might agitate the whole third estate. Such a moral epidemic, like the plague at Constantinople, said the author, would require a general quarantine.

It is to these last years of the eighteenth century that both the revolutionary and the counterrevolutionary traditions of modern Russia can be traced. At the popular level, Professor Shtrange has counted almost three hundred serf rebellions from 1796 to 1798 alone. At the top, Catherine's grandson Alexander I, La Harpe's pupil, surrounded by men like Stroganov, attempted after 1801 to liberalize the empire. On the other hand, the fear of new ideas and of Western Europe also continued, condemning Russia for a long time to an alternation between the two poles.

To summarize, the period of the First Coalition, formed in 1792–93 to counteract the revolutionary disturbances in France and Poland, closed in the mid-decade with the revolution still alive in France but killed off in Eastern Europe.

[6]

The Sister Republics:
The Revolution Expanded

BEGINNING IN 1795 a set of new revolutionary republics sprang up beyond the borders of France. They were revolutionary in being entirely different from the older republics long familiar to Europe, such as Venice and Genoa or the Dutch Netherlands and the Swiss cantons. All looked for inspiration to the French Revolution, incorporated the principles of 1789, and formally modeled themselves on the French constitution of the Year III, that is, the regime of the Directory, which in these new republics was commonly called "democratic." They were revolutionary also in being brought about by rebellious native leaders—Dutch, Swiss, and Italian—who were impatient of their own inherited institutions and joined with the French to reorganize their own countries. All were small, none having much over a tenth of the French population. They were dependents or satellites of the French Republic, or in the language of the day its "sisters." Had events turned out differently, or had diverse radical groups been successful, there might have been new republics on the German left bank of the Rhine, in south Germany, in Ireland, or briefly in Belgium in 1792. In fact, by 1799, there were six sister republics—

the Batavian, Helvetic, Cisalpine, Ligurian, Roman, and Neapolitan, which was also called Parthenopean.

It was in the sister republics that the expanding wave of the French Revolution was most manifest. The metaphor of the wave is not altogether exact. If a wave means a disturbance entirely generated by a central force, then the appearance of these republics was not merely a wave. Each arose in large part from forces within its own territory, in some cases continuing an internal revolutionary movement that antedated 1789. Each represented, on its local scene, a reaction against the Old Order and a response to the intellectual revolution, or Enlightenment, as described in Chapter 1. The sister republics all belonged to what was there called the second zone of Europe, the region of urban civilization, a developed middle class and a free landowning peasantry, with exceptions for south Italy, where the new republicanism showed little strength. The observation was also made, in the first chapter, that certain ecclesiastical and social arrangements, involving established churches and legal estates, were more widespread in Europe than the institutions of monarchy. The observation applies to the area of the sister republics, none of which, except in Naples, had a native monarch to dethrone, but all of which menaced the former legal position of the church and the older sociopolitical ruling elites.

But if the republics represented indigenous forces, all were byproducts of the French Revolution. Or rather, they were byproducts of the war that began in 1792, and which after the spring of 1794 the French happened to win. In the course of these hostilities, the French wanted to use the resources of the regions in question for their own purposes, whether by setting up new republics or not. Reformers and revolutionaries of these same regions wanted to use the French victories for their own advantage. If there was an excited sense of expanding revolution and universal liberation, there were also self-interest and then disillusionment on both sides.

The French government, under both the Convention and the Directory, was generally skeptical of "foreign" revolutionaries and hesitant about sponsoring republics outside France. It never at any time, for example, supposed that unconditional surrender and total collapse of an enemy government were necessary to the terms of peace. Only extreme radicals talked this way at that time. Neither the Convention nor the Directory ever conspired with émigrés as Catherine II did with the Targowica Poles. Sporadic incidents excepted, there was no "underground war" conducted by the Convention or Directory against the old governments of neighboring states. No counterpart could be written to the recent book on *The Underground War Against Revolutionary France*, in which Harvey Mitchell traces the British involvement with French royalists in the years from 1794 to 1800.

The plans of Dumouriez for a Belgian republic in 1792 have been already described. There had been a real Belgian revolution in 1789; the Belgians had themselves expelled their Austrian overlord; the French, at war with Austria, had annexed Belgium in 1793, then had been driven out in the debacle of Dumouriez's defeat and defection, then returned in 1794, and again annexed Belgium in 1795. A good many Belgian businessmen of the kind interested in new developments and enlarged markets, together with anticlericals, favored this solution as at least better than the archaic old regime, or better than an independent Belgium everlastingly torn by its Statist and Democratic parties. Belgium remained part of France for twenty years. As a result, the old localistic towns and provinces of the Austrian Netherlands and the Bishopric of Liège were thoroughly transformed by the effects of the French Revolution. Without this fusion of the old entities the nineteenth-century kingdom of Belgium could never have been created.

The French Jacobins, at least after the expulsion of the Brissot group, usually scoffed at the foreign revolutionaries as no more than visionaries and agitators. They rightly perceived that these would-be revolutionaries could accomplish nothing without French aid. Robespierre believed in the reality of no revolution but the French, and it was at the height of the Revolutionary Government, on Robespierre's initiative, early in 1794, that the exponents of international revolution who had been active in Paris since 1792 were silenced, and their various legions, conventions, and committees were dissolved.

With the French victories that began with the Battle of

Fleurus in June, 1794, the hopes of potential revolutionaries in other countries were aroused. The French showed no particular sympathy. Not only did they give no encouragement to Kosciuszko, and rebuff the secret messenger, already mentioned, from the "Jacobins" in Vienna, but they showed little interest in revolutionaries nearer home. At Oneglia, in Sardinia, occupied by French troops, French civilian representatives included the Italian-speaking Buonarroti, Babeuf's companion of two years later. Robespierre's own brother was stationed nearby. Various Italians wishing to overthrow the kingdom of Sardinia sought their aid. They attracted no notice. At Geneva, the *égalisateurs* set up a Revolutionary Tribunal and executed fourteen persons in July, 1794. The French *Conventionnels* observing these events from Grenoble, dismissed them with scorn. In Belgium, the invading French army was accompanied by returning Belgian refugees. The French made no attempt to cooperate with them, believing them to be too intent on their own vengeance against fellow Belgians. The same army was also accompanied, like Dumouriez in 1792, by Dutch refugees who were eager to revolutionize Holland. The Dutch émigré General Daendels offered to make a secret trip to Amsterdam to produce a revolution there in favor of the French. The Committee of Public Safety was evasive; it would welcome a revolution made by the Dutch against the House of Orange, since the existing Dutch regime was at war with France; but it gave no promise of aid and would make no commitments. As Carnot said, the Dutch were thinking only of their own country, and "we who are French must think of ours."

Nevertheless, as will be explained, the French in 1795 recognized a revolutionary Batavian Republic. Thus removing the Dutch from the list of its enemies, the Convention also in its final months made peace with Prussia and Spain, in effect breaking up the First Coalition. With Prussia remaining neutral for a decade, with the British army withdrawn from the Continent, and with the Batavian Republic and even the Spanish Bourbon monarchy soon allying with the regicide Republic, the French concentrated their war effort against Austria, with which Sardinia was still cooperating. The result was the brilliant campaign conducted by Bonaparte in north Italy in 1796 against Sardinia and the Austrian forces in Lombardy.

The Directory not only oscillated between Left and Right in internal affairs. It also blew hot and cold on the plans of foreign revolutionaries in their own countries. Coming into office despite the royalist uprising of Vendémiaire and the attempted Anglo-royalist invasion at Quiberon, it at first inclined to work with neo-Jacobins at home and to look with some favor on the projects of activists abroad. Early in 1796 the French foreign minister, Delacroix, encouraged Buonarroti and other Italians in their plans for a republican revolution in Italy. He befriended a secret group in south Germany who worked with an adventurer named Poteratz to set up a republic there. He permitted the Poles to organize a legion of several thousand Polish exiles with the French army in Italy. He laid plans with the Irish revolutionary Wolfe Tone for the liberation of Ireland and assembled information on the possibilities of revolution in England itself. He allowed the South Carolina adventurer, William Tate, to land a party of several hundred Frenchmen in a raid on the coast of Wales. He sponsored the most vehement democratic and anti-British party in the new Batavian Republic and maintained relations with the Sultan of Mysore against the British in India.

He even turned his attention to North America. There were Franco-Spanish talks on the retrocession of Louisiana to France, and the French General Collot, in 1796, on the pretense of a scientific expedition, made a trip from the East Coast as far as St. Louis (then a French town under Spanish rule) to study the state of opinion in the American West. There seemed some possibility—enough for Washington to warn against it in his Farewell Address—that the settlers beyond the Alleghenies, disaffected toward the East, might accept French sponsorship for an independent Western Republic. George Rogers Clark was commissioned (for the second time) as a brigadier general in the French army to rally the westerners. Since the Americans after Jay's Treaty of 1794 seemed to be allied to England, Delacroix even favored a "revolution" in the United States, in the mild sense of preferring the election of Jefferson to that of Adams as president.

The French minister to the United States, in public speeches, threatened the displeasure of France if Jefferson was not chosen. Jefferson himself, in a letter of April, 1796, to his friend Mazzei in Europe, said that good republicans in America were being stifled by a selfish combination of Anglophiles, monocrats, and aristocrats. The letter caused a commotion in America when published in the Paris *Moniteur* a few months later.

But these tendencies to export revolution, some of which were not very serious, were gradually reversed. For one thing, Buonarroti was found in May, 1796, to be conspiring with Babeuf to overthrow the Directory. For another, the French began to win military victories in Italy. In proportion to military success it was less necessary to threaten the enemy with subversion. The Directory took alarm at the Babeuf conspiracy, more probably for its insurrectionary intent than for its utopian projects on the abolition of property. Support for the Poteratz conspiracy in Germany was withdrawn. Buonarroti went to prison, and the Directory decided, in July, 1796, that it was contrary to French interests to set up "democratic republics" in Italy, since the revolutionaries in that country were not strong enough to stand on their own feet. Meanwhile, when a group of Italians proclaimed the republic at Alba, near Turin, intending to do away with seigneurial dues, the nobility, and the Sardinian monarchy, they received no aid from the French. Bonaparte, in fact, made an armistice with the king of Sardinia, thus knocking the country out of the war but recognizing the monarchy. The Directory tended to revert to an old-fashioned diplomacy of mutual concessions and balance of power. French conquests in Italy might, for example, be returned to Austria at a peace conference in return for recognition of the transfer to France of the Austrian Netherlands, or acquisition by France of territory along the Rhine.

Nevertheless, first the Cispadane Republic was organized in the Po valley in 1796, then the Cisalpine and the Ligurian Republics in 1797. The Cisalpine was built around the Austrian Milanese; the Ligurian replaced the ancient and aristocratic Republic of Genoa. It was not the French government that brought these developments about. They arose more from the personal policy of Bonaparte and the wishes of some of the pro-French Italian reformers and revolutionaries themselves.

In 1797 the Directory engaged in prolonged peace talks with the British. The fact that Belgium was now part of France and that a Batavian Republic, allied to France, had come into being was very difficult for the British to accept. Even so, pressed by internal troubles, Pitt was on the point of recognizing these innovations, if only Britain could acquire the Dutch colonies in Ceylon and at the Cape of Good Hope. But the Directory, in response to the internal royalist revival, which was favored by Britain, executed the coup d'état of Fructidor, by which the French government moved leftward toward a reassertion of revolutionary purpose. Peace talks with Great Britain were broken off. Bonaparte made peace with Austria by the treaty of Campo Formio. The Cisalpine Republic was now a fact. The Austrians could no more be happy with a pro-French revolutionary republic in north Italy than the British could be with one in Holland. Peace prevailed on the Continent in 1798, only France and Britain remaining at war. But the peace was generally understood to be temporary.

At this time various Swiss—La Harpe of the Vaud, Ochs of Basel, Usteri of Zurich—decided that the time had come for a reconstruction of Switzerland. They met in Paris with members of the Directory and with General Bonaparte. The result was a series of uprisings in Switzerland against the old governments, conducted under the protection of the French army. The Helvetic Republic was proclaimed.

At Rome, some of the citizens wished to get rid of ecclesiastical government and the temporal power of the pope. Other Italians, excited by the Ligurian and Cisalpine Republics (which many Catholic bishops had accepted), believed that a republicanization of the papal states was in order. The French government hesitated; it was not eager to provoke a renewal of the war by a supposed liberation of the Romans. Pius VI was not a dangerous enemy; he had in a way accepted the existence of the French Republic *de facto*; he knew that his political domains were threatened by the territorial ambitions of the monarchs of Naples and Austria as much as by French or Italian republicans. Nothing might have happened except for an unfortunate incident. The French General Duphot, attached to the French embassy in Rome, was killed in a street riot. A clamor for intervention arose in France and Italy. The Directory could not resist it, and early in 1798 Rome was occupied by French troops from Milan, soon reinforced by Poles and north Italian Cisalpines. A Roman Republic followed.

A few months later, as a Second Coalition was forming against France, the king of Naples sent an army into the new Roman Republic and occupied its capital. The French, assisted by Cisalpine troops, soon turned the tables, drove off the invaders, and occupied Naples. In Paris, the Directory positively disapproved the creation of a new republic in south Italy. With the renewal of war, it supposed that a mere occupation might be more advantageous to France as a means of utilizing the wealth of the country, and that mere military occupation would set up no obstacles to a later negotiation for peace. Nevertheless, thanks to the disobedience of the French General Championnet, and upon the insistence of native Neapolitan enthusiasts, the Neapolitan Republic was proclaimed early in 1799.

So the six sister republics came into being with or without the wishes of the government in Paris. They reflected a European and not merely a French revolutionary upheaval. Indeed, by their existence, the French Revolution became captive of a revolution of greater geographical scope. It had, indeed, been locked into a supranational conflict from the beginning. The first émigrés of 1789 had found sympathizers abroad; national feeling was least pronounced in the upper classes, and a kind of fraternization among dynasties and aristocracies existed long before the Convention, in November, 1792, offered "aid and fraternity" to the "peoples." The offer was not made in a void. There were, in fact, persons from Dublin to Naples who were more eager to have French support than the French proved willing to give it.

There is no doubt that the post-Robespierrist Convention and the Directory would have preferred to make peace and stabilize or terminate the Revolution. They did, in fact, make or impose treaties with all powers except Great Britain. It was well under-

stood that continuing war carried the danger of military dictatorship; it had been understood since the days of Dumouriez, Robes-
pierre had warned against it, and Bonaparte after 1796 became an
object of similar fears. The Convention had gone out, and the
Directory had come in, under military protection, when troops had
been used against insurrection on the Left in Prairial, and on the
Right in Vendémiaire. Again, in 1797, by the coup d'état of
Fructidor, the Republic put down the royalists with the aid of
Bonaparte and the army. It was largely to assure his position in
Italy, to keep alive his new Cisalpine Republic, that Bonaparte
joined with the Directory to check counterrevolution. The Directory could with difficulty resist the generals, even if military
dictatorship could be foreseen. There were other differences between 1797 or 1798 and 1792. The advanced democrats now
favored the victorious generals. They rejoiced in the triumphs of
their citizen armies, in the disarray and wholesale collapse of aristocrats, and in the proliferation of new republics from Holland to
Italy. The Directory could not discourage foreign republicans
without being accused of "moderatism" in Paris. It could not
restrain Bonaparte in 1797 or Championnet in 1799, as the Convention had restrained Dumouriez, without raising a storm of
protest in France which it was not strong enough to risk.

Victorious in the war, the French government became the
victim not only of its generals but also of its foreign admirers. It
could neither check the ideological passions aroused in neighboring countries nor disown the sister republics once they were born.
To reject friends would be to give comfort to enemies—strengthen
the most conservative anti-French elements in the Netherlands,
Switzerland, and Italy—turn the Dutch over to the British influence and the Italians to the Austrian, and leave the Swiss to the
combined Anglo-Austrian intervention to which Swiss conservatives looked for help, not only against France, but against other
Swiss who desired to modernize the old confederation.

For the French, it was not a necessity of the war to set up
dependent republics. They could have treated the invaded regions
as occupied areas, requisitioned in them at will, confiscated the
property of the enemy governments, churches and privileged
classes, and so supported their armies and enriched themselves

during hostilities, while making no commitment that might inter-
fere with a peace settlement. This was precisely what the Belgians
and Dutch did not want in 1792 or the Neapolitans in 1799. It
was the strength of revolutionary sentiment in the invaded regions,
when combined with the programs of French generals or other
agents in the field, that produced the sister republics as a solution to the French problem. The policy in the invaded regions
would be not requisitions alone, but *liberté et réquisitions*, as
Professor Godechot has expressed it. Each republic, under French
direction, but technically independent, would maintain its army,
make payments to France under treaty, or otherwise share in the
war against the counterrevolution, which if successful would
destroy them all.

In addition, the French "lived on the country" by direct
requisitions to support their own armies in the invaded areas.
To official requisitions was added the burden of informal pillage
by French soldiers and the schemes of private fortunemaking, in
which French officers and civilians, from Bonaparte on down,
widely engaged. In one estimate, offered hesitantly by Jacques
Godechot, the sums raised by the French in the occupied regions,
from 1792 to 1799, reached a total of at least 360 million livres.
It was a substantial amount, but only half as large as the French
annual budget of 1791, and only half as large as the indemnity imposed upon France by the allies after the defeat of Napoleon.
What made such levies unpleasant was not their gross amount,
nor the purpose for which they were raised, since the existence
of the lesser republics depended on the success of the French
armies. It was the disorderly and sporadic way in which money
and supplies were collected, injuring some more than others, the
arbitrary demands of an irresistible foreign power, the exactions
of a conqueror who claimed also to be a liberator and a friend, all
compounded by private graft and corruption that could not be
controlled, and, in Italy, by the spectacular hauling away of famous
paintings and statuary to grace the museums of Paris. Roughly, it
seems that Italy suffered the most, Switzerland next, and Holland
the least from these depredations. As for the Belgians after 1795
and the German Rhinelanders after 1797, once organized as de-

partments of France, they paid, in principle, only what French citizens paid. The burden was heavy enough to cause disaffection and to turn some sympathizers into enemies of the French. It offered a rich field for propaganda for the Counterrevolution. For the most part, the revolutionary republicans from Holland to Naples accepted it as a necessity of their position, and better than unrelieved foreign occupation. Requisitions, for them, were better with liberty than without it.

The existence of the sister republics after 1795 made peace impossible. Britain could never accept, short of total defeat, an international revolutionary republicanism installed in Belgium and Holland, threatening Ireland, and attracting sympathy in England itself. As for Austria, the Directory was willing to compromise. In return for its territories lost to the Cisalpine Republic, the Hapsburg monarchy received Venice and its mainland possessions, and in return for French acquisitions on the Rhine it was to absorb certain states of the Holy Roman Empire. The Austrians could accept drastic change, including the extinction of the Holy Roman Empire, the Kingdom of Poland, and the Republic of Venice, three of the most ancient structures in Europe. They could not accept drastic change brought about by revolutionary action. Already engaged in pacifying their portion of Poland, and in governing a disaffected Hungary, the Austrians after 1797 had the unwilling Venice and Venetians in their empire. They could hardly tolerate the Cisalpine and Roman Republics on the Venetian border.

As the Italian historian Zaghi has said, peace was impossible in 1798 because the revolution had become a diffuse force in itself, by no means localized in France, and certainly not in the Directory, but "in the very existence of the Cisalpine, the Roman, the Batavian and the Helvetic Republics." The Directory did not even believe in these new creations. It agreed with a long state paper drafted by Talleyrand, now the foreign minister, in July, 1798, which concluded that the sister republics were on balance a nuisance to France, drawing off French resources for their protection, unwilling to fight in their own interest, and standing in the way of any lasting peace or stabilization of the new order in

France. He made an exception only of the Batavian Republic, which had its own internal strength and was a willing and useful ally against England.

Fathered by the war, though with internal conditions in their own countries as their mothers, the sister republics were infant democracies born into a quarrelsome European household. They provided early sketches or models of a kind of democracy known on the Continent, as distinct from the democratic development of the United States or Great Britain.

Each republic had its constitution, corresponding to the French constitution of the Year III, itself derived from the constitution of 1789–91. Each constitution began with its declaration of the Rights of Man and Citizen. Each proclaimed the sovereignty of the people or citizen-body. Each pronounced its territory to be "one and indivisible," and each then divided the territory into uniform "departments," thus affirming territorial unity and internal geographic equality. Each provided for an elected bicameral legislature, with equality of numerical representation, for limited terms of office, and with salaries to be paid from the public treasury to the members. These provisions were in themselves enough to supplant the Old Order, in which representation, where it existed, was a privilege of some (but not all) towns, boroughs, or historic districts regardless of size, and was exercised either by inherited right or by persons who largely selected themselves, often for life, and who far from being "wage servants of the people" were expected to draw income from other sources. The actual suffrage in the various republics was almost universal for men, though combined with a system of secondary electoral assemblies, without which popular elections would hardly have been feasible, at a time when most voters were barely literate if at all, lacked the leisure for the week-long public deliberations, and had no political parties to explain issues or tell them for whom to vote. In all the republics the executive was a collegiate body chosen by the legislature. All gave citizenship to persons of any religion or of no religion and dissociated the clergy from public authority and from education. All abolished nobility, and redefined landed property to deprive it of its manorial or jurisdictional features. In all the republics, citizens became liable to the same taxes, the same law courts, penalties, and legal procedures. In all, there was an active participation through political clubs. In all of them the periodical press was more lively than it had been under the Old Order, even in Holland. All took steps for the advancement of public schools.

Changes projected on the local scene were even more significant than those at the upper levels, so much so that contemporaries often spoke of the revolution as a process of "departmentalization." France had been departmentalized in 1790. Savoy after 1792, the Austrian Netherlands and Liège after 1795, and the Left Bank of the Rhine after 1797 were departmentalized in the course of annexation to France. The Dutch Netherlands, Switzerland, and Italy were departmentalized in the Batavian, Helvetic, and various Italic republics. The effects were similar everywhere. The department, unlike the old province, was the creation of the new state. The state itself, whether large or small, whether France or the Cisalpine Republic, was unitary and centralized. There was reason for the association between democratic objectives and a centralized unitary and departmentalized public power. In the United States of the time, by way of contrast, it was the democrats who were most suspicious of centralization, and most insistent on local autonomy, because local authority had been democratic from the beginning. In the Old Order in Europe, local authority meant the power of hereditary status groups, manorial lords, benches of judges, exclusive town councils, guilds, and miscellaneous corporate or privileged bodies, reinforced by the parish clergy of an established church. The monarchies of the Old Order, like the old Dutch and Swiss federations, had been put together from these pre-existing parts, which in turn derived from the very different world of the Middle Ages. To have a democratic or even a modern state required the liquidation of these older units. In a society so deeply aristocratic, oligarchic, or ecclesiastical, democracy could not simply well up from below, as it supposedly did in America, or as some have supposed that it did in Great Britain. It required that the "nation"—a new revolutionary conception—act through both the central and the local machinery of a unitary state. The departments, along with the newly created municipalities, with their elected or appointed officers, were the organs by which the elites of the Old Order were met on their own ground. They were the channels through which new legislation could be imposed, the arenas in which resistance could be combated. It was here, on the local stage, but under national sponsorship, that "feudalism" gave way to the civic community conceived along new lines. It was a community in which the possessing and professional classes at first enjoyed the advantages, and participated most actively, but which in design and principle made room eventually for wider segments of the population.

[7]

The Batavian, Helvetic, and Italian Republics

THE DUTCH REVOLUTION was a continuation of the Patriot movement of the 1780s. It was a continuation with a difference, for the former Patriots had been made more radical by the negativism and repressiveness of the Orange regime as restored under Anglo-Prussian auspices in 1787. Some had emigrated to France and lived through the experience of the French Revolution. More had stayed at home, secretly awaiting the chance to renew their efforts.

It may be wondered what "revolution" could signify for so utterly middle-class a country, which had no genuine monarchy, no hierarchic church, few nobles, and few poor. The answer is that, like others, it had its privileged and unprivileged classes. Small hereditary circles of self-perpetuating regents enjoyed the emoluments of government. These were considerable; the thirty-six members of the governing council of Amsterdam, who chose themselves, also chose the burgomaster, elected the deputies to the Estates of Holland, and had 3,600 offices at their disposal as a source of income. A good many bankers, shipowners, merchants, professional men, and journalists, as well as tradesmen and artisans, stood outside these ruling groups. Almost half the population was not of the Reformed church. Mainly Catholic,

163

but with some Protestant sectaries, the religious outgroup, which included both rich and poor, was tolerated but not admitted to the best society or to higher political appointments. Very advanced in some ways, the country was "medieval" in others, a bundle of localistic provinces and towns, each with its estates and its councils over which no centralized government apparatus had been created. Foreign relations also were an old subject of controversy; there had long been pro-French and pro-British parties. The chronic dependency of the Orange family on England, the sympathy of many Dutch for the American Revolution, the British habit of seizing Dutch colonies, most recently in 1783, the role of Britain in the Orange restoration of 1787, the unpopular war with France in 1793, all added fuel to the Anglophobic fires.

The revolutionary party was, therefore, very mixed. It included some of the regents who believed that the country required administrative reform if it was to survive. It drew in wealthy commercial men outside the regent aristocracy. It appealed to Catholics and to the minority Protestants. It attracted intellectuals and the youth. While the lower half of the population generally favored the House of Orange, a good many shopkeepers and handicraft workers were discontented. In general, the leading revolutionaries were men of substance. The most prominent of the Dutch émigrés in 1794, for example, was General Daendels, a former brick manufacturer, doctor of laws, Patriot of 1787 and officer in the Batavian Legion of 1792. Both millionaires and workingmen could be found on both sides in the Dutch Revolution.

The French victories of the summer of 1794 brought the restless elements to life. By June there were thirty-four political clubs active in Amsterdam and twelve in Utrecht, disguised as reading societies, discussing Paine's *Rights of Man* and Paulus' *Menschenvriend*, exchanging delegations, communicating with the Dutch émigrés, and secretly storing arms. One of their members, I. J. A. Gogel, who worked for an Amsterdam business firm, wrote secretly to the French—at the height of the Terror, and with his government at war—urging the French to invade Holland, abolish the existing privileges, guilds, provinces, monopolies, magistracies and law courts, and introduce a new constitution along with a revolutionary tribunal and guillotine. On July 31, as the French crossed the frontier, the clubs from seven provinces met at Amsterdam. They sent a messenger to French headquarters to ask on what terms they might be spared the fate of a "conquered country," such as they feared was being dealt out to Belgium. The French replied that they would treat the Dutch as allies if they would first stage their own revolution.

That the Dutch clubs found this reply disconcerting is significant not only for Holland but for all the sister republics. The situation was typical of them all. The Dutch clubs wanted a revolution, but not the popular violence and turmoil that revolution might involve. They wanted a revolution supervised by the French army, an orderly and safe revolution in which the Old Regime would be overthrown, a new constitution introduced, and counterrevolutionaries driven away, but in which anarchy and bloodshed would be prevented by the armed forces of the French Republic. It is in this element of prudence and readiness to depend on outsiders that the revolutions in the sister republics were not true revolutions at all.

As the French advanced, the country fell to pieces. By stipulating only that the House of Orange must go, and that Holland join in the war against England, and by refraining from revolutionary threats, the French appealed to a wide stratum of Dutch opinion. Moderates joined with incendiaries. Committees formed by the clubs moved in to replace old burgomasters and councils. Riots in Amsterdam and elsewhere unseated the older authorities. The Orange regime seemed helpless; no one was willing to fight for it; it made no concessions to enhance its popularity. It tried to proclaim a *levée en masse* to repel invasion. It obtained no response. The regime could not, like the French Convention in 1793, proclaim an ideal of liberty and equality to recruit a citizen army. This too was typical; for in all the sister republics (as indeed in France in 1788) the revolution could be explained more by the weakness of the Old Order than by the power of its opponents.

In January, 1795, in a memorable operation, the French cavalry rode into Amsterdam on the ice, and Dutch revolutionaries proclaimed the Batavian Republic. From the beginning, the Batavians showed an ardor that in France was already beginning to subside. For example, it was the Batavian Republic that first made official use of the magic triad—Liberty, Equality, Fraternity—not employed in this exact form in France until 1848. The Prince of Orange fled to England. The Batavian Republic signed a severe treaty with France, by which it declared war on England, paid an indemnity of 100 million florins, agreed to support the French occupying army, accepted the French annexation of Belgium, and ceded the mouth of the Scheldt. A few Dutch revolutionaries were enraged by the treaty. Most of them thought it acceptable; they were willing enough to fight England, and wealthy enough to pay the costs.

For three years the French stood by, in military occupation but refraining from interference in Dutch affairs, waiting for the Dutch to decide for themselves on the form of their new republic. The Dutch found it difficult to devise a constitution, or even to call a constitutional convention, because of profound differences on "unitary" as against "federal" principles. The difference reflected concrete social realities. Federalism held that provinces and towns, whether large or small, should preserve their old identity and be represented as such. Unitarism held that these corporate entities should be disregarded; that only real individuals and human beings should count; that influence should be in proportion to numbers. Federalism protected the position of men who already enjoyed influence, prestige, or office in existing political units. It was conservative in effect. Unitarism was the doctrine of democrats. The problem arose also from the very great disparity between the existing units. For example, the Union consisted of seven provinces, but Holland had half the population. Hollanders, therefore, were unitarists, wanting numbers of inhabitants to count in a unified Batavian nation. Most of the enormous Dutch public debt was also in fact the debt of Holland. Hollanders wanted this debt to be assumed by a unified Batavian state. People in the less populous and less indebted provinces thus inclined to federalism. To Hollanders and democrats it seemed that federalism was an excuse put up by the most rustic, backward, traditional, and old-fashioned people in the country, including the former elites.

At first, the federalists insisted on maintaining the framework of the old Estates General, in which the seven provinces were represented as such. The democrats demanded a true "convention." They became menacing and tumultuous. The French, in this Thermidorian phase of the last months of the French Convention, considered the Dutch democrats to be dangerously radical, *véritables sans-culottes*, and even forbade French soldiers to associate with them. Months passed in struggles at local levels between obstreperous democrats on the one hand, and federalists often supported by secret Orange and British agents on the other, until in 1796 it became possible for a convention to assemble. For its election, the seven provinces and the two areas of Drenthe and North Brabant, which had never received provincial rights, were replaced by 124 equal electoral districts. The convention thus elected found itself still stalemated on the same unitary-versus-federalist question. After more than a year, it produced a constitution which it submitted for popular ratification in August, 1797. The most notable innovation was disestablishment of the Reformed church, with admission of Catholics, Jews, and minority Protestants to equal rights. But the constitution was a compromise that satisfied no one. In populous Holland and Utrecht the unitary democrats voted against it. In the more conservative inland provinces the voters rejected it for its radicalism. A second convention was thereupon chosen, but it too seemed unable to reach any agreement.

At this point the French intervened. What they wanted was an organized Dutch government that could play a positive role in the common war against England. In this aim the Dutch democrats fully concurred. Britain, for them, was the real force behind the House of Orange, which hardly at that time enjoyed its later popularity among the Dutch. As the Princess of Orange, writing from England, observed to her son: "No one will make a man budge for us without British money." And the Orange family was proving as counterrevolutionary as any royal dynasty. William V rejected all proposals of compromise with his own people, even proposals made by his own son, who was a leading conciliator, and in 1814 became the first king of the Netherlands. To all approaches from moderates, William V replied by insisting on restoration of the Reformed Religion, "hereditary honors and offices," and the "privileges of provinces, towns and bodies of nobles." "I am positively decided," he said in 1797, "not to return on any conditions founded on the democratic basis of alleged rights of man and equality." In short, William V took the same position as Louis XVIII. Moderates in the Netherlands, as in France, were driven to support the Republic.

After the Fructidor coup d'état in France, and after the breakup of the peace conferences with England, the French laid plans for an invasion of England and assembled a large *Armée d'Angleterre* on the channel coast. The assistance of the Dutch navy and transports was vital. The Dutch fleet, however, was defeated in October by the British at Camperdown. Dutch democrats denounced incompetence and possible treason among the Batavian moderates. They demanded a Dutch Fructidor, which with French support they obtained in the coup d'état of January 22, 1798. Twenty-two moderates or federalists were expelled from the Batavian Convention.

The convention now speedily adopted a unitary and democratic constitution, using a draft prepared in Paris by a combination of French and Dutch, and adding a few features to make a more democratic document than the French at first favored. It provided for manhood suffrage, and set up a bicameral legislature and an Executive Directory of five persons, as in France. It thus abolished the old Estates General and the stadtholderate. It likewise abolished all guilds, monopolies, "staples," and other barriers to the circulation of goods and persons. It completed the disestablishment of the Reformed church. And it provided for a unified civic community, or "nation," consolidating the debt and the revenues, and extinguishing the old provinces, which it replaced with eight departments of equal population. The older bases of political position were thus swept away. Submitted for popular ratification in a population of about 400,000 adult males, the constitution received 165,520 affirmative as against only 11,597 negative votes.

The five months from January to June, 1798, saw the height of the democratic movement in the Netherlands. There was a scramble for office on the part of people not yet seen in public life, such as barrelmakers and warehouse keepers, apothecaries, and shipping clerks. Various persons of higher station were ejected; some feared for their careers or their property, though not really for their lives. Even men in the government known for democratic opinions thought the populist agitation went too far. But the course of Batavian politics really depended on the French. The French Directory underwent a new oscillation in May, when it quashed the democratic or neo-Jacobin successes in the French elections of 1798. It also decided in May, secretly, to give up the invasion of either England or Ireland. Bonaparte took an army to Egypt instead. The French had less need for the most zealous anti-British feeling among the Dutch. They allowed the Dutch democrats who had turned "moderate," men like Daendels and Gogel, already mentioned, to carry through a second coup d'état in June, by which the more fiery democrats were driven out of the government.

In 1799 the British and Russians landed a sizable army in north Holland. They imagined from information given by secret agents and by Orangist émigrés that the Dutch in the Batavian Republic, supposedly oppressed by the French and by a few Dutch collaborators, would rise to greet the invaders in a great surge of liberation. It was expected that the true Dutch people, or at least the better sort, allying with the Anglo-Russian force, and in conjunction with other armies coming by way of Switzerland and Italy, would converge in a grand invasion of France, join with French royalists rising in insurrection, and at last after ten years put an end to the French Revolution. Nothing of the sort happened. The Dutch did not stir. They did not want William V back, or the old Union of Utrecht. A combined French and Batavian army soon forced the humiliated Anglo-Russians to take to sea.

The Batavian Republic underwent a succession of changes, turned into the Kingdom of Holland under Louis Bonaparte in Napoleon's empire, and then in 1814 into the Kingdom of the Netherlands with the last stadtholder's son as the first Dutch king. The most basic changes made by the Batavian revolution and the constitution of 1798 were retained throughout: territorial uniformity, fiscal consolidation, modernized administration and law courts, religious disestablishment, and equality of civil rights.

Switzerland before 1798 was even more amorphous than the United Provinces. There were only thirteen cantons, all German-speaking, and united in a loose confederation called an *Eidgenossenschaft*, or "oath-fellowship." The trilingual Switzerland of modern times did not yet exist. Geneva and Neuchâtel did not belong to the confederation. The French-speaking Vaud and Valais, like the Italian-speaking regions to the south, were dependencies of this or that canton or combination of cantons. Most of the German-speaking peoples lived in "allied" or "subject" districts, not in cantons. Some of the high Alpine cantons were small folk-democracies which settled their affairs in public meetings and wished to preserve their isolation. They had remained Catholic at the time of the Reformation. These "primitive" cantons, however, the fabled country of William Tell, comprised only a twentieth of the population. Essentially, the confederation was a league of busy Protestant towns, of which Bern, Basel, and Zurich were the most important. Rights were town rights, or burgher privileges. "To be born in Switzerland," said Peter Ochs in 1796, "gives no rights whatsoever."

Never having been brought under a monarchy, the Swiss had indeed escaped royal despotism but also the accompanying effects of modernization. Medieval liberties flourished. There was no uniform law, coinage, or weights and measures. There were about a hundred "internal" tariffs. The roads were poor. Guilds in each town regulated business and labor within local horizons. The rural people in many places were subject to manorial dues and a seigneurial jurisdiction which no monarchy had restricted. Each canton was free to have its own religion, but there was no religious freedom for individual persons. Torture was used in criminal cases, newspapers were censored, and political undesirables were sent to prison. Except in the small "democratic" cantons, government was in the hands of a few families that filled the various town councils from one generation to the next. The famous nineteenth-century historian Burckhardt, for example, with his distaste for the mass age, came from one of the old ruling families of Basel. It is true that Switzerland had none of the wealthy, haughty, and ostentatious aristocracy that congregated at Vienna or Versailles. But the image of Switzerland as a land of simple equality and innocent liberty was mainly a literary dream to which the facts hardly corresponded.

Always fearful of contamination, the Swiss governments took especial pains after 1789 to keep out news of the French Revolution. There was, however, much dissatisfaction in Switzerland. It was most openly expressed by Swiss who knew the world outside. Paulus Usteri, a Zurich doctor, wrote for journals in Leipzig and Augsburg. The Zurich educator Pestalozzi was in full touch with the European Enlightenment. La Harpe before 1796 had tutored the grand dukes of Russia. P. M. Glayre, a Vaudois like La Harpe, had been adviser to the king of Poland. Peter Ochs, a Basel patrician, owned property in France and had the first Revolutionary mayor of Strasbourg for a brother-in-law.

Men of this kind began to correspond and to lay plans in the 1790s. With the war of 1792 it became doubtful whether the neutrality of the country could be preserved. Against such a hive of French émigrés and British agents, actively conspiring against the new government in France, and against the ancient ambitions of Austria, it seemed likely that the French might intervene. Even the separate existence of Switzerland, or its territorial integrity, such as it was, was in doubt. In 1792 the French had occupied the Bishopric of Basel, in 1793 they took the semi-Swiss Savoy from Sardinia, in 1798 they annexed Geneva. In 1797 the southern region of the Valtellina went to the Cisalpine Republic. After this new state was created in north Italy, the French-speaking Valais, already disaffected against Bern, and controlling the approach to the Simplon pass, became of interest to Bonaparte as an avenue of communication between France and Milan. It was possible that Switzerland, like Poland, might be partitioned.

Ochs, La Harpe, Bonaparte, and the French Directors, meeting in Paris in December, 1797, decided to sponsor a revolution in Switzerland. Ochs prepared a constitution, which the Directors Reubell and Merlin de Douai considerably amended. In the following weeks revolts broke out in various of the cantons and subject districts. Patriots in the Vaud, the region about Lausanne, captured the château of Chillon and proclaimed a "Lemanic Republic" independent of Bern. In the Thurgau the rural subjects of the city of Zurich, many of them weavers who worked for Zurich businessmen, rebelled against the city. The French, with the Swiss as with the Dutch, would have preferred the revolution to be indigenous, or at least to seem so, especially since Switzerland was not a combatant in the war. They agreed with La Harpe, however, on the wisdom of using military force before the shaken Swiss governments could concert their resistance, or Britain or Austria come to their aid. The French army occupied Bern. Its commander, Brune, on orders from Paris, first proclaimed three separate republics—the Rhone Republic for the French and Italian districts, the Helvetic Republic for the German towns, and the Tellgau Republic, named for William Tell, for the rural and old-fashioned "democratic" Alpine cantons that preferred to be left out of any future arrangements. La Harpe and other Swiss patriots, thus faced with the prospect of actual dismemberment, then urged the imposition, by the French, of a unitary republic in which the ethnic groups should be for the first time on a plane of equality. The Directory changed its orders to Brune, who in March, 1798, proclaimed a single all-embracing Helvetic Republic, under the constitution of which Ochs was a principal author.

The constitution was published in German, French, and Italian. It was unitary and consolidationist, as a protection against secessionism, linguistic divergence, and counterrevolutionary efforts. As among the Dutch, conservatives were "federalists" and the unitary principle was "democratic." A Directory and a two-chamber legislature, as in France, began to function. Ochs and La Harpe became Directors. The constitution introduced the modern forms of liberty and equality in place of old burgher privileges and subject status. It provided for religious freedom and national citizenship. Legal differences between town dwellers and rural people disappeared. The largest of the old cantons, Bern and Zurich, were reduced. New cantons were created, so that the whole territory was laid out in legally equal cantons. The new cantons were in effect "departments," in the new language of the Revolution; they were called cantons, or in German *Orte*, as a concession to Swiss traditions. All the twenty-two cantons of modern Switzerland (except Geneva and Neuchâtel), and indeed the principle of cantonal organization for the area as a whole, though much changed and modified by decentralization, date in effect from the revolution of 1798.

Switzerland was thus saved from dismemberment but hardly from foreign influence. "Switzerland today," wrote Talleyrand to Ochs, "must be either Austrian or French." Or as the British agent William Wickham observed in 1799, when he was working with Swiss émigrés to restore the Old Order, the Swiss must "be delivered, *bound hand and foot* [his emphasis]—they cannot have a will of their own."

Since it was French influence that prevailed, the Helvetic Republic set about an energetic program of reform along the general lines of the international revolution. In some ways it was the most conservative of the sister republics; for example, it was the only one to withhold equal rights from Jews, it required twenty years for naturalization (as against ten in the Batavian Republic and seven in France under the Directory), and in the attempt to please the conservative cantons of the high mountains it allowed Zug, with 20,000 inhabitants, to have as many representatives as Zurich, with 150,000. But it worked at abolition of seigneurial dues and tithes. Despite compromises, it thus won support from the rural people. The Helvetic Republic, in fact, differed from the other sister republics, and from France itself, in that the rural population (outside the "primitive" cantons) tended to be more radical than the formerly privileged cities. The country people gladly threw off their "subject" status. Many were advanced enough to appreciate the advantages of abolition of guilds, freedom of occupation and enterprise, development of schools, and equal access to educational facilities. It was the Helvetic Republic that enabled Pestalozzi to run his famous school near Bern. Land law was modernized, tariffs, and tolls were simplified or abolished, monasteries closed and their property confiscated. There was not much violence against religion, but the abbot of St. Gallen lost his 100,000 temporal subjects, who were reorganized as a canton, and the new laws provided for civil marriage and for mixed marriages between Protestants and Catholics. Torture was abolished, the courts were reformed, and the press set at liberty.

There were of course many Swiss who opposed the Helvetic Republic and all its works. There were about 5,000 Swiss émigrés, led by the abbot of St. Gallen and the former chief magistrate of Bern. These men, like the most irreconcilable of French and Dutch émigrés, sought British and Austrian help and insisted on a total restoration of the Old Order. The old "democratic" cantons also resisted. These were Uri, Schwyz, Zug, and Unterwalden, the nucleus of the original confederation, tiny communities in the high valleys which had long managed their own affairs undisturbed by the outside world. They objected to the taxes, the bureaucracy, the higher courts, and the military service that membership in a "big" Switzerland would entail. They complained also that, as Catholics, they were being robbed of their "holy religion." They reflected the conflict between an ancient direct democracy, meaning essentially the independence of the folk meeting, and the modern, or "representative," democracy, which the Helvetic Republic explicitly claimed to introduce. They therefore rebelled, and the Helvetic government, having no armed force of its own, requested the French army to put them down. This it did, whereupon the Helvetic authorities dissolved the four small cantons and recombined them into one of more normal size. The inhabitants remained hostile. The British, the Austrians, and the émigré Swiss patricians turned these events into propaganda against the democratic pretensions of the Helvetic Republic.

Opposition was generated also by the French. The occupation was harder on the Swiss than on the Dutch. Beginning by removing the "treasure" of Bern, the French proceeded through a long series of official levies and requisitions, which were made worse by pillaging and by the private self-enrichment of various French agents and officers. Many who had favored the original intervention by the French now turned against them. The French also demanded an offensive and defensive alliance. Some Swiss, including Ochs, believed the request reasonable, since the survival of the Helvetic Republic depended on defeat of the European Counterrevolution. Most, however, including La Harpe, took a more characteristic Swiss attitude, insisting that Switzerland remain neutral, or fight only within its own frontiers and only if attacked. The French, after a coup d'état, forced acceptance of the treaty anyway.

The French also asked the Helvetic Republic to raise its own army, like the Batavian and the Cisalpine. Only a force of 18,000 was requested, not a large number, considering that at least 11,000 Swiss mercenaries had been in the French service before the French Revolution. The French proposed conscription and Ochs agreed: "Nothing would better serve kings than for republics to renounce compulsory service." The Helvetic legislature flatly refused, on the very eve of the Austrian and Russian invasion of 1799. There were about 4,000 voluntary enlistments, and one young lieutenant of 1799 lived to be commander in chief of the Swiss Federal army in 1830. On the whole, however, the very Swiss who favored the Helvetic Revolution believed that it should be the French who defended it. On the other hand, attempts to raise a counter-revolutionary Swiss force, at British expense, were even less successful. The Swiss, with the whole future regime of their country at stake, simply preferred not to be involved.

In July, 1799, Marshall Suvorov brought a Russian army across the St. Gotthard pass. He had just destroyed the Cisalpine Republic; he meant now to destroy the Helvetic, and then to move into eastern France, join with the Russian army from Holland, and, with Austrian support, proceed to stamp out, once and for all, the center of revolutionary conflagration in Paris. The abbot of St. Gallen and other Swiss émigrés expected to return. But a French general, Masséna, and a French army, supported by the small Helvetic contingents, defeated Suvorov at the second battle of Zurich.

So the Helvetic Republic—as well as the French—survived. Switzerland went through many vicissitudes in Napoleonic and later times. But the Helvetic Republic had the same kind of lasting significance as the Batavian. The transmutation which it brought proved lasting. In Switzerland, as in the United Provinces, the constitution of 1798 was the vehicle by which an archaic system of medieval liberties moved on to become a modern state, with the kinds of legal rights, territorial nationality, and individual citizenship which the Revolution offered to Europe.

Italy before 1796 consisted on the map of some ten principal states. Adjoining France in the northwest was the Kingdom of Sardinia, shut off from the coast by the independent Republic of Genoa. Milan was the capital of a duchy attached to the Hapsburg empire. From a point only twenty miles east of Milan, and running on into Dalmatia, were the territories of the Republic of Venice. Parma, Modena, and Tuscany were independent duchies, of which Tuscany, by far the most important, belonged to the Hapsburg family but not to the empire. The Papal States ran from the mouth of the Po to a point south of Rome. All the south, including Sicily, formed the Kingdom of Naples.

The most important units of social life, however, were not these territorial states but the cities. They were the lasting realities around which political boundaries fluctuated. City life had continued in Italy even during the true feudal period north of the Alps. As a result, the contrast between noble and commoner, or between lord and burgher, was less distinct than in northern Europe. Nobles lived in town, and urban patricians owned country estates. Revolutionary feeling in Italy was not an affair of a third estate against nobles; it was characterized, in fact, by the large number of noblemen who took part in it. The revolutionaries were city dwellers, noble or not, but recruited, as elsewhere, from lawyers, doctors, engineers, government servants, and officeholders, merchants, journalists, writers, free intellectuals, and persons who simply lived on income from their own property or annuities. The mass of the population remained unaroused or conservative. Urban workingmen took less part in the revolution in Italy than in Holland, and there was nothing in Italy like the rural support for the new regime that could be found in the Helvetic Republic. In the north, the country people were free farmers who suffered heavily from French requisitions and pillaging. In the south, where agriculture was unproductive, an impoverished peasantry worked on huge estates whose owners lived in the cities. Since the *giacobini* were urban, this rural proletariat was suspicious of "Jacobinism."

Revolutionary sympathizers included also in Italy a surprising number of priests, and even bishops. The very fact that Italy was so Catholic, and the seat of the papacy, produced dissatisfaction among the clergy. There was a strong current of what was called Jansenism. This term covered a variety of attitudes: the opposition of some bishops to the papal power; the opposition of some governments to ecclesiastical influence; the actual religious beliefs of some priests and some laymen, who saw a danger to the church in its wealth, its pomp, and its administrative complexity, who favored a more apostolic simplicity, and who found in the modern message of liberty, equality, and fraternity, "rightly understood," a restatement of the Christian faith. The revolutionary disturbances saw anti-Christian outbursts in Italy as elsewhere, but they were less violent than in France, and the area of agreement between Christianity and the Revolution was greater than in France or than in the predominantly Protestant sister republics north of the Alps. Certainly neither the Anglican nor the Dutch Reformed establishments showed any such receptiveness to the Revolution. Fourteen cardinals were present at the birth of the Roman Republic; the future Pius VII, then Bishop of Imola, gave the Cisalpine Republic his blessing; and the French Cardinal Maury reported with disgust, during the reaction of 1799 at Naples, that "ninety-year-old priests, on being hanged, have preached democracy and invoked the French at the steps of the gallows." When the Counterrevolution prevailed temporarily in north Italy in 1799, almost five hundred clergy were suspended in Lombardy for revolutionary activity in the preceding years, and a list of 4,300 "dangerous Jacobins" in Piedmont included 742 priests.

It was a restless and expectant country that the French army entered in 1796. Italy too had had its "philosophers," its Enlightenment, its reading clubs, and its rapid growth of the press. The Italian universities were more alive than those of France or England. While Italy had long since lost its primacy in long-distance trade, there was a good deal of commercial development in Tuscany and the north. Many merchants and enterprising landowners found the localism of guilds and towns an obstruction to their ambitions. Italy had had its reforming governments. The most striking example was Tuscany under Leopold, where so many changes had already been introduced that the Revolution attracted little support. Even Pius VI had attempted reforms and sold off church properties to laymen to mend his finances. There had been many proposals at Milan to reform the tax structure, the land law, the law courts, and the governing councils. These had failed, not because of the Austrian overlordship, which had in fact pressed for reform before 1790, but because the conservative Milanese patricians had sensed a threat to their established customs and privileges. In the Italian cities, as elsewhere, there were inbred and hereditary ruling families which disliked new men and new ideas. The old municipal feeling itself also made for discontent. Bologna and Ferrara objected to government by papal legates. Verona and Padua resented the supremacy of the city of Venice, in whose affairs even their own patricians could play no part. Instead of a system in which one city ruled over another, many Italians wanted a modern state. It need not be the unified Italy of literary imagination, but it should have an enlarged territorial base, individual citizenship, an expanded trading area, and means of overcoming the opposition between town and town, and between town and country.

Various revolutionary conspiracies were at work before the French arrived. Two clubs had been formed at Naples at the time of a visit by the French fleet in 1792. Though repressed, the agitation continued in secret until the French army arrived in 1799. In 1794 a conspiracy at Bologna against the government of the pope resulted in trials, torture, and execution. In 1793 Sardinia went to war with France, supported by a grant of £200,000 from Britain, and two revolutionary clubs were formed at Turin, supported by the French envoy at Genoa. The more moderate of these clubs was led by a banker; the other, more definitely republican, included medical students and doctors, one of whom was Carlo Botta, later famous as a historian. The plots were discovered; the plotters fled. Some sought out Robespierre's brother, stationed on the Italian frontier in 1794; but, as already noted, the Committee of Public Safety took no interest in them. It was with men of this kind that Buonarroti was in touch during the Babeuf conspiracy of 1796, one of whose objectives was the liberation of Italy.

Bonaparte routed the Austrians at the bridge of Lodi in May, 1796. The French then occupied Milan, where various liberal patricians like Melzi d'Eril and Pietro Verri came out to meet them, the populace cheered, and middle-class persons formed a Society of Friends of Liberty and Equality. The aim of the French was to pursue and defeat the Austrians, and to support their army by local requisitions. For this purpose they first set up a Military Agency of three Frenchmen, which was soon replaced, as a more effective instrument for French purposes, by a General Administration of Lombardy composed of sympathetic Italians. The French were more concerned with logistics than with revolution. But as the Italian historian Ghisalberti has said, "The battle of the bridge at Lodi imposed on all actors on the political stage the problem of the democratization of Italy."

The General Administration (like the Belgians and Dutch before it) had no desire to administer a mere occupied area. It began to work for a Lombard or even an all-Italian republic. It sponsored a famous essay contest, which the economist Gioia won, on "Which form of free government is best suited to Italy?" Gioia and many other contestants favored a unitary democratic republic. It was the General Administration, also, that organized a Lombard Legion, to which it gave a new flag of red, white, and green stripes. Thus the modern Italian tricolor, like the Polish national anthem, first sung by the Polish Legion, appeared in the Po valley in 1796. Meanwhile there were revolutionary outbreaks beyond the boundaries of the Austrian Milanese. Republicans again rose in the Kingdom of Sardinia. Modena and Reggio revolted against the pope. Padua, Verona, Vicenza, Bergamo rebelled against Venice. In Venice itself a group of democrats overthrew the historic Venetian oligarchy. Each city acted on its own. Bologna provided itself with a constitution, regarded as the first modern constitution of Italy. Various cities sent their separate delegations to Paris to solicit aid. Rejecting the old, yet jealous of each other, they as yet had no plans for a larger territorial unit.

In the face of an Austrian counteroffensive, audiences in the Milan theater sang the *Marseillaise*, and in November, in a great demonstration before the cathedral, the Milanese patriots proclaimed the independence of Lombardy and demanded "primary assemblies" for election of a constituent assembly. The French army suppressed this uprising by force. Bonaparte, still actively engaged against the Austrians, was not ready for a republic in Lombardy. South of the Po, however, he concluded that French interests would be served by bringing together the insurgent cities, so that deputies from Bologna, Ferrara, Modena, and Reggio met in an assembly, drafted a constitution, and set up an entity called the Cispadane Republic at the end of 1796.

The Cispadane, with its Directory, its Legislative Body, and its new judicial, administrative, fiscal, military, and electoral apparatus, was modeled on the French constitution of the Year III. Of all the republics proclaimed in Italy in these years the Cispadane was born with the least interference from the French. Its constitution was in this sense the most purely Italian, and yet of all the constitutions of the *triennio* (three years of the revolution) it most resembled the French. It was when least pressed by the French that the Italians most fully agreed with them, since they drew on a body of thought, in the Enlightenment, which was not so much French as supranational or European. There had been much constitutional thinking in Italy, and one member of the Cispadane assembly, Compagnoni, was appointed, at Ferrara in 1797, to what is called the first professorship of constitutional law in a European university.

By the spring of 1797 Bonaparte defeated the Austrians and made a truce with them at Leoben. He turned his mind to the revolutionaries by whom all northern Italy was being shaken. His decisions settled their fate. He refused to sponsor those in Sardinia, where the monarchy survived. He withheld support from those in Venice and most of its mainland cities, which in fact he turned over to the Austrians as a kind of exchange for Milan. He decided to make Milan the capital of a Cisalpine Republic, with which the Cispadane was merged in 1797. For his "betrayal" of the Venetian and Sardinian revolutionaries he was loudly denounced by the advanced democrats of both Italy and France. It was the sacrifice of Venice, indeed, more than the Terror itself, which turned Wordsworth and other foreign sympathizers in England against the French Revolution, and contributed to the reputation of the Directory for "cynicism." But by his creation of the Cisalpine (and of the Ligurian at Genoa) Bonaparte also became the hero of republicans everywhere. They flocked from all over Italy to Milan, now a center of revolutionary journalism, club meetings, and general agitation, where talk of overthrowing the pope and the king of Naples began to be heard. It was to protect his new Cisalpine Republic, as already noted, that Bonaparte joined with the republicans of the French Directory to repress royalism in the coup d'état of Fructidor, and a few months later to sponsor revolution in Switzerland. Even the distant Americans saw something sensational in the Cisalpine Republic. To the young John Quincy Adams it seemed that the insatiable French were determined to republicanize and hence ruin the world. But for American "republicans," as democrats were then called, the auguries were more favorable. Andrew Jackson, in 1798, hoped that Bonaparte would next go to invade and republicanize England itself.

The Cisalpine Republic (which became the Italian Republic in 1802 and the Kingdom of Italy in 1805) marked an important step in the Italian Risorgimento, and offered a brilliant example of what the Revolution meant to eighteenth-century Europe. Unlike the other sister republics, it was a wholly new territorial formation. It was put together from fragments of six former jurisdictions: the duchies of Milan, Mantua, and Modena, the northern papal states (Bologna, Ferrara, Imola), western Venetia (Bergamo, Brescia), and the Italian-speaking Valtellina, formerly subject to the Swiss Dreibünde. These miscellaneous regions were reorganized into twenty legally and administratively uniform departments, which mostly received the names of rivers, as in France after 1789. Above them were the usual Executive Directory and Legislative Body. The first incumbents of those offices, however, were not elected but simply appointed by Bonaparte from among the Italians in whom he had confidence. The higher structure of government in the Cisalpine was of little importance. It was repeatedly subjected to revisions and coups d'état. The importance of the Cisalpine lies rather in the program that it pursued, and in the rounds of activity that it promoted—the outburst of political journalism, the public meetings and speeches, the administrative activity in the departments, the attempts to instruct the people and the projects, debates, and enactments of the Legislative Body.

To review the efforts of the Cisalpine Republic in a mere two years (before it was temporarily crushed and abolished by the Austro-Russian reaction of 1799) is to repeat the program of the Revolution wherever it came into power. Nobility was abolished. Torture disappeared. The press was freed. Jews received equal rights. An Italian peculiarity, the use of castrated men as singers, was prohibited as an indefensible outrage to human dignity. Guilds and internal tolls and tariffs were done away with. Taxes were simplified, and budgets introduced. Education was removed from the control of the bishops, and there was much discussion of a system of state-supported public schools, since the constitution specified, as in France, that after twelve years literacy would be required for voting. Family trusts on *fidecommessi*, the equivalent of the English primogeniture and entail, were suppressed, so that younger sons were able to inherit, the market for real property became more mobile, and the economic basis of an aristocratic family system was undermined. An army of 15,000 troops was created, with a mild degree of conscription in 1798. Military service had long been virtually unknown in Italy, but it was a doctrine of the Revolution that a free state must possess its own citizen army.

The Cisalpine Republic, though recognizing a certain preponderance for Catholicism, took a firm attitude toward the church. It was the only sister republic to use the French republican calendar. It was "secular" in the sense that religion had nothing to do with political and civil rights. It confiscated and resold properties of the church, which were generally bought up by middle-class city people. Monastic vows were prohibited. Civil marriage was provided, and divorce permitted under certain conditions. Religious processions were put under strict controls, church bells were not to ring at night, images of the saints were removed from the streets, and streets named for saints received new republican designations. The government named the bishops, and citizens elected their parish priests. No ecclesiastical document originating outside the Republic could be admitted against the will of the government.

It is noteworthy, in these circumstances, that a great many of the bishops in the various cities of which it was composed accepted and approved of the Cisalpine Republic. Most memorable in retrospect is the case of Chiaramonti, the bishop of Imola in the former Papal States, who became Pope Pius VII in 1800. He was not the most collaborationist of the bishops. He never conceded the right of the government to appoint churchmen or to exclude papal communications. But he accepted the annexation of Imola to the Cisalpine, used the republican calendar in his letters and the printed words Liberty and Equality on his letterheads, waived the title of Monsignor and allowed himself to be addressed as "Citizen Cardinal." He complied with a request from the Cisalpine government to deliver a Christmas sermon, in 1797, in support of the new regime. What he gave was a genuine religious message, in which he insisted that democracy was more in need of Christianity than other forms of government because it required a subordination of selfish interests. But he recognized the Republic and the principles which it expressed. "The democratic form of government adopted among us, dear brethren, is not contrary to the Gospel. . . . Be good Christians, and you will be excellent democrats."

Despite this record, Chiaramonti was elected pope hardly more than two years later, and lived through a long and troubled pontificate. His Christmas sermon was soon buried in oblivion; under conditions of the nineteenth century neither conservatives nor democrats, neither clergy nor anticlericals, wanted to remember that there had ever been a citizen cardinal or an almost Jacobin pope. Only in recent years have Catholic historians in France and Italy brought to light the true situation of 1797.

The French Directory, never forgetting that its real enemies were Austria and Great Britain, and never fully persuaded that revolution in Italy was desirable or viable anyway, soon came to regard the Cisalpine Republic as something of a problem. The Italians, for their part, became increasingly anti-French, even those Italians who remained most favorable to revolution in Italy. The

French imposed, as with the Batavian and Helvetic republics, a treaty guaranteeing financial and military support in the war against the common foe. The Cisalpines were divided on the propriety of the treaty. The burden of French requisitions was heavy, and a great many individual Frenchmen, from Bonaparte on down through both military and civilian echelons, made considerable private fortunes through various forms of plunder. The Directory attempted to control the private depredations of French army officers, if only to keep the flow within official channels. It tried also to restrain the most vociferous Cisalpine democrats, and the firebrands from all Italy who congregated at Milan, who made trouble by their antireligious excesses or noisy threats against the pope and the kings and dukes from Sardinia to Naples. As a result, disaffected French generals and Italian superrepublicans both turned against the Directory in Paris, accusing it of moderatism, timidity, and betrayal of the revolution.

When, therefore, General Duphot was killed in Rome, in the course of an anti-French demonstration, in December, 1797, a clamor arose throughout Italy, and was echoed in Paris, for French intervention against the insufferable and incompetent government of the Papal States. The Directory ordered French troops to occupy Rome. The pope was driven out of the city. A crowd of Romans assembled in the Forum by the French General Berthier gave their acclamation to an act of independence of the Roman people. Four Frenchmen then hastily wrote a constitution for the new Roman Republic.

Though created under these unpromising auspices, the Roman Republic actually enjoyed considerable support in Rome itself. As elsewhere, especially in Italy, the most depressed classes were the least attracted to new ideas. In Rome they believed that the pope had been outraged. Since Rome had a numerous Jewish colony, which threw off the ghetto badges on the day the French entered the city, the latent anti-Semitism of the populace was aroused against a revolution that seemed suspiciously "Jewish." But among persons sufficiently enlightened to perceive the difference between the pope's temporal and spiritual powers—both laymen and ecclesiastics—there was more inclination to accept the new regime, which replaced the pope's government, but did not in principle question his spiritual authority. It was only a few weeks since Chiaramonti, himself a former subject of the Papal States, had spoken in favor of Cisalpine democracy. There were other north Italian bishops less guarded in their enthusiasm for revolutionary republicanism than the bishop of Imola. Seen in this light, it is the less surprising that half the cardinals then in Rome lent their presence to the opening ceremonies of the new state, though all but two of them soon departed. A canon of St. Peter's became finance minister of the Roman Republic, two friars became battalion commanders in the National Guard, and a Dominican scholar joined the new National Institute. There were many sympathizers with the new regime among regular clergy who taught in the schools. A well-known theological writer, G. V. Bolgeni, who had been a Jesuit in former days, wrote a pamphlet to argue that the church must adapt itself to modern conditions, and to explain that Catholics could be loyal both to the exiled pope and to the Republic, to which he himself took the oath.

Laymen of the upper and middle classes had long been restive under the papal government, in which the highest positions were reserved for elderly ecclesiastics, and which at best was devious, inefficient, and cumbersome. Attempts at reform made by Pius VI himself, attempts to correct the chronic evils of nepotism, inflation, debt, and agrarian landlordism, had been generally unsuccessful. Persons interested in reform were therefore willing to give a chance to the Republic. They included many nobles of the Borghese and other families. Doctors were active; one of them became a "consul," corresponding to Director in the other sister republics. Lawyers practicing in the papal courts, and lay officials and administrators generally, were well disposed. Among leading Jews in the city, several joined the National Guard and one was elected a senator. In favor of the Republic were also various artists, including the younger Piranesi and the famous sculptor Ceracchi, whose democratic opinions had been reinforced by two professional visits to the United States.

The Roman Republic, which lasted hardly more than a year, was never sufficiently stabilized to produce any organized program.

Its adherents soon divided between moderates and extreme democrats. The moderates were mainly actual Romans, the extremists included excitable newcomers from other parts of Italy, assorted journalists, intellectuals, and veterans of the revolutionary club at Milan. The moderates wanted tangible reforms on the local scene, practical improvements in taxation, administration, law courts, and police powers, with opportunities to advance their own careers or to buy up land confiscated from clerical bodies. Among the extreme democrats, some called for a breaking up of the vast estates from which rich absentees who lived in the city drew their income. They favored not Babeuf's "communism" but the creation of a peasantry of small independent proprietors. Others engaged in anticlerical demonstrations; on one occasion a pile of cardinals' hats, the minutes of the Inquisition, titles of nobility, and the golden book of the Capitol were burned before an altar of Liberty. Most of all, the extremists clamored for a general uprising throughout all Italy, a grand overthrow of crowned heads from Turin to Naples, from which a vast popular unified all-Italian democratic republic might come into being. In such a vague and all-devouring Italian republic, the moderate Roman revolutionaries had no interest, and the French Directory was positively opposed to it. The moderates, therefore, strong in the Consulate and Senate, sympathized with the French Directory and its civilian commissioners. The radicals, strong or at least articulate in the lower house, found their friends among the ardent republicans of the French army, especially some of the generals. The generals, impatient of the Directory, and remembering what Bonaparte had done in the Cisalpine, were inspired both by the thought of making fortunes for themselves and of acting as liberators for the Italians who pleaded for their support.

In these circumstances, the Roman Republic accomplished little, beyond abolishing the *fidecommessi*, launching discussion of education, taxation, and the penal code, and confiscating some properties of the church, most of which wound up in the hands of governmental, landowning, and mercantile personages who owned agricultural land already. Outside Rome, in the Papal States, the new government was never able to assert its authority, and confusion reigned across the peninsula to the Adriatic, with the French and their supporters prevailing temporarily in a few towns such as Ancona, and the peasants everywhere sullenly hostile, both to Italian "Jacobins" and to the French armies which brought pillage and requisitions. In any case, the life of the Roman Republic was darkened by the expectation of war, and ended by war itself.

Extremists in Rome clamored for war against the king of Naples, who reciprocated by awaiting the moment to kill the ephemeral regime in the Eternal City. Ferdinand IV, of the Spanish Bourbon family, was married to a Hapsburg, Maria Carolina, who was a sister of Marie Antoinette of France. In their hearty detestation of republicanism, both French and Italian, they were abetted by a coterie of English advisers, for the king's chief minister was an English expatriate, Acton, and the queen's confidante was the famous adventuress, Emma Hamilton, wife of the British ambassador. They were joined in September, 1798, by Admiral Horatio Nelson, who had just destroyed the French fleet in Egypt, isolated Bonaparte and a French army in that remote country, and was now transferring his operations to the western Mediterranean for a resumption of hostilities against France itself. That Naples was technically neutral, or at least out of the war, made no difference. Both the British government, which was patiently trying to construct a Second Coalition, and the Austrian, which was still at peace, warned Ferdinand IV against premature action. They preferred to wait until the French attacked Naples, after which an anti-French coalition might be more readily formed. The Directory in Paris had no intention of attacking Naples. It was Nelson and the English colony that persuaded Ferdinand IV to act without delay. A Neapolitan army in November attacked the Roman Republic. It occupied Rome without difficulty. King Ferdinand had barely time to appear in person, promising a restoration of order and true religion, when the French general Championnet, hastily assembling a small force, threw the Neapolitans violently and speedily back across the frontier. In January, 1799, a mixed force of French, Poles, and Cisalpine Italians occupied the city of Naples. The king and queen, together with Lord and Lady Hamilton, escaped under Nelson's protection to the island haven of Palermo. Championnet, exceeding his orders (as Nelson had done), combined with the local revolutionaries to set up a Neapolitan Republic.

South Italy offered an unpromising terrain for the eighteenth-century revolution. And, indeed, the significance of events in south Italy in 1799 is not so much in showing the meaning of revolutionary republicanism, as in illustrating the lengths to which the Counterrevolution could go where it was successful.

Naples itself was one of the largest cities of Europe and the home of many refined and enlightened men and women, but most of its population was composed of wretchedly poor, under-employed, and wholly uneducated *lazzaroni*. There were many small and ancient cities throughout the kingdom, but their upper classes, like those of the capital, drew their incomes mainly from the possession of rural land, which was infertile and unimproved, worked by a miserable peasantry, and productive of large revenues only because the owners held it in large amounts. The Kingdom of Naples, though urbanized, was hardly a center of what is thought of as urban civilization. The rural proletarians and urban *lazzaroni* hardly had the makings of sans-culottes. Not only were they shut off from the currents of the day by extreme poverty, they were isolated even from each other by language, since they spoke local dialects hardly known except to their own priests. The upper classes, among whom earlier distinctions between nobles and burghers had tended to fade, shared in a somewhat bookish culture, but had a minimum connection with any modern political or economic interests, and lived in the cities from the proceeds of a backward agriculture to whose advancement they had nothing to contribute. It was these upper-class circles that furnished the revolutionaries in Naples. The rural population saw them as distant and half-known alien beings.

The drama of 1799 at Naples was a kind of fast-moving shadow play. Both republicanism and royalism were lacking in substance. There was neither a solid revolutionary movement nor a solid conservatism. The Bourbons, installed in Naples only since 1733, commanded no strong allegiance. The rural masses, sunk in poverty and neglect, hardly knew in some places that they belonged to a Kingdom of Naples or even to a universal Catholic church. The educated classes felt no strong attachment to the monarchy, and none of the satisfaction with their own traditions from which a positive conservatism, as in England or Germany, could arise. With the hasty flight of the king and queen to Sicily, and their continuing involvement with their English friends and dependence on British power, a great many of the urban elites were willing at least for a moment to accept the Republic.

The Republic also, however, was insubstantial, though it had its constitution, its bicameral legislature, its Directors (called "archons"), its revolutionary clubs, and its democratic political journals. Its leaders included princes Caraciollo and Pignatelli, various marquises and counts, diverse archbishops, bishops and priests, and the usual array of doctors, pharmacists, lawyers, judges, professors, and intellectuals of independent income. They enacted the usual "abolition of feudalism," put an end to the *fidecommessi*, and made plans for popular education. They did and could do nothing about the abject poverty, which was the main social problem, and paid no attention to proposals, made by Vicenzo Russo, for division of great estates and transfer of property rights to the peasantry. More than elsewhere, the men and women prominent in the Neapolitan Republic (one of whom was a noble lady Eleonora de Fonseca Pimentel, who edited the *Monitore napoletano*) were high-minded, generous, and idealistic, genuine friends of humanity, and inspired by good will toward their own unfortunate social inferiors, with whom, however, they were never able to form any effectual contact. They had with them no interests in common, nor common enemies in the form of *seigneurs* or privileged classes that could be readily identified and singled out. Their interests were in fact opposed; the "Jacobins" were the very absentee landowners on whom the rural workers blamed their troubles.

The French never had many troops in Naples, and within three months, with the renewal of war with Austria, they withdrew these few. The Neapolitan republicans were left defenseless. The peasants broke out in amorphous and disconnected insurrections. Their insurgency was organized by Cardinal Ruffo, who emerged as the most capable figure on either side. Ruffo was not a priest; he had been a chief minister to Pius VI in the Papal States some years before, but his reforming program had offended the land-owning interests of central Italy, so that Pius VI had dismissed him, while granting him a cardinal's hat in recognition of his services. Settling at Naples, Ruffo had advised Ferdinand IV against retreating to Sicily in January, 1799, but had nevertheless followed him there. In February he landed in Calabria with only eight companions, and set about the reconquest of the mainland kingdom. He organized the incipient peasant insurrections into an *Armata Christiana,* commonly called the Army of the Holy Faith, or San Fedists.

The *Armata Christiana,* or San Fedism, was not exactly a re-ligious crusade. At least a good many priests were later punished for resistance to it, and Cardinal Zurlo, the archbishop of Naples, disapproved of it in the beginning. The peasants, to be sure, infused it with their own fanatical hatred of city people and godless republicans. But Ruffo rallied the peasant bands by essen-tially social appeals, and the fury of the peasants was as much sociological as religious, reflecting a struggle of rural proletarians against the urbanized and "Jacobin" landowners. Ruffo, like the idealistic republicans in the city of Naples, pronounced the "aboli-tion of feudalism," but he went further in likewise canceling unpopular taxes, getting rid of certain local offices, allowing peasants to occupy common lands, and trying to throw the burden of his requisitions on the landlords rather than on the rural workers. He thus rallied the country, and the hordes once assem-bled poured angrily into the smaller cities, looted the homes of bourgeois and nobles alike, and put to death many persons who could be discredited as Jacobins. In May Ruffo occupied the city of Naples. The last remnant of determined republicans took refuge in the fortress of St. Elmo.

"We wish no mercy shown to any rebel against God and Me." Such, in grandiose royal language, were the instructions of Fer-dinand IV, still safely in Sicily, to his representative Ruffo in the field. Ruffo, nevertheless, promised the republicans, whom he besieged at St. Elmo, that if they surrendered, their lives would be spared. They surrendered on this understanding. The king and queen believed Ruffo to have been disgracefully lenient. They left the honoring of Ruffo's terms to Nelson's judgment. But they gave him advice; as the queen wrote to Lady Hamilton (of whom Nelson had become enamored, but that is another story), "I recommend to Milord Nelson to treat Naples as if it were a rebel Irish town." Rebel towns in Ireland, since the unsuccessful Irish rebellion of the year before, were undergoing severe treatment, nor did the implacable Maria Carolina wish anything better for the people of her own capital.

Nelson agreed. A convinced monarchist and passionate adversary of the French or any other revolution, he believed that civilization, from Ireland to the Straits of Messina, required the extermination of Jacobinism. He dismissed the more tolerant Ruffo as a "swelled up priest." When Ruffo called the republicans "patriots," Nelson thought he had "prostituted" the word. That Catholics might be Jacobins in Naples only proved to the British admiral that both were bad. "Your news of the hanging of thirteen Jacobins," he wrote to one of his British officers, "gives us great pleasure; and the three priests, I hope, [will] dangle on the tree best adapted to the weight of their sins." Nelson, in short, carried out King Ferdinand's desire to ignore Ruffo's terms with complete personal agreement. He had the republican prince and former admiral, Caracciolo, hanged from the yardarm of the *Minerva*. Another 118 republicans were put to death at Naples in the following months. They included fifteen clerics, another prince, four marquises, and two women of high social station.

The repression of republicanism at Naples was only part of the general counterrevolutionary triumph in Italy in 1799. This in turn was only part of a larger movement which, as already remarked, brought the Russian army into Switzerland and an Anglo-Russian invasion force into Holland. The general aim was to crush all the sister republics, and then the French Republic itself. The movement was successful only in Italy. But the Counterrevolution in Italy suggests what was in store for other places where the republican regimes might be overthrown.

In Italy, the War of the Second Coalition went unfavorably for the French. In the Second Coalition, unlike the First, the Russians were active. Marshal Suvorov led a Russian army into Italy. The Turks, brought into the war by Bonaparte's expedition to Egypt, also contributed a few forces to the operations in Italy, which thus received the armed attention of Moslems for the first time in centuries. The combination of Austrians, Russians, Turks, and the British fleet proved more than the French and their Italian supporters could withstand. First Naples fell, then Rome, then Milan. All the new republics in Italy, except the Ligurian, were wiped out.

What the Italians call the *triennio*, or three years of the revolution, was followed by the *tredici mesi*, or thirteen months of the Austro-Russian reaction. Actually it was an Austrian reaction, since the Russians soon departed for Switzerland, where Masséna defeated them. The Austrians preserved some features of the new order. They kept Venetia while regaining Milan. They neither restored Bologna and Ferrara to the pope, nor returned the church property confiscated in the Cisalpine Republic to the clergy. All other innovations were abrogated. The apparatus of the Cisalpine Republic was dismantled, and thousands who had taken part in it either fled to France or were interned in Austria. Schools and universities were closed, but the old school for teaching German at Milan was reopened. The *fidecommessi*, the seigneurial dues, and the old hunting rights were restored. Jansenists were repressed; Jews and non-Catholics lost their equal rights. Religious holidays were made obligatory. Censorship was imposed, "bad books" were burned in public squares, and anti-French literature was introduced. Meanwhile the Austrians supported themselves, as the French had done, by official requisitions mixed with private pillage. The economist Melchior Gioia, in 1801, estimated that in the material burdens that it imposed the Austrian occupation had been heavier than the French. The burden of censorship and police activity was far worse.

With Italy thus gripped by reaction, France in 1799 saw a kind of Jacobin revival against the imminency of danger to the Revolution. A conspicuous victim of the new crisis was Pius VI. At first, when the Roman Republic was proclaimed, he had only been forced out of the city and had settled in Florence. He was in fact a prisoner of the French, and with the renewal of war in Italy, the French defeats and the collapse of republicanism throughout the peninsula, the French became increasingly brutal toward him. They moved him from city to city, deprived him of his advisers,

and finally transported him, at the age of eighty-two, partly para-
lyzed and almost alone, through a frozen Alpine pass into France,
where he died. For fervid anti-Catholics, the heirs of Voltaire, it
seemed that the century of Enlightenment had at last seen, in its
final year, the crushing of the *infâme* and the death agony of
Rome itself. For Catholics, the year 1800 was the low point of the
papacy in modern times. With the disorders in Rome, a conclave
was held at Venice under Austrian protection, but the cardinals
were deadlocked for three months among the French, Austrian,
and Spanish parties, and in the end, by a surprising compromise,
elected Pius VII, who two years before had accepted the revolution in Italy.

In France, a combination of neo-Jacobins, advanced democrats,
and disaffected and indeed disobedient generals, such as Championnet, who had fathered the Neapolitan Republic, prepared to
set up a new Revolutionary Government against attack by the
Second Coalition. The French victories in the Helvetic and
Batavian Republics blunted the danger. But various men of 1789
and of 1793, who were now essentially moderates, found in the
sensational General Bonaparte the man they needed. By the
coup d'état of Brumaire the Directory gave way to the Consulate,
with Bonaparte as First Consul.

Bonaparte's defeat of the Austrians at Marengo in 1800 brought
the Cisalpine Republic back to life. It also confirmed the destruction of the Second Coalition and assured the continuation of a
New Order in France and Western Europe. The New Order, if no
longer revolutionary or democratic, was assiduously reformist.
Granting only the mildest of compromises, its face was set against
the Old. In France, the Republic turned into the Consulate,
which in effect codified much of the Revolution of 1789. The
sister republics underwent corresponding changes. When Bonaparte became Napoleon, and France an empire, the Batavian
Republic turned into the Kingdom of Holland, the Cisalpine into
the Kingdom of Italy, and what had been the Neapolitan Republic in 1799 reappeared as the Kingdom of Naples, first under
the emperor's brother Joseph, then under his brother-in-law
Joachim Murat. It was essentially the programs first launched in
the sister republics, without the machinery for democratic elec-

tions, that were carried forward in the Napoleonic states, sometimes by the very same persons. More generally, while policies remained the same, the personalities were different, the revolutionary enthusiasts of the 1790s being succeeded by more pragmatic administrators and servants of the state.

[8]

The English-Speaking Countries:
The Revolution Acclaimed
and Detested

BRITONS AND AMERICANS, whom the French persist in grouping together as Anglo-Saxons, enjoyed a peculiar relationship to each other at the close of the eighteenth century, which the French Revolution and ensuing war made even more complicated. Most Americans at the time were quite consciously of English descent, and there had been a large recent immigration from the Protestant north of Ireland. These Anglo-Saxons traded with each other with only a brief interruption during the American Revolution. The Americans used British credit and capital. Both peoples looked back to the same history, especially the long period from the real Anglo-Saxons to Oliver Cromwell. They read the same books; or rather, until after 1800, Americans mostly read books which had been written in England, except indeed for the Bible, which Americans absorbed in the King James version, and with the important additional exception of the ancient classics, from which so many disturbing ideas could be derived.

At the time of the French Revolution, the American Revolution was in the recent past. It had been part of a civil struggle within the English-speaking community as a whole. Far more than a mere movement of independence, it had rejected the very principles of hereditary monarchy; the hereditary House of Lords, the eccentric methods of selection of the House of Commons, the theory of "virtual representation," and the mysteries of a traditional and unwritten constitution. It was critical of the established Anglican church, the impressive apparatus of upper-class sinecures, dignities and emoluments and the whole aristocratic ethos of English life.

The American revolutionaries found their transatlantic friends not in Edmund Burke, whose praises of America antedated the break of 1776, but in the Dissenters in England, the more extreme parliamentary reformers in England and Scotland, and the Volunteers of Ireland, who at their height about 1783 were mainly Presbyterians, many of them with relatives in America. Once the Loyalists were repressed or resettled in Canada, the Americans came out of their revolution with a pronounced Anglophobia. To have a national character they must be un-English; Noah Webster even insisted upon the existence of an American language. To some extent the Americans were even pro-French, thanks to French aid in the War of Independence. They gave the name of Bourbon to one of their new counties in Kentucky, in gratitude to Louis XVI, thus perpetuating the fame of a European dynasty in the word for an American beverage. The British reciprocated by looking on the Americans as ungrateful and wayward children. Except for Dissenters and radical reformers, the British, unlike Continental Europeans, saw little to learn from the American Revolution and the new American state and federal constitutions.

The French Revolution had a powerful impact upon both Britain and America. The war, the spread of the Revolution, the French annexation of the Austrian Netherlands, the appearance of the Dutch, Swiss, and Italian sister republics, had an influence perhaps even greater than the Revolution in France itself. Most persons of conservative outlook in England, those less aroused than Burke, would probably have tolerated a revolution, however violent, that was confined within the borders of France. The spread of the Revolution, signalized in November, 1792, by the opening of the river Scheldt, made them sense a menace to British interests. Among positive sympathizers with the French Revolution in the English-speaking countries there was an inclination to excuse even the Terror as a passing frenzy or necessity provoked by foreign intervention. But when the dismantling of the guillotine was followed by continuing French victories, by occupation of neighboring countries, and proclamation of new revolutionary republics, even many friends of the French Revolution were dismayed.

There was very little knowledge or understanding in the English-speaking world of actual conditions in Belgium, Holland, the German Rhineland, Switzerland, or Italy. It was not seen that the opening of the Scheldt reflected Belgian wishes as well as French. How much genuine unrest existed in the areas occupied by the French was not known. The Dutch and Swiss confederations, in particular, were already republics, among the classic republics of modern Europe. What use had republics to be revolutionized? The Dutch and Swiss were seen also as Protestants, with whom the English, Scots, and Americans had a fellow feeling going back over two centuries to the Reformation. Was revolution necessary in countries where there was no longer any popery to overthrow? That such attitudes arose from ignorance and misapprehension should be evident from the preceding chapters. But after 1798 even the partisans of France in Britain and America were embarrassed. They had difficulty in refuting the claim that the French had become mere plunderers and conquerors of weaker peoples, or that they were deliberately embarked on a mad program to revolutionize the world. What is called the disillusionment with the French Revolution in Britain and America came as much in 1798 as at any previous time, and was a response to developments in the European revolution as much as in the French.

It was in 1792 that excitement both for and against the French Revolution became acute. Both the radical-republican and the conservative-aristocratic tendencies were accentuated in the United States and in Great Britain. For an exact date, 1794 may be selected. It is to that year, when the conservative or Portland Whigs joined in a coalition in the government of William Pitt, with the remaining Whigs led by Charles James Fox being antiwar and pro-French, that the origins of the later Conservative and Liberal parties have been traced. It was Jay's Treaty of 1794 between the United States and Great Britain, or rather the popular opposition to it in America, that differentiated the Jeffersonian Republicans, or "democrats," from the socially more conservative Federalists.

Throughout the British Isles the same Dissenters, English reformers, restive Scots, and militant Irish who had been most sympathetic to the American Revolution now favored the bid for liberty made by the French. In America those who thought their own revolution incomplete, who feared an Anglophile reaction, and wished to move further in a democratic direction, became enthusiastic for the French Revolution. The most ardent cheered for the attempted revolution in Poland, they viewed the revolutions in Italy with satisfaction (Switzerland and Holland were more puzzling), they wished well to the United Irish, and some even hoped, like Andrew Jackson in 1798 (who was to be president in the era of "Jacksonian democracy" thirty years later), that England itself might be republicanized by a French invasion. But such turbulence and excitement also produced a contrary feeling. In England there was a hardening of the conservatism that had already shown itself against the American Revolution. In America, and notably in New England, men who formerly had been vehemently anti-British, now alarmed by the French Revolutionaries and by the American democrats, began to feel the ancestral stirrings of their English background, to dwell on the wisdom of the British constitution, and to admire some of those peculiarities of eighteenth-century British life that they had in fact repudiated. Though declining after 1798, Gallomania and Anglomania both swept the United States, while in the British Isles Gallomania was offset by an increasing self-satisfaction with British institutions.

The two countries were obviously very different, and developed in different ways. By 1800 Pitt's government had silenced the radical movement in Britain and crushed the United Irish. In 1800 Thomas Jefferson, friend of France and notorious "Jacobin," was elected as the first "democratic" president of the United States. In Britain, an aristocratic conservatism triumphed; in America, the native revolutionary tradition. But the undercurrents remained. British radicalism reappeared immediately after Waterloo. In America, although true conservatism never prevailed, the sympathy for French and Continental democracy diminished. As France went through a succession of empires, revolutions, and republics, and as England became slowly democratized, a new situation was created. In the twentieth century the two most celebrated Democratic presidents of the United States, Woodrow Wilson and Franklin Roosevelt, felt an affinity for England that would have astonished Jefferson or Jackson, but they had little patience with France or understanding of the French Revolution.

News of the fall of the Bastille was at first received with unanimous pleasure in England, for the British were willing enough to see the French enjoy the liberties associated with constitutional monarchy. The events of the following weeks in France soon broke the consensus. It was on "equality" that British opinion divided, and on the role to be assigned to organized religion in civil society. The dramatic surrender of privileges on August 4, the Declaration of Rights both in its substance and in its dogmatic style, the rising power of the lower classes as shown in the peasant revolts and in the march on Versailles, the confiscation of the property of the church, the abolition of nobility, the Civil Constitution of the clergy, the granting of the vote to over half the adult male population, the cutting up of historic provinces into eighty-three uniform departments, the disrespect to the king, his arrest at Varennes—all these developments, by 1791, shocked and alienated some people in England, but were greeted with excited approval by others.

For the former, Burke wrote his *Reflections on the French Revolution*. For the latter, Paine replied with the *Rights of Man*. It is estimated that Burke's book sold 30,000 copies, Paine's 1,500,000. The difference is significant, even if the figure for Paine is discounted by a half or two-thirds. (If half a million copies of the *Rights of Man* were sold in English, there would be one for every forty men, women, and children in England, Wales, Scotland, Ireland, the United States, and Canada at that time.) Burke's book was actually the more original of the two. Amplifying the arguments he had used against the British reform bills half a dozen years before, he developed a kind of preromantic, antirationalist, anti-individualist, and organic philosophy to justify the existing order and rule by the landed interests in Britain. The book was soon read in translation on the Continent. In England it provoked numerous refutations, and even in the governing classes Burke was thought to be slightly mad. The *Rights of Man* was less original because it expressed a critical spirit, a dissatisfaction and an idealism that were widespread. It too was translated into many languages. Drawing on Paine's observations in America, France, and England, it was the most widely known, powerfully stated and successful book of the whole international revolutionary upheaval. It is the fate of revolutions, however, to go out of date, or to lose their appeal when the conditions against which they are directed are forgotten, so that in later times Burke was considered a philosopher, and Paine a pamphleteer.

By 1792, with the outbreak of war on the Continent, the division of opinion in Britain was clearly marked. The government, especially after the fall of the monarchy and the September Massacres, had no sympathy with the French, but it also had no desire to enter the war against them. Against the French, on the whole, were the Anglican, aristocratic, agrarian, and most of the professional interests of the country. In an occupational analysis, sympathy for the French Revolution was less wide in England than on the Continent or in Scotland and Ireland. On the Continent, it was usual to find lawyers, doctors, university professors, professional civil servants, occasional nobles, and even priests and bishops favorable to the Revolution. At Dublin the United Irish Club in 1792 (before it became fully revolutionary) had about 300 members, about half of them Catholic and half Protestant, including 99 merchants, 30 attorneys, 26 barristers, and 16 physicians. In Scotland the Whig Club of Dundee sent an address of congratulations to the French Assembly (this was in the mild year 1790), signed by 33 merchants, 11 "esquires," 11 clergymen, 3 surgeons, a doctor, and various teachers. In England, where the professions were closely geared to the ruling elite, few legal or medical practitioners had any inclination to the Revolution, the Anglican clergy even less; there was hardly any class of career civil servants; and as for the academic world, the only universities were

Oxford and Cambridge, which were both Anglican establishments, hardly attracted by novel ideas.

In England, therefore, the friends of France, in 1792 and for a few years thereafter, were the poets—Wordsworth, Coleridge, Southey, and Blake (with the Scottish poets Burns and Campbell)—Dissenters in general and Dissenting intellectuals in particular, like the famous Priestley—and independent spirits from the upper classes, including half a dozen peers, and from fifty to a hundred Whigs in the House of Commons who followed Charles James Fox. The latter formed in 1792 the Society of the Friends of the People. With its dues of two-and-a-half guineas a year it was limited to the well-to-do, and indeed desired no popular membership; but even after Britain became involved as a combatant, the Society boldly opposed the war. In England the sympathizers with the French Revolution came mainly from what were called the industrious classes—that is, the people "in trade," the businessmen, the new factory owners and their employees, and the world of artisans, small shops, and skilled labor. The real poor, especially the rural poor, remained more staunchly conservative.

The radical movement was far from revolutionary. It fell far short of what even the Americans, not to mention the French, had done. It was unfriendly to royalty and to the Lords, but did not propose to abolish them. It had no idea of re-creating the state by a constituent convention and a written constitution, as in America and on the Continent. It did mean to raise the stature of the people, and it demanded "reform" of the House of Commons. What it wanted, however, was more than mere reform, if reform means a gradual, careful, and partial readjustment of existing institutions, as later happened with the passage of the Reform Acts of 1832 and 1867. The radicals offered a totally new theory of political power and representation. Their theory corresponded to the new theory in France and in the sister republics— that is, the "people" should be "sovereign," and legislators should only be their representatives. These representatives (an un-English term) should be chosen by a nationally uniform suffrage, they should represent approximately equal numbers of constituents, and all towns and rural areas without exception should take part in the choice of deputies, who were to serve for brief terms and be paid salaries from the public funds. While the peculiarities of recruitment to the House of Commons in the eighteenth century are too complex for brief description, it may be said that they reflected none of these newfangled desiderata. The House (though four-fifths of the seats were for "boroughs") was composed overwhelmingly of country gentlemen, many of whom had close ties with the Lords. The House elected in 1790, in a membership of 558, included 85 baronets and 121 persons who were the sons of peers or Irish peers themselves. Two-thirds of the members were the sons or close relatives of former members; 278 had been educated at Oxford or Cambridge, and 115 at Eton. Over a hundred, though it was a time of peace, were either career officers or holders of temporary commissions in the army or navy. There were 72 lawyers, who mainly served the landed interest, 27 bankers, and another half hundred who were heavily involved in commerce. The House, while concerned for the welfare of the country, recognized no actual dependency on the electorate, or rather on the varied assortment of persons—the crown, the borough patrons, the county freeholders, and the actual populace in a few boroughs —to whom they owed their seats. In principle, the "burgesses," who sat for the boroughs, were legally required to have an independent income from land of £300 a year, or about 7,500 French livres. In France, by way of contrast, the democrats in 1791 objected to a corresponding requirement of a few hundred livres a year as "aristocratic."

The industrious classes did not believe that they were properly represented in the House of Commons. The discontent was most evident in some of the urban agglomerations that had grown up recently in the course of industrialization, such as Manchester, which now had 75,000 people, but was not a borough, preserving instead its medieval manorial organization, with its inhabitants participating in elections to the House only as freeholders in the county of Lancashire. In Manchester, Birmingham, Sheffield, Leeds, and elsewhere the wealthy and prosperous manufacturers inclined strongly to the radical ideas. They regarded the aristocracy as idlers, drones, and parasites on the public purse. Such men were especially enraged by the Birmingham riots of 1791, when a mob shouting its loyalty to church and king attacked the home of Joseph Priestley, who was disliked as a Dissenter, a Unitarian, a reformer, and an apologist for the American and French Revolutions. His house, furniture, and scientific instruments were destroyed. In these circumstances, the ideas proclaimed by the French Revolutionaries appealed strongly to the new industrialists, including James Watt and Matthew Boulton, the manufacturers of steam engines, John Wilkinson, the famous ironmaster, and Thomas Walker, the boroughreeve (or mayor, as it were) of Manchester, who sponsored Thomas Cooper in publishing the pro-French and antiwar *Manchester Herald*. As late as 1795, after two years of war, two textile manufacturers at Manchester who became prominent later—Robert Peel, who initiated factory legislation, and Robert Owen, who became known as a socialist— signed a petition urging immediate peace.

As the war went on, however, as resistance to it became more clearly unpatriotic, and as the government intensified its campaign —it disgraced and impoverished Walker by a trial for subversion in which he was in fact acquitted—the men of the middle and business classes, who had too much to lose, dropped out of the radical movement. For reasons already suggested, they also lost their sympathy for France. Radicalism in England, more than the revolutionary and republican movements in France and its sister republics, came to settle at the level of the "lower-middle" or "upper-working" classes.

The year 1792 saw the sudden apparition of a great many political clubs. Beside the aristocratic Friends of the People, there appeared the Society for Constitutional Information, which was favored by intellectuals such as Thomas Paine and the poet-engraver William Blake. The master shoemaker Thomas Hardy organized the London Corresponding Society. From his observation of the failure of parliamentary reform during and after the American Revolution, when various of the rural gentry and even a prime minister had urged it in vain, Hardy decided to appeal, as he said, to "tradesmen, shopkeepers and mechanics." His new society charged dues of only a penny a week, and before the end of 1792 had about 2,000 members in London, organized in neigh-

borhood units which held their own meetings. Similar clubs took
form at Sheffield, Norfolk, many other English towns, and in
Scotland. It was to correspond with these clubs, and to unite
them in common political action, that Hardy called his new association a Corresponding Society, though some of his enemies
circulated the fallacious idea that it was meant to correspond with
the French. It did send a few unsolicited and complimentary
messages to Paris. But despite the most careful inquiry by
Parliamentary Committees, carried on until 1799, no one was
ever able to reveal the name of a single Frenchman involved in
the British clubs, the reformist mass meetings, the radical press,
or the naval mutinies of 1797. The French seem to have had no
more to do with the English Jacobins than with those of Vienna.

The clubs, while they talked of reforming Parliament, had more
in mind than a mere constitutional rearrangement. They aimed at
reform of the tax structure, which fell heavily on the poor through
indirect taxes, and at the whole regime of "privilege" by which
the aristocracy was supported. Thomas Paine, for example, in 1792
published the Second Part of his *Rights of Man*. He proposed
a progressive income tax, by which incomes of £12,000 a year
should be taxed at 50 percent, and all income over £22,000 confiscated *in toto*. (£22,000 was about the income of the fabulously
wealthy bishop of Strasbourg before the French Revolution; and
in Pitt's famous income tax of 1799 the progression stopped at the
£200 income level, above which it stood at 10 percent.) Paine's
purpose was in part to take the tax burden off the poor, and in
part to oblige the very rich to divide their estates at death, to
force the rich, so to speak, to share with each other through making
primogeniture fiscally suicidal. Such ideas struck at the foundations
of the prevailing family and social system. Faced with an indict-
ment, Paine fled to France, where he was made an honorary
citizen, elected to the Convention, befriended by the Brissot
group, interned by the Robespierrist government, and given leisure
to write the *Age of Reason*. This vehement tract was as much an
attack on Christian credulity as on Christianity itself. It arraigned
all revealed, professionalized, and established religion. Written
in France, it seemed to show that the French Revolution was
appallingly atheistic. It helped to turn respectable churchgoers in

Britain and America against modern republicanism at the very moment when the future Pope Pius VII was accepting it. A fervent moralist and pious deist, Paine was remembered as a "filthy little atheist" a century later by President Theodore Roosevelt.

In April, 1792, France and Austria went to war. In May the British government issued a proclamation against seditious writings. Radical tracts continued to come from the presses and the clubs continued to multiply. Their members watched the unfolding drama on the Continent with horror, hope, admiration, and suspense—the Austro-Prussian invasion, the Brunswick Manifesto, the rising in Paris, the dethronement of Louis XVI, the September Massacres, Valmy, the proclamation of the Republic, Jemappes, and the French victories in the Austrian Netherlands and in the Rhineland. These events turned the British upper classes against the Revolution. They had no such effect on the popular clubs. Bonfires were lit at Sheffield in October to celebrate the Prussian retreat after Valmy. A thousand people rioted at Dundee and burned two landowners in effigy. A mass meeting in Kensington Common, near London, applauding France, was broken up by dragoons. Club members collected shoes and firearms to be sent to the sans-culotte army. Five clubs—at London, Manchester, and Norfolk—sent a joint address to the French Convention, expressing the hope that Britain would remain neutral or even ally with France against "tyrants." A group of English, Scots, Irish, and Americans residing in Paris presented a similar declaration to the Convention in November.

At the end of 1792 the government called up the militia, not so much in expectation of war as to preserve order in Britain itself. It favored also the organization of counterclubs. In November John Reeves, a writer on English law, organized the Association for Preserving Liberty and Property against Republicans and Levellers. Provided with secret service money, the association issued thousands of copies of pamphlets against reformist and "French" ideas. Similar groups sprang up throughout the country under the auspices of local gentlemen and Anglican clergy. They warned booksellers who sold radical literature, threatened innkeepers who allowed radical clubs to meet on their premises, burned Thomas Paine in effigy, persuaded people of the "lower orders" to sign loyalist petitions, and spread derogatory rumors about persons whose opinions they disliked. Wealthy donors gave funds so that literature in praise of the British constitution could be circulated at no charge.

It was also at the very end of 1792 that the Scottish radical clubs held a meeting at Edinburgh. Scotland had a distressed population of weavers and of rural workers on great landed estates, for whom the existing political system offered no means of expression, since in a population of 1 million there were only about 1,300 freeholders qualified to vote for the House of Commons. Delegates from eighty clubs in sixty-five Scottish towns and villages held a convention at Edinburgh in December, 1792. The very word "Convention" was inflammatory, the delegates addressed each other as "citizen," and on disbanding they took the French oath to "live free or die." They focused their demands on a more equal representation in Parliament, and laid plans for an all-British Convention.

Although faced with such disaffection at home, and also in Ireland, where the United Irish began to form in 1792, the British government, as the French threatened Belgium and Holland, concluded that another of the many wars with France was inevitable. The French further outraged the upper classes by executing Louis XVI in January. They declared war on Great Britain on February 1, 1793. Pitt's government found itself at war over the strenuous objection of thousands of its own people, who remained pro-French, pro-Revolutionary, and vehemently hostile to the ministry and the Parliament as then constituted. Radicals blamed the war, as they had blamed the loss of America, on the closed and aristocratic character of the Parliament. Protests and petitions for reform poured in from all over the country. The one from Sheffield had 8,000 signatures, one from London and Westminster 6,000, one from Norwich 3,700. Those from Scotland were proportionately even more numerous. The one from Edinburgh stretched "the whole length of the floor of the House."

The government first acted in Scotland, where the law gave less protection to accused persons than in England. In particular, it tried and deported to Australia, in 1793, two men who had been active in the Edinburgh Convention, Thomas Muir and Thomas Fyshe Palmer, the latter an Englishman who had assisted the weavers at Dundee in framing an address to Parliament. The trial was remembered for the arbitrary conduct of its presiding judge, Braxfield. "In this country," said Braxfield, "the landed interest alone has a right to be represented." He added that he had never liked the French anyway, but could "now only consider them as monsters of human nature." Despite the fate of Muir and Palmer, the Scottish clubs held another convention in April, and a third, a British Convention, in November, 1793. Among those in attendance were delegates from the London and Sheffield clubs, and Hamilton Rowan from the United Irish. Its feeling was strong and its language violent, but it had no real program or leadership, and thirty constables were able to break it up. Further trials followed, in which Braxfield sentenced three more persons to deportation to Australia. By 1794 most of the Scottish clubs were extinguished.

The agitation continued in England, where the clubs were incensed by the proceedings in Scotland. The London Corresponding Society, at a general meeting in January, 1794, defended the Scots, denounced the war, and declared that if the government tried to crush liberty in England the Society should issue a solemn call for "a General Convention of the People." The reaction was similar in other towns. A meeting at Sheffield adopted an Address to the British Nation. It rejected "virtual representation," as the Americans had done two decades before. It complained that plain people could get no hearing from "gentlemen." It declared that since petitions were useless, a "complete revolution in sentiment" must occur. "What is the constitution to us," asked the Sheffield meeting, "if we are nothing to it? The constitution of Britain, indeed, is highly extolled as the greatest effort of human wisdom— so is the constitution of Turkey at Constantinople." Less ironically, the Sheffield mechanics demanded Equality of Rights—not a "visionary Equality of Property" but the equality that makes "the Slave a Man, the Man a Citizen, and the Citizen an integral part of the State, to make him a joint Sovereign, and not a Subject." Here was the very language of Rousseau and the French Republic. The author of the address, Joseph Gales, soon emigrated, or rather fled, to America.

Since the British government conducted the war by financial grants to Continental allies and by use of its navy, requiring only a small professional army (there was never any conscription in England until 1916), it could carry on hostilities even in the face of vigorous opposition. It was nevertheless awkward to have such disaffection in wartime, so much pro-French spirit, and so much disbelief in those very institutions which the war against France was supposed to protect. In 1794 the government moved against radicalism in England, as in Scotland in 1793. Thomas Hardy of the London Corresponding Society, Thomas Walker of Manchester, Horne Tooke, John Thelwall, and other radicals from many years back were indicted for treason. They were defended by Thomas Erskine, who had defended Paine *in absentia* in 1792. The English law gave less advantage to the prosecution than the Scottish, in which Roman and Continental jurisprudence was more influential. Erskine was able to show that some of the evidence adduced by the government was fabricated, and that no collusion of his clients with the French could be proved or was even likely. A jury of London businessmen acquitted Hardy and all the others. But the fear, the disgrace, and the expense resulting from such state trials drove most middle-class persons out of the radical movement.

The movement, however, as a more purely working-class phenomenon, reached its height in 1795. Encouraged by the acquittals of 1794, and under the pressures of the food shortage and high prices which afflicted England as well as France, the London Corresponding Society increased its membership to about 5,000. It staged public demonstrations and mass meetings with fiery political speeches but usually without disorder. In October, 1795, a crowd estimated at 200,000 swarmed in the streets—if its size was exaggerated, it compared with the 80,000 said to have besieged the French Convention at the time of the expulsion of the Girondins. The people had assembled to watch, less approvingly than in later times, the procession for the opening of Parliament. With jeers for the parade of peers and bishops, and cries of

"Bread! Bread! Peace! Peace!" they pressed closely against the king's own coach, in which a window was broken by some flying object, said by a contemporary to be a small pebble or a bullet. The king was extricated with difficulty.

The government, now at war for almost two years, concluded after this assault on George III that firmer steps must be taken against the "clubbists," "levellers" and "anarchy men." It was now reinforced by the coalition with the Portland Whigs—the duke of Portland, William Windham, Sir Gilbert Elliott, all favored by Edmund Burke—the most ideologically aristocratic and bellicose of what may be somewhat inaccurately called the Whig party. Parliament passed two bills: the Treasonable Practices Act, which enlarged the definition of treason, and the Seditious Meetings Act, which made it unlawful for meetings to hear speeches except in the presence of officers of the law. Some seventy Foxite Whigs voted against the two bills in the Commons, upheld the innocence of the London Corresponding Society in the affair of the king's coach, and even hinted at the need of parliamentary reform. Most of the House strongly favored the bills. Windham pointed to the continuing seductions of the French Revolution as seen most recently in the United States and in the new Batavian Republic. Every country in Europe, he said, was threatened by the poison from France, "this great democracy."

With the enforcement of the two acts, the radical clubs declined. The substantial workingmen now followed the prudent middle class out of the movement, which was left in the hands of small groups of temperamental extremists. Even so, as late as November 1796, some five hundred persons sat down to an eight-shilling dinner, at the Crown and Anchor Tavern in London, with the radical Earl of Stanhope in the chair, and listened to demands for reform. In 1797 Charles Grey introduced another reform bill in the Commons; it failed, but the same Grey obtained passage of the First Reform Act a generation later. Under pressure, the London Corresponding Society became secret. It established vague relations with the nebulous "United English" in the region of Sheffield and Manchester, and with the United Irish, who rebelled in 1798. What relations it had, if any, with the naval mutinies of 1797 has never been ascertained. The mutinies in themselves, coming in time of war, and of actual threats of invasion, were a serious evidence of disaffection. In 1798 Pitt suspended *habeas corpus* and committed various organizers and agitators to prison without trial. In 1799 the radical clubs were simply prohibited. The protest movement was silenced for the duration of the war.

In all this commotion the British lost a number of their more articulate democrats to other countries—Paine by flight to France, others by transportation to Australia, and still others by emigration to the United States. Of the latter, the most famous was the scientist Priestley, who lived for many years in Pennsylvania. Joseph Gales, the author of the Sheffield address, went to North Carolina. Thomas Cooper, of the *Manchester Herald*, and Benjamin Vaughan, who had defended France in the *Morning Chronicle* of London in 1793, also settled in the United States. For fugitive radicals, they fared well: Cooper became president of a South Carolina college, and Vaughan received an honorary degree from Harvard.

It was the counterrevolutionary writers who won the war of words in England in the 1790s. John Bowles, of the Association against Republicans and Levellers, published his *Real Grounds for the Present War with France* in 1793. He argued (and it was even long believed) that the French Convention, in offering "aid and fraternity" to all peoples in its decree of the preceding November, had actually meant to overthrow the British and all other governments. John Reeves, of the same Association, wrote a pamphlet comparing the French Jacobins to English Puritans. The French Revolution and the Protestant Reformation, he said, were the twin sources of all modern evils. John Robison of Edinburgh University, alarmed by Scottish radicalism, produced in 1797 his *Proofs of a Conspiracy against all the religions and governments of Europe, carried on in the secret meetings of Free Masons, Illuminati and Reading Societies*. A similar book by the French émigré Barruel, with a conspiratorial thesis, was published in English before it appeared in French. Burke wrote his *Letters on a Regicide Peace*, and George Canning edited his *Anti-Jacobin Review*. Mallet du Pan was subsidized with British funds to attack the French Revolution in his *British Mercury* in London, and Friedrich Gentz to do the same in his *Historisches Journal* in

Berlin. Archdeacon Paley published his *Reasons for Contentment,* and Mrs. Hannah More her *Cheap Repository Tracts* to cure English working people of French delusions. Even the first edition of Malthus's *Essay on Population* began as a refutation of Condorcet. More ephemeral was Anthony Aufrere's *Cannibal's Progress: Or the Dreadful Horrors of French Invasion,* in which the wars in Germany were described. A translation appeared of a book by a disgruntled Prussian count, who had left the Prussian service because of its policy of neutrality after 1795. The count's *Anecdotes and Characteristic Traits respecting the Incursion of the French Republicans into Franconia* was a long tale of atrocities. The republicans were "Huns"; they frequented "Jew taverns"; they violated women in the streets, and butchered their brothers and fathers; their commanding officer, Bernadotte, was a monster who dismissed such crimes as "trifles" to be condoned in time of war. It was not then known that this Bernadotte was to become the king of Sweden.

Most of these books spread to America, where they colored the understanding of the French Revolution. But if the British upper classes were so aroused, it was in part because of the attempted revolution in Ireland.

Ireland in the 1790s was half as populous as Great Britain, as populous as the United States, and more so than the Batavian, Helvetic, or Cisalpine Republics. Its formal institutions were modeled on those of England. Its established church was Anglican, its Lords owned estates in both islands, and its House of Commons resembled that of the British, but was even less representative, since the Catholic majority was excluded from it. In Ireland, as in Britain, there had been a movement for parliamentary reform, closely related to the American Revolution. Its failure has been noted in Chapter 3. The frustrated reformers hailed the French Revolution with enthusiasm—not only the fall of the Bastille, but the more significant revolutionary actions that followed.

The English ascendancy, though dating from the Middle Ages, had mainly arisen in the seventeenth-century conquest and occupation, and was strategically justified by the recurrent menace of the French. After the English Revolution of 1689, Louis XIV had landed an army in Ireland to support James II. The victory of William III at the Battle of the Boyne was the rock on which both the Irish and the British eighteenth-century political and social systems had been built. The same threat of French invasion of Ireland reappeared in later wars, notably in the War of American Independence. With France a republic, and a growing Irish movement for independence, the threat was even more serious in the War of the French Revolution.

The agricultural workers were among the most poverty-stricken in Western Europe. They suffered from high rents, absentee land-lords, poor yields, precarious tenures, and frequent evictions. They formed secret and sometimes violent protective associations, such as the Catholic Defenders and the Protestant Peep-of-Day Boys. While these groups joined in the rebellion of 1798 when it came, they were not its leaders or organizers. Ireland, too, had its dis-affected middle classes in the towns. Dublin, with 200,000 inhabi-tants, was by far the largest city in the English-speaking world after London. Even under the disadvantages imposed by tariffs and trade laws, enacted in England, an active mercantile and professional community including both Catholics and Protestants had grown up in the eighteenth century. These people, more than the agricultural masses, felt the weight of discrimination and knew what was happening in America, in France, in Holland, and in England itself.

It was in 1792, in Ireland as in England and Scotland, just as war began on the Continent, that the new disaffection began to show itself. There had long been an informal and unofficial organi-zation called the Catholic Committee, dominated by a few Catholic bishops. In 1792 they were outvoted by a more militant group of Catholic laity, who expressed a wish to cooperate with Protestants in working for concessions from the Anglo-Irish ascendancy and the British government. They employed as their agent a young Anglican lawyer named Theobald Wolfe Tone, who had recently founded at Belfast a Society of United Irish-men. The Belfast group, mainly Presbyterian merchants, trades-men, and lawyers, meant in using the word "United" to join forces with Catholics. United Irish lodges were founded through-out the island. They were at first entirely open and legal, like the societies in London or Sheffield, or the *sociétés populaires* of the French Revolution, or the democratic clubs that were appearing at this same moment in the United States. The United Irish pressed for parliamentary reform, denounced the war against France, circulated Paine's *Rights of Man*, published the semi-weekly *Northern Star* at Belfast, and called for an Irish Convention. Without at first questioning the connection with England, they proposed drastic changes for Ireland, as illustrated by a draft reform bill published by the Dublin group in 1794. This proposal envisaged 300 equal electoral districts in place of the existing boroughs and counties, each to send one member to the Irish Commons, elected by universal male suffrage, for one-year terms; each member of the House was to be paid, and be under no requirement to own property. There would be no limitation of civic rights on account of religion. The United Irishmen of Dublin, far from having in mind only formal constitutional principles, meant to go on with such a parliament, to abolish tithes and primogeniture, reduce pensions and sinecures, and review the whole system of taxes and tariffs—that is, to make economic changes of the kind that could most readily be effected by legislation. Such changes, if made, would revolutionize the social structure of Ireland.

The authorities offered a few concessions. The British ministry was more willing than the Anglo-Irish ascendancy to loosen the old restrictions. Under pressure from Westminster, the Irish parliament allowed Catholics to become members of borough corporations, to take degrees from Dublin University, and to vote for members of the Irish House of Commons (though not to be elected to it) if they met the usual requirements, such as the forty-shilling freehold. These measures were designed to discourage "Jacobinism" in Ireland by preventing the merger of Catholics and Presbyterian Dissenters against the Anglican ascendancy. Few Catholics, however, were in a position to benefit from the new rights now granted, so that the agitation continued. Arguments heard in the Irish parliament, when another reform bill was defeated, were taken as insults to the Irish people. Some, like the Dutch clubs in Amsterdam, entered into secret correspondence with the French in 1794, seeking aid from the enemy in time of war. The Committee of Public Safety sent a secret agent to Dublin to report on the chances for revolution. This agent was William Jackson, a veteran radical, who had published and praised the American state constitutions, and other documents of the American Revolution, in a London edition ten years before. Jackson was arrested as a spy and executed in Dublin. Wolfe Tone, Hamilton Rowan, and Benjamin Vaughan fled to America. The United Irish societies were pronounced subversive and illegal. They therefore, after 1794, turned conspiratorial and revolutionary.

Tone, with his family, settled on a farm near Princeton, New Jersey, from which he was abruptly summoned to Philadelphia by the French minister to the United States, who invited him to proceed to France to work with the Directory for the liberation of Ireland. In Paris in 1796 he was sponsored by the American minister and future president, James Monroe, and worked with the foreign minister, Delacroix, for an invasion of Ireland. Meanwhile the United Irish lodges were holding clandestine meetings, re-cruiting members, imposing oaths, collecting weapons, and plan-ning rebellion. They now aimed at an independent republic, along the general lines of the French Revolution, and under French protection, for which the Batavian Republic offered a welcome model.

Tone's years in Paris were a time of agonizing procrastinations and disappointments, recorded faithfully in his diary. The Direc-tory, irresolute as ever, could not commit itself fully to a massive invasion of Ireland. Partly it feared the uncertainty of a maritime operation against the British fleet. Partly it felt that if the risk were to be taken, the objective should be England itself, which had so small an army that the landing of a few tens of thousands of troops might force the British government out of the war. If it seemed feasible, an Irish Republic might then follow. There might even be revolution in England, or at least the tumults in England and Scotland, the reports of a handful of extremists, the loud alarms voiced by British conservatives, the State Trials, the two acts, the naval mutinies of 1797, and suspension of gold payments by the Bank of England seemed to indicate such a possi-bility. The French, therefore, reinforced by the Dutch, laid plans for a direct assault on England in 1797. Tone and the United

Irish, so far as they knew of such plans, regarded them as a diversion, probably doomed to fail, and ruinous to their cause.

The French, nevertheless, made three attempts to assist the United Irish. The first two, on a considerable scale, came to nothing; the third landed a force of French troops that was too small and came too late to accomplish anything. In 1796 a force of 15,000 French soldiers, including Tone in a French uniform, reached Bantry Bay, on the southwest coast of Ireland. The United Irish were not yet organized in the southwest, so that no preparation had been made to receive the invaders, who were prevented from landing by continuing storms, and withdrew after waiting for sixteen days. In 1797 a Franco-Dutch force of 15,000 assembled in the Texel, from which the Batavian fleet was to escort them to points on the Scottish and Ulster coasts. It so happened that the British fleet was disabled at this very moment by the mutinies. Weeks of dead calm, however, prevented the Franco-Dutch force from seizing the opportunity. The British naval victory at Camperdown ended the chance a few weeks later. On these two occasions, as Tone remarked, the weather had saved England from its greatest danger since the Spanish Armada.

The expedition to Bantry Bay, though unsuccessful, gave confidence to the United Irish leaders that the French really meant to lend aid. Mass recruitment with a view to insurrection went rapidly forward in 1797, until there were 100,000 United Irishmen in Ulster alone. Local lodges sent delegates to regional bodies, which formed a kind of shadow government with a Directory, ready to take over at the proper moment as one of France's sister republics. The British reacted by reinforcing their garrison, until they had about 140,000 troops in the island, half regulars and half militia. It was about five times as many as the British were to have at Waterloo. The "British"—by which must be understood the Anglo-Irish ascendancy, and other Irish favoring the British connection, as well as actual Englishmen—took a variety of effective measures against the now fully revolutionary lodges. "Nothing but terror will keep them in order," reported the British commander. There were searches, interrogations, arrests, imprisonments, seizures, burnings, hangings, deportations, and miscellaneous barbarities inflicted in part by the official government and in part by antagonistic bands of armed civilians, on both sides, who detested each other. It was not, like later Irish troubles, an affair between Catholics and Protestants, or between Saxons and Celts, or between North and South. It was a struggle for and against an independent Irish Republic.

The United Irish, like the Poles in 1794, were obliged to come out in open rebellion before they were ready, because of the countermeasures taken against them. Unknown to them, the moment was unfavorable so far as French aid was concerned. Insurrection began in Ulster in April, 1798, and soon spread throughout the island. In May Bonaparte took a French army to Egypt, using troops that had formerly been assembled on the Channel coast. The glamour of this expedition—which began the modernization of the Near East, virtually founded the science of Egyptology, and brought a flow of mummies and obelisks to Western Europe—has obscured the possibility that it may have been a colossal strategic and political error. The French soon lost a fleet and an army in Egypt, anyway. Even with such a loss, had it been sustained in connection with a large-scale landing in Ireland at the height of the Irish rebellion, the effect might have been very different. The Second Coalition might never have been formed if Bonaparte had not gone to Egypt, and if Nelson had been in British waters instead of at Naples in 1798. With no Second Coalition, Britain and France might have made an uneasy peace (in which indeed the Irish might have been sacrificed), the Directory might have maintained itself, and a moderate regime might have survived in France—speculation is endless. Such is not what happened.

In fact the Irish revolutionaries, at the height of the rebellion, were assisted only by a party of a thousand French landed by General Humbert on the western coast. A force of 10,000 additional French troops was ready to follow if Humbert had any success. His cavalry, joined by Irish allies, penetrated the country for fifty miles; but the Gaelic-speaking west of Ireland was the part least affected by the United Irish organization. Hopelessly outnumbered by British forces, Humbert was obliged to surrender. Exchanged and returned to France, and disapproving of Napoleon a few years later, Humbert too withdrew to America. He fought against the British again under Andrew Jackson in the War of 1812.

Fighting raged in all parts of Ireland, but was most serious in Wexford, in the southeast. The Irish Catholic bishops, more conservative than those of Italy, offered no encouragement to the uprising, but a great many priests joined in it, enough for the future Lord Castlereagh, who was there, to call it "a Jacobinical conspiracy pursuing its object chiefly with Popish instruments." In fact it was not "popish" alone; twelve Presbyterian ministers are known to have been involved, of whom three were executed. The most conspicuous of the clerical rebels, however, was a certain Father John Murphy, who emerged as a military leader in Wexford, directing the movements of a confused host of poorly armed Catholic peasants against overwhelming odds. The movement had been decapitated before the outbreak by the flight of its leaders to the Continent or their confinement in British jails. When the fighting came, there was widespread participation but no central direction. Nothing could be coordinated, communications broke down, local successes could not be exploited, nor local danger points reinforced. The expectation of French support faded away. By the end of the summer the wave of insurrection had turned into a wave of systematic repression. The ferocity of this counter-revolution, as conducted by the Anglo-Irish, the partisans of the threatened ascendancy, shocked even the English Commander Cornwallis, and was long remembered in Ireland. The English-speaking world was expanded by the transportation of about two thousand United Irish to Australia. Various leaders were executed for treason. Wolfe Tone, facing the same fate, having slipped in from France during the fighting, cut his throat in prison. He was the chief figure in the United Irish rebellion, which, if successful, might have placed him among more memorable leaders of liberation. The difference between rebellion and revolution lay in the outcome; as Tone put it, "Washington succeeded, and Kosciuszko failed."

The consequence of the rebellion, or of its successful repression, was the Act of Union of Great Britain and Ireland, enacted in 1801 after two years of discussion in Parliament. The Union lasted until the First World War. Strategically, it was originally designed for security against the French. Socially, Pitt and others intended it as a constructive solution to the Irish problem. By abolition of the Irish parliament, and direct representation of the Irish in a unitary Parliament of the United Kingdom, Pitt hoped that the old Anglo-Irish oligarchy would be weakened, and that the Irish Catholics, by becoming a minority in a larger whole, could be safely entrusted with political rights. As it turned out, the Union was carried but no political rights were conferred on the Irish (or English) Catholics until 1827. Pitt's program collapsed before the resistance of George III, supported by the most conservative, anti-Catholic and anti-Jacobin opinion in both Britain and Ireland. For such people the Union was less a means of bringing the Irish into a larger community than a measure to be taken against international Jacobinism. As Sir Gilbert Elliott, now Lord Minto, said in the British House of Lords in 1799, an Ireland separate from England would become a "democratic republic, or rather anarchy," which would infect England itself. For him, the Union was necessary to preserve the old Anglican supremacy in Ireland in a new form, and indeed the existing order in England itself. Thus the Union became an additional grievance for most of the Irish. Irish radicalism, though silenced, continued to exist. Ireland became a kind of Poland of Western Europe. Discontented Irish, settling in Lancashire to work in the factories, or emigrating to the United States, played a role in the democratic movements of both England and America in the following century.

In the United States in the 1790s all the principal towns were Atlantic seaports. They were small by European standards— Philadelphia, the largest, had only 70,000 people—but they were in close and frequent contact with Europe. Though connections with the Continent had grown rapidly since the American Revolution, by which the Americans had thrown off the old colonial trade restrictions, the principal contact was still with England, both in the exchange of merchandise and in the receipt of news. In the journalism of the day it was easier to copy foreign papers than to employ local reporters, so that the press of Boston, New York, Philadelphia, and Charleston carried a large volume of European news. Most of it was mediated through the British press. When Thomas Jefferson returned from France at the end of 1789, he was dismayed to find American ideas of the French Revolution distorted, as he thought, by this dependency on British sources, and took steps to have one of the New York papers supplied with information from the *Leyden Gazette* of Holland.

The impact of the French Revolution in the United States was therefore a complex phenomenon. To the direct French influence was added a concurrent influence from Britain, from both the radical and the conservative, the pro-French and anti-French ideas and movements in what was still the Mother Country. Lesser influences came by way of two other parts of America— Canada and the French West Indies. In a word, British conservatism in Canada stoked the democratic fires in the United States. The collapse of slavery in the French sugar islands, by revealing new consequences of Liberty, Equality, and Fraternity, gave strength to American conservative sentiment.

As for Canada, its French-speaking population, led by its priests, was hostile to the French Revolution, but not wholly reconciled to the British rule under which it had lived since 1763. The English-speaking population was mainly composed of conservative Loyalist refugees from the American Revolution. The British Parliament, by the Canada Act of 1791, set up governments in Upper and Lower Canada (the later Ontario and Quebec) that were expressly designed to avoid the "democratic excesses" of both the American and the French Revolutions. In addition, the British had not yet fully accepted the western boundaries of the United States as drawn in the treaty of 1783. The governor of Upper Canada felt that his authority really extended beyond the Lakes and into the Illinois Country, and even believed, in 1794, that these almost untrodden wildernesses were penetrated by "Jacobin emissaries." Distrusting the French Canadians, fearful of the French of France and the troublesome Americans south of the border, the British Canadians and the British authorities were very much attached to British traditions. Loyalty Associations arose, as in England in 1792; and an Alien Act against dangerous foreigners was adopted, as in the United States in 1798. One or two revolutionary conspiracies were in fact discovered. An American, David McLane, who was actually implicated in one of them, was executed for treason by hanging and "drawing" in 1797. This was more than happened at the time in either England or the United States. The pronounced anti-Americanism that emanated from Canada heightened the Anglophobia of American democrats.

The effects in the United States of the revolution in Saint Domingue, the later Republic of Haiti, are very difficult to assess. Undoubtedly they sharpened the fears of whites living among Negro slaves in the American South. As early as 1791 the Constituent Assembly had decreed equal rights for the free blacks in the French colonies. The white *colons* had objected, the black slaves had become restless; revolt and civil war followed, punctuated by the total abolition of slavery by the Convention in 1794. That Toussaint l'Ouverture, a Negro and former slave, should emerge as a leader, be commissioned a general in the French army, and wear the uniform of the French Republic, was hardly more palatable to most Americans than to the French whites in the French colonies. Most of the latter abandoned the islands, especially Saint Domingue, the largest, some returning to France, some settling on the American mainland. In 1797 it was estimated that there were 20,000 French refugees in the United States, mainly from Saint Domingue. A few notables, including Talleyrand, made more temporary sojourns during the Terror. Most of these French refugees were not very well disposed toward the Revolution. On the other hand, given the war between France and Great Britain, and the hopes for a moderate settlement under the Directory, they felt themselves to be French and so were viewed with suspicion in conservative American circles. Most of the foreign democrats in the United States were in fact English, Scottish, or Irish. They were hard to distinguish from Americans. Like the events in Saint Domingue itself, the presence of the French refugees, who were very numerous in Philadelphia, the capital city, to which they brought the foreign accents associated with Jacobinism, contributed to conservatism in America.

In 1789 the government of the United States was just beginning to organize itself under the new federal Constitution. A large measure of harmony prevailed in the country, for even those who had criticized or opposed the new Constitution, while it was still only a project, were now willing to accept it. The differences that soon developed, and which became very bitter, were not a continuation of former differences of opinion. There were no counterrevolutionaries in America, in the sense known in France, or in Holland; no one wished to restore King George or to revive the regime that had preceded 1776. The differences were merely incipient or potential. Some favored development under the Constitution in a more democratic direction, some did not. The differences, which the influence of the French Revolution was to crystallize into two political parties, at first manifested themselves in response to the policies of the new federal government.

For some, led by Alexander Hamilton, what the new country needed was economic development and a more unified central authority. Economic development required investment and borrowing, at home and in Europe, since Europe was economically more highly developed than America, and was the source from which capital could be obtained. In particular, Europe meant England, for England, along with Holland, was the country where fluid wealth was most plentiful and banking facilities most available, and with which Americans were most accustomed to doing business in any case. Hamilton therefore undertook to make the United States into a country in which creditors would risk their money. He insisted that the older debts, which went back to the Revolution, and for which the securities had often changed hands at falling prices, should nevertheless be paid at their face value, even though such payment produced a windfall for the present owners of depreciated paper. He insisted also—like the advanced democrats of the Batavian Republic of 1795—that the various state debts should be consolidated into a national debt for which the new central government would make itself responsible. The government would therefore require an income, to be drawn from excise taxes and customs duties, and the flow of customs duties should be enlarged by a growing volume of foreign trade. Hamilton, in short, to develop the country economically, and to strengthen it politically against the many centrifugal forces within it, proposed to work through the apparatus of capitalism, of which Great Britain was the main center.

Others, for whom Thomas Jefferson eventually became the

leader, were less eager to see America "developed" along such lines, or to become more like Europe, with its huge cities, its class distinctions, its very rich and its very poor. Still less did they want a government that made its appeal to the moneyed interests. To pay off depreciated paper at par, to raise money by taxing the people, and then turn it over to speculators who had bought the paper at much lower rates, seemed inexcusable and unnecessary. The critics of Hamilton preferred in any case that the country should remain mainly agricultural, with trade and finance kept in a merely auxiliary role. For such a purpose no great strengthening of a remote central government would be needed. Liberty, as vindicated in the American Revolution, would be the better preserved if government remained mostly local or at the state level. Equality, as known in the past, and characteristic of America since the earliest settlement, would likewise be maintained in a society of yeoman farmers, each owning his own land, managing his own affairs, content with a comfortable livelihood, and not dependent on the decisions of far-away and unknown persons, whether employers, merchants, creditors, tax collectors or other public officials. Such a society also, in this view, had the best chance of maintaining the national independence so lately won against England.

Hamilton, supported by Washington, managed to get his policies adopted during the first two or three years of the new government. His supporters were mainly in the towns, in the growing business and commercial community, and among farmers who lived near the towns or along the rivers, which put them in touch with the outside world. His followers called themselves Federalists, meaning that they wished to strengthen the federal union. The word had an opposite sense to "federalism" in Europe, where it signified, first in France and then in the sister republics, a desire to prevent the concentration of power. Hamilton himself was a great centralist, who would have preferred to abolish the existing states, especially such agrarian giants as Virginia, and to replace them (like the democrats in Europe) with *départements* created by a national government.

Opponents of Hamilton gradually came to call themselves Republicans. They were in effect democrats. The suffrage itself was not at issue. The battle waged by reformers in Britain and Ireland, and by friends of the "passive" or nonvoting citizens in France in 1790–92, had already been won in the United States, where in most states a very extensive male suffrage already existed. What the Republicans wanted was a more active participation, more interest in politics, more frequent actual voting, by plain men whose right to vote was not in question. They wanted these ordinary voters to elect plain people like themselves to office, and not to be content, as in the past, to choose upper-class persons to represent them. They were made more class conscious by Hamilton's inducements to creditors, to bankers, to men of wealth and magnates of commerce, those who had money or were determined to make it. They saw themselves as the "people," threatened by new forces of aristocracy. In strong government they sensed the danger of tyranny. They feared the evils of special privilege in any ruling elite, in favors by government to business, in chartered banks or indeed in any large organizations.

Men of this kind sympathized with the French Revolution. In 1792 and 1793 they formed a good many popular clubs. Though these clubs soon disappeared because they were replaced by more definite units of the emerging Republican party, their appearance signified the birth of a new democratic movement. Over forty such clubs have been identified, chiefly in the seaports and along the frontiers. On the whole, about half their membership was truly popular, and about half was composed of lawyers, doctors, merchants, and landowners above the level of simple farmers. Their attitude was one of vigilance against persons in established position, or in the language of the Ulster Democratic Club of upstate New York, "against designing men in office and affluent circumstances, who are forever combining against the rights of all but themselves." They upheld the "many" against the "few." The "few" responded by talking like the upper orders of Europe. Timothy Dwight, president of Yale College, compared the club members to a herd of swine (echoing Burke on the English democrats), and another New England notable, Oliver Wolcott, called them "the lowest order of mechanics, laborers and draymen."

While the Americans were thus becoming divided, on purely domestic grounds, France was invaded and became a republic, and then went to war with Britain. Americans took sides, for Britain or for France, to a degree never paralleled in connection with any later war or revolution in Europe. There was something paradoxical in the situation. Hamilton, the great Anglophile and hater of the French Revolution, was actually more of a revolutionary than Jefferson, or at least more oriented to the future, more impatient of the American past, more eager to see a new central power obliterate existing states and institutions. Jefferson, with his sympathy for the French Revolution, was a landed gentleman, essentially a moderate, who disliked both the bourgeoisie and the unruly populace of great cities. In upholding liberty and equality, he meant to conserve certain features of the American past, a liberty which meant the virtual absence or weakness of government, and an equality that reflected a simple and rural society. Agrarians in Europe were the most consistent adversaries of the French Revolution; in America, its most enthusiastic supporters. The urban and business interests which in Europe, and even in England, were inclined to see merit in Revolutionary or radical ideas, in America generally opposed them. Such a transposition of attitudes arose from the very great differences between the two sides of the Atlantic. Class perceptions were different, because the social structure of America was in fact different. No American saw to what extent the French Revolution was a "bourgeois" movement. With no true aristocracy or royal court above them, the American men of affairs who followed Hamilton saw themselves as the uppermost level of society. They readily identified with the landed aristocracy of Britain and Europe, by which, in fact, they would probably have been thought to be too much "in trade." They supposed that the Revolution in Europe was the work of an ignorant rabble. As for the democrats in America, who knew little of the sans-culottes, not to mention Babeuf, they exaggerated the resemblance between themselves and the democrats of Europe, who were by no means simple farmers and country attorneys. The American democrats, whose ideal of government was to have as little of it as possible, did not see that popular government in Europe must be strong if it was to accomplish anything, or even to survive against the onslaughts of its opponents.

In April, 1793, just as news of the war between Britain and France was reaching America, a new French minister disembarked at Charleston, South Carolina. He was Edmond Genêt, a young man of noble birth who had served in the French Foreign Office before the Revolution, where he had worked with Benjamin Franklin in Paris. More recently, having enthusiastically accepted the Revolution, he had contended with "aristocrats" in Russia and Holland as well as in France. He received a tremendous ovation from the American democrats on his long overland journey from Charleston to Philadelphia. He began to contend with aristocrats in America, mixed with the admiring democrats, sponsored the formation of new democratic clubs, and recruited frontiersmen for expeditions in the West and in Florida against the British and Spanish, with whom France was at war, but with whom the United States was at peace. Genêt tried to take advantage of the Franco-American treaty of alliance of 1778, which was still legally in effect. President Washington issued a Proclamation of Neutrality instead. The American democrats were offended by the proclamation, in which they saw a pro-British and a Hamiltonian maneuver. The clubs, on the other hand, seemed to the Federalists to be merely pro-French, "Genêt's clubs"; and the whole democratic commotion was seen as a French frenzy, if not the product of an actual French Revolutionary conspiracy. The clubs were dismissed as mere unauthorized centers of agitation; Washington called them "self-created," as if to be unofficial were a reproach. The democrats were outraged at such a rebuke. They feared, with some justice, that the very principles of popular sovereignty, self-government, and the American Revolution were being questioned.

Genêt's mission was soon terminated by his own government. Since he was a friend of the Girondins expelled from the Convention on June 2, 1793, the emerging Revolutionary Government in France found him undesirable anyway; but it also expected to profit from maintaining United States neutrality, and readily complied with Washington's request for his recall. Genêt soon married the daughter of a leading Republican, and lived in New York State for forty years.

The crest of the wave of enthusiasm for France continued through the most violent phase, undeterred by the Terror. It showed itself in the clubs, in public meetings and ceremonies, in sermons and patriotic orations, and in the newspaper press. Native journalists were reinforced by those from Britain and Ireland. The most in view of these newcomers was William Cobbett, who took sides with the Federalists, since at this time he detested all democrats (his more famous radical phase coming much later after his return to England); but most of the newly arriving journalists were vehemently Republican, inflamed by their unpleasant experiences in the British Isles. Thus the Irishman John Daly Burk edited the Boston *Polar Star*, and then the New York *Timepiece*; Joseph Gales from Sheffield put out a paper in North Carolina; and Thomas Cooper from Manchester wrote a number of pamphlets. But most of the vehement democrats were native born. Even many of the Congregationalist clergy of New England and Presbyterian clergy of the Middle States spoke up in favor of the French Revolution, and were disposed to suspend judgment on its "excesses." In their view, the evils of monarchy and of Roman Catholicism could hardly be cured without convulsions.

In January, 1793, a meeting at Plymouth, Massachusetts, celebrated the victories of the French Republic at Valmy and in Belgium. The pastor of the Plymouth congregation, using abundant quotations from the Bible, pronounced a eulogy of the French Revolution. Selections from Robespierre's speeches were published at Philadelphia, and in western Pennsylvania the Pittsburgh *Gazette* fumed against the English, and the novelist and western landowner Hugh Brackenridge asked rhetorically: "If kings combine to support kings, why not republics to support republics?" In 1794 the Massachusetts Constitutional Society resolved that the happiness of "the *whole world of Mankind*" depended on the success of the French Revolution. Even Noah Webster, who favored the Federalists, could not bring himself to wish well to the "vile league of tyrants" with which the French were at war. "Perhaps," he said in a speech in New York, and referring to the Terror, "other circumstances not known in this country may serve to palliate the apparent cruelty of the ruling faction." Even Jedidiah Morse, clergyman, geographer, Federalist, and Congregationalist luminary, in November, 1794, by which time full news of the Terror had reached New England, thought that the "irregularities" in France, including the atheism and the guillotinings, should be in large measure "excused." In July, 1795, a year after the death of Robespierre, in a Fourth of July oration at Boston, the orator gave his highest praise to the French and not to the American Revolution, for the American struggles, he said, "were but as the first achievement of Hercules in his cradle compared to the wonderful labors reserved for his manhood."

A great many democrats, though not Jefferson and other responsible leaders, would have welcomed the chance for another war against England. The United States, however, signed a treaty with England in 1794. Agreeing only to withdraw from the Northwest, the British refused all other concessions. The treaty was denounced by democrats as a shameful appeasement. The American Congress heatedly debated the legislation needed to implement it, which was finally enacted in April, 1796, by a narrow margin of only 51 to 48.

Defining themselves in the debates and voting on Jay's Treaty, that is, essentially on attitudes to be taken toward the French Revolution and the war in Europe, two clearly delineated parties, Federalist and Republican, prepared for the presidential election of 1796, which, with the retirement of Washington, was the first contested presidential election. The candidates were, respectively, John Adams and Thomas Jefferson. Each was denounced by the opposition as the tool of a foreign power. Adams, to the Republicans, was a monocrat and an aristocrat, "the champion of rank, titles and hereditary distinctions," an Anglomaniac absurdly enamored of "the British Monarchical form of Government." Jefferson, to the Federalists, was an irresponsible Francophile, a leveler, a libertine, an atheist, and a Jacobin. Such caricatures were gross oversimplifications, but it was true that Jefferson had more faith in liberty and equality, and more tolerance for the French Revolution, than Adams did; and that Adams, though he despised Hamilton and disliked moneyed men, had become extremely respectful of the British constitution as he understood it.

The French, as noted earlier, interfered in the election of 1796 to the extent of expressing an obvious preference for the election of Jefferson. Adams was nevertheless elected by a narrow margin of 71 to 68 electoral votes. As a result, under the Constitution as it then existed, Jefferson became vice-president, and the administration was internally divided. The French Directory took Jay's Treaty and the election of Adams to mean that the United States was now in effect allied to Britain, and even formed the impression, from publication of Vice-President Jefferson's "Mazzei letter" in the *Moniteur*, and from the continuing outcries of American democrats, that the United States government did not really represent the wishes of its own people. Concentrating its forces against England at the end of 1797, after making peace with Austria and laying plans for an invasion of England or Ireland, the Directory began also to attack American shipping in the Atlantic, since it was now England that benefited from the American merchant marine. American vessels defended themselves; Adams created a Navy Department. France and the United States were embroiled in a "quasi-war."

In these circumstances the tide of Francophile sentiment began to recede. In addition, the American clergy were far more scandalized by Paine's *Age of Reason*, which appeared in 1795, than by the Worship of Reason in Paris in 1793. It now seemed that not only Catholicism and monarchy but New England Congregationalism and Christianity itself might be swept away. For Americans in the Reformed tradition the French invasion and revolutionary developments in Holland and Switzerland, after 1795, seemed like wanton violence against innocent victims. The counter-revolutionary writings composed in England began to reach the United States. Burke's *Reflections* had only two American printings in the 1790s; it was too ornate, and too traditionalist, to suit American taste at the time. In 1795 William Cobbett brought out an American edition of Playfair's *History of Jacobinism, Its Crimes, Cruelties and Perfidies*, to which he added a resounding appendix on the American democrats. English translations of Mallet du Pan, Barruel, and other Continental opponents of the Revolution appeared in America. John Quincy Adams, the son of John Adams, sent as American minister to the Batavian Republic, viewed the spread of revolution in Europe with alarm; he discovered Friedrich Gentz's *Historisches Journal*, edited at Berlin with a British subsidy; and he published in America, to combat the election of Jefferson in 1800, a translation of Gentz's comparison of the American and French Revolutions, which was designed to show how evil the French Revolution was. Jedidiah Morse changed his opinion, and far from "excusing" the French, as in 1794, preached two sermons in 1798 revealing a vast secret revolutionary conspiracy. The Illuminati, Morse now said, had been working for years to undermine all government and religion. He got the idea from the Scottish Presbyterian Robison, who had drawn upon German sources, and had published his *Proofs of a Conspiracy* in 1797. Thanks to Morse, the United States was briefly gripped in 1798 by its first revolutionary scare.

President Adams, who discounted much of these frenzies, sent a commission to France to attempt a settlement of the quasi-war. Someone in the French government, probably Talleyrand, the foreign minister, offered to facilitate the negotiations in return for what amounted to a bribe. The American commissioners refused. Adams, hoping to throw cold water on the persistent democratic ardor for France, published the documents of this abortive negotiation. In place of the French names he put X, Y, and Z. The XYZ papers caused a tremendous furor. Actually, the French Directors were not themselves involved; diplomatic bribery was an old story in Europe, and Pitt himself in 1797 had seriously entertained a similar proposal. But the American moral sense was outraged. The Republicans were shocked and disconcerted. The Federalists gloated in their easy triumph. They found that the French had "insulted America and demanded of her a tribute."

With undeclared hostilities going on at sea, Hamilton and the "high" Federalists—those who found Adams too moderate—labored to bring the United States into a full-scale war. They dreamed of allying with Britain in a crusade against an atheistic and Jacobinical French Republic, a war in which American Republicans would be exposed, and in which conquests might be made in the Spanish American empire, to which Cuba, Florida, New Orleans, Texas, and Mexico still belonged. Adams resisted the war spirit, in which the Republicans saw a direct menace to themselves. A Federalist majority in Congress, in 1798, enacted

a series of four different laws, known as the Alien and Sedition
Acts: the Naturalization Act, the Alien Act, the Alien Enemies
Act, and the Sedition Act. The first three reflected the Federalist
belief that democratic ideas were a foreign importation—that the
clubs of 1793 had been "Genêt's clubs," that most critics of the
government were "fortune-hunting foreigners," that the newly
risen Republicans were "the vile organs of a foreign democracy,"
to quote the Federalist press. The Naturalization Act raised the
residence requirement for naturalization from 5 to 14 years. The
Alien Act provided for the deportation of troublesome foreigners.
No one was ever deported under this Act, though many of the
French refugees felt threatened by it and left the country. The
Alien Enemies Act authorized the president, in time of war or invasion, to imprison or banish any foreigners he believed to be a
menace to public security. The Sedition Act was palpably used
for partisan purposes. There was no sedition in the United States,
either in the true sense of attempts to overturn the government, or
in the extended sense, then current in England, meaning radical
disapproval of the very Constitution and form of government
itself. What the Federalists meant by sedition was disagreement,
often indeed expressed in extravagant language, with their policies,
programs, and conduct in office. Fifteen persons were indicted
under the Sedition Act, and eleven convicted. They were all
active Republicans, including a congressman and six newspaper
editors.

The Republicans naturally took alarm. While an argument
could be made, given the behavior of the French government toward the United States since 1796, and the actual hostilities at
sea, for precautions against the pro-French elements in the
country, it was clear that the three acts were being used to crush
the criticism of government, to destroy the new Republican party,
and even, for some, to sweep the country into a real war on the
side of England. The Republicans defended themselves with
dangerous weapons, which if long used would have been fatal to
the ten-year-old Constitution and to the very existence of the
United States. That is, through the state legislatures of Virginia
and Kentucky, guided by Madison and Jefferson, they took the view
that laws threatening "liberty," in this case the Alien and Sedition

Acts, were simply null and void and of no effect in the protesting states.

In the words of President Adams, who knew a great deal about Europe, the United States was sinking into the "corruption of Poland." He meant that it was torn by an internal dissension in which groups of its people felt closer to foreigners than to their own fellow citizens; and that these foreign powers, England and France, if unchecked, would manipulate and ruin the United States in the course of their struggles with each other. Much as he disliked the French Revolution, he did not believe that the British or anyone else would soon put an end to it. Nor did he relish the thought of a militarized America dominated by Hamilton. He therefore sent another peace commission to Paris. The French, now that the Second Coalition had formed against them, proved more tractable than in the days of the XYZ affair. They stopped their attacks on American shipping. Peace was restored between the two republics. Hamilton and the High Federalists were enraged. At this moment, with Suvorov's victories in Italy and the Anglo-Russian landing in Holland, with the collapse of the Italian republics and the expected "liberation" of the Batavian, the American Federalists seem to have believed, like the extreme counterrevolutionaries of Europe, that with a little more effort the whole wretched episode of the French Revolution might at last be closed. They denounced Adams as a traitor to their principles and virtually a Jacobin himself. He failed for re-election in 1800, retired from public life, and spent the next twenty-six years in sarcastic comment on the foolishness of the Federalists, and eventually in renewing the classic friendship with Jefferson that had begun in the American Revolution.

Jefferson took office early in 1801. While shuddering at the "Jacobin" president, the Federalists raised no rebellion or conspiracy against him. It was the only peaceable and lasting transfer of power to Republican hands in the whole eighteenth-century revolutionary upheaval. The new federal constitution, rejected by neither party, took on the features of permanency and legitimacy— also the only such case. The country had been furiously divided, but it escaped the fate of Poland. It might have been less fortunate if France or Britain had been actually on its borders. The very heat of the controversy generated by the French Revolution, though it seemed almost to throw the new country into dissolution, actually served in a roundabout way to consolidate it. It was decisive in the formation of a two-party system on a national scale, with each party reaching throughout the whole territory, and composed not only of leaders but of mass followers, men in every locality who were aroused by great visible and dramatic issues on a larger stage.

As France passed under the sway of Napoleon, as the reform movement was extinguished in Britain, and as war continued in Europe, the Americans ceased to be fascinated by foreign struggles. They began instead to feel a sense of fortunate isolation, and even of superiority to an afflicted and benighted Europe. But the United States, in the form it took after 1800, was not the product of isolation, nor of the American Revolution alone, but also of the whole revolution of Western civilization which accompanied the Revolution in France.

[9]

Germany: The Revolution Philosophized

THE DISTINCTIVE THING about Germany in the revolutionary world of the 1790s was the lack of any revolutionary experience, or indeed of political experience of any kind. In France, above all, but also in Poland and Ireland, as in America in 1775, men had taken matters into their own hands and defied their rulers in open rebellion. In the sister republics from Holland to Naples, in Great Britain, and in the United States in the 1790s, there was a great deal of organized agitation and counteragitation. In all these countries, men of similar views tried to work together for public purposes over a large area. In all of them, in one way or another, the politically interested either joined clubs, or formed associations, or attended conventions, or sat in assemblies, or issued manifestoes, or projected new constitutions, or cast votes in elections, or joined national guards, or milled about in demonstrations or mass meetings, or at least delivered or listened to public speeches. Hardly anything of the sort happened in Germany.

On the other hand, the Germans were far from indifferent to current developments. Their feelings were aroused for the Revolution or against it. They did a good deal of reading, for the number of books and magazines published in Germany was possibly greater than in any other country. They gave the Revolution much thought. The generation of 1789 was also the supreme age of

German literature and philosophy, the age of Goethe and Schiller, of Kant, Fichte, and Hegel, of Herder and Schleiermacher, Tieck and Novalis, the Schlegels and the Humboldts. All these men had views on the age in which they lived. All remained essentially spectators. There were no German revolutionaries, but there was a host of commentators on, or philosophers of, the Revolution. A divorce between thought and action has often been said to be characteristic of German culture. Beyond their mere separation, it was the near absence of action and the overwhelming presence of thought, that marked Germany in the world of the French Revolution.

Thinking in Germany, as elsewhere, about 1770, or 1780, turned increasingly to questions of government and society. It became politicized, but in a strangely nonpolitical way. There was a new eagerness to consider the state in the abstract, but not to plan courses of action, assume responsibilities, judge in terms of alternatives and consequences, appeal for support from real human beings, or form alliances by means of tactical compromises. Political thinking became idealistic and absolute. It concerned itself less with empirical problems than with essences—the state itself, liberty, right, law, human dignity, or the general movement of history. The Germans had almost a popular liking for metaphysics. The philosophy of Kant reached far beyond the lecture hall. The conception of a Categorical Imperative, an absolute inner voice of duty as such, without much scrutiny of specific duties or choices, became almost a national doctrine. For some, it provided a kind of austere religion; for others, an ethical equivalent to the French idea of the Rights of Man and Citizen.

That the Germans remained inactive politically was due to the nature of their governments and the relations obtaining between their social classes. "Germany" was a mere geographical or ethnic expression. Politically, there was the Holy Roman Empire, which had virtually no powers. It embraced about three hundred states, some ruled by lay princes, some by bishops or abbots, along with fifty free cities and a thousand imperial knights. The latter were of aristocratic families which had managed, over the centuries, to avoid coming under any effective government at all. The free cities were mainly closed oligarchies of hereditary patricians. In the princely and ecclesiastical states the government was carried on by professional civil servants untroubled by public opinion. In a few places the estates on the late medieval model continued to meet, and gave a semblance of parliamentary life, notably in Württemberg, where, however, the nobles did not attend the assembly, having long ago individually seceded, so to speak, and set up as independent knights of the empire.

The fragmentation of Germany was most extreme on the side toward France. A hundred and fifty separate jurisdictions crowded the Left Bank of the Rhine. The East was occupied by the only two significant German powers, the Prussian and the Austrian monarchies. Both included a great many Poles, especially after the interventions and partitions of 1793 and 1795, as already described. Both had vigorous governments. The rise and fall of reform in the Hapsburg dominions has been traced in Chapter 5. A spirit of innovation remained more active in Prussia. It was found, however, not in any public opposition to government, but in the agents of the Prussian state itself.

In Prussia the middle classes had confidence in the monarchy, so that while generally sympathetic to the French Revolution they had no feeling that anything of the kind was necessary in Prussia. And in truth, the monarchy was not averse to new ideas. The British envoy Lord Malmesbury, in 1794, believed the Prussian officer corps to be infected with "a strong taint of democracy." In 1795 Prussia withdrew from the war against France; it remained neutral for eleven years. The king abolished serfdom where he had enough power—that is, on his own crown domains. Much reforming attention was directed to the army. One officer, in 1797, used American, Dutch, and French examples to argue that men having a positive emotional commitment to their political system made better soldiers. Another advised against floggings and degrading punishments, believing that to injure the soldier's self-respect was to undermine the sources of his courage. A third thought that Prussian soldiers should be "actual citizens" (not outside mercenaries), and that middle-class persons should be admitted to the officer ranks. It is true that a certain von Ribbentrop warned against the admission of Jews, that much of this discussion remained confidential and unknown, and that little was done until after the disaster at Jena in 1806. There remained a certain confidence in the intentions of the government. Most Prussians would have agreed with what the Minister Struensee said to a French visitor in 1799: "The salutary revolution which you made from below will take place gradually here in Prussia. The king is a democrat in his way; he is working constantly to limit the privileges of the nobility." In fact, however, the new Prussian code of 1794 defined the rights of all Prussian subjects, not as "citizens," but by estates and classes. It gave separate treatment to nobles, burghers, and others. In this sense it was contrary to everything that happened in France from the Declaration of 1789 to the Napoleonic codes of 1804–10. In Prussia it was accepted with satisfaction as guaranteeing a rule of law and rational government. That it allowed for neither political liberty nor legal equality seemed not to matter.

Both in Prussia and in the smaller states there was a great respect for authority, a disposition to trust the rulers and their expert advisers, to believe that public clamor, pressure, or even criticism was unseemly. There was also an acceptance of the existing structure of social classes. The classes mixed less than in Italy and Western Europe. Except in the East the peasants were legally free, and sometimes even prosperous, but they had no common interests with the towns, whose very privileges kept them asunder. Nobles seldom intermarried with burghers or joined with them in business. Burghers were literally townsmen, whose towns remained rather quaint and archaic. Hamburg was an exception in being a busy and modern commercial seaport, but its wealthy citizens looked outward to the world rather than inward to Germany. At Hamburg and in the other free cities the burgher patricians governed themselves, the lesser townsfolk, and their neighboring rural subjects. But neither in the free cities, nor in the towns of Prussia, any more than in the diet of Württemberg, did the burghers have occasion to act on a wider stage, or to seek alliance with landed nobles for a common purpose. Except at Hamburg, the middle class was hardly associated with capitalism or any large-scale enterprise. In Prussia the economy was dependent on the state. Most middle-class Germans were of modest station: local functionaries, professional men, small merchants or guild-masters, university professors, writers, musicians, publishers, editors, clergymen, and government employees. They might occasionally complain of individual nobles, or yearn for more recognition for themselves. But relations between the two classes were distant. Neither provoked the other. German burghers favored the Rights of Man, they wished well to humanity, they shared in much of the European Enlightenment. But they felt no potentially revolutionary asperity toward anyone in particular. Generally sympathetic to the Revolution in France, they attributed it to specifically French causes, without application to themselves.

In a country so divided, thought on abstract questions leaped over the barriers, but any movement that might arise on a practical matter, reflecting some grievance or proposing some course of action, broke against political boundaries only a few miles away. What might be relevant in one place was less so in another. There was no capital, no common ruler or superstructure, no central target at which to aim. Nobles, burghers, and peasants stood apart. Half the Germans were Protestants, half Catholics, and still sensitive to the difference. In short, Germany was not a "nation," at a time when the nation, or civic community, was one of the chief Revolutionary conceptions. A nation, whatever else it may be, is a vehicle for collective human action. This vehicle Germany lacked.

On the level of action, the principal disturbances were in the Rhineland, but a few other places may be considered first. As early as 1790 there was a mass rebellion among the peasants of Electoral Saxony. With long-standing grievances of their own, they had heard the news of agrarian revolt in France the year before. Roughly arming themselves, they threatened their lords, who took refuge in Dresden. For a few weeks the peasants controlled an area of over a thousand square miles. Then localism and social isolation asserted themselves. No one in the towns made common cause with the peasants, nor did the agrarian insurrection spread outside the Electorate. The Electors' troops restored order. Three years later, in 1794, similar troubles broke out in Silesia, a part of Prussia that adjoined Poland. A rumor circulated, perhaps inspired by Kosciuszko's Polaniec proclamation abolishing serfdom, that the new Prussian code was about to put an end to forced labor. The rumor was false, for the Prussian code took a conservative view of the rights and functions of social classes. Order was restored by the Prussian army.

Hamburg, commercially the most advanced city of Germany, was also the most eagerly sympathetic to the French Revolution. It was said to have forty-one millionaires, one of whom, Heinrich Sieveking, turned his house virtually into a political club. It was much frequented by French, Dutch, Irish, and American, as well as by German patriots. Wealthy though they were, Sieveking's group befriended the more truly radical and even "socialist" writer A. G. Rebmann when he passed through Hamburg in 1797. There was also a radical press in Hamburg, and clubs were formed for more modest people, such as the young diarist Ferdinand Beneke, who was to live to see the Revolution of 1848. Beneke confided to his diary in 1794 that inwardly he was a "staunch republican, even a democrat," while outwardly only a *Weltburger*. There were many such *Weltburger* in Germany at the time— that is, burghers who felt cramped by the old barriers, who longed to become citizens, but in the absence of a German state could find citizenship only in a free world of somewhat indefinite character and location.

The Rhineland in the 1790s was a sleepy byway, untouched by the maritime trade of Hamburg, nor yet affected by an industrialism that was still to come. Its towns were numerous but old-fashioned. Aachen and Frankfurt were free cities; Mainz, Trier, and Cologne were the seats of archbishops and capitals of their temporal states; Bonn and Coblenz belonged to the archbishops of Cologne and Trier, respectively. The impact of the French Revolution was immediate. French émigrés began to concentrate at Coblenz as early as 1789. While their frivolity and *hauteur* turned some Rhinelanders into sympathizers with the Revolution, their tales of anarchy and horror made conservatives of others. In some places the peasants began to refuse payment of seigneurial dues. In the diets of the territories belonging to Trier and Cologne there were disputes over equality of taxation as between clergy, nobles, and third estate. At Aachen the Protestants were annoyed at the refusal of equal rights by the Catholic town authorities. To

Edmund Burke, writing in 1791, it seemed that "a great revolution is preparing in Germany," and that the Rhineland in particular was infected with the theory of the rights of man.

In the absence of economic development, the middle class in the Rhineland was heavily weighted with intellectuals—Catholic ecclesiastics, teachers in schools, university professors and students, librarians, editors, and writers. Some were in trouble before the French arrived. A. J. Dorsch was ejected from a chair in philosophy at Mainz in 1791 for his Kantian opinions. He became a zealous collaborator with the French. Eulogius Schneider was removed from a chair at Bonn in 1791 for questioning the divinity of Christ. He plunged into the Revolution in France itself, at Strasbourg, where he was later executed as an extremist. In 1792, at Mainz, Georg Forster, librarian of the University, and well known as a writer and traveler, formed a political club. Its first members included a doctor, the head of a Protestant school, and four professors at the University, including A. J. Hoffmann, who was to attempt revolution in southwestern Germany in 1798, and live to see the Revolution of 1848. These were the original "Mainz Jacobins." They were necessarily a secret society, at a time when Austrian and Prussian forces were passing through Mainz on their way to the invasion of France.

In October, 1792, a month after Valmy, the French Revolutionary armies entered the Rhineland. Their commander, Custine, turned to Forster's group as a useful association of local adherents. The Mainz Jacobins emerged from obscurity. They found hundreds of like-minded persons in the multifarious principalities of the Left Bank. In March, 1793, a gathering of such patriots assembled in a Rhenish-German Convention. The Convention claimed to represent the sovereignty of a "free people" in a new state, which, having no pre-existing identity, was simply described as the "region from Landau to Bingen." Three days later the Convention voted for incorporation of this newly sovereign people into the French Republic.

These proceedings were simultaneous with the annexation to France of the neighboring Austrian Netherlands and Bishopric of Liège, which were also states of the Holy Roman Empire without much political vitality of their own. It was less strange than it seemed in later times for disaffected persons in these areas to seek union with France. Neither a Belgium nor a Germany yet existed as a real political organization. National feeling was unformed; French was a familiar language, and if Netherlanders and Rhinelanders detested the memory of Louis XIV, they could the more readily identify with a revolutionary French people who had rejected their monarchy and seemed to represent the liberation of mankind. Revolutionary Rhinelanders, like Belgian Democrats, expected more recognition of their own ideas, and more personal security for themselves, as citizens of the great Republic than as subjects of their respective town councils, estates, or princelings. Those who took any initiative in seeking annexation to France were an infinitesimal minority. Those who strongly opposed it, or who would take action to defend the Old Order in their own countries, were not numerous. The future reformer of Prussia, Freiherr von Stein, was then stationed in the Rhineland. "The spirit in these countries could not be worse," he reported to Berlin in 1792. "The magistrates at Worms sent a deputation to the French, to give them the keys to the city."

The situation was abruptly reversed by Dumouriez's defeat at Neerwinden. The Rhineland, like Belgium, was evacuated by the French, and throughout 1793 it seemed to the more optimistic counterrevolutionary observers that republicanism would soon collapse in France itself. The efforts of the Rhenish-German Convention came to nothing. Nor were they put to any test.

The French soon returned, and by 1797 another flurry became evident in the Rhineland. It took the form of demands for a Cisrhenane Republic, to be modeled on the Batavian or the Cisalpine, and to include the whole Left Bank from Alsace to the Dutch frontier. The articulate "Cisrhenanes" never numbered more than two or three thousand. They included the Mainz Jacobins of 1792, to whom others were now added: men disgusted with or imperiled by the intervening restoration, those compromised by working with the French occupying authorities, those excited by the spread of revolution in Holland and Italy. "Citizens!" cried the Cisrhenanes at Bonn, "Italy is ahead of us; it has proclaimed the Rights of Man and become a free and independent state. We wish valiantly to follow their lofty example. The power of France protects us, so that the revolution of humanity that has become necessary for us will cost no tears." These Germans thus used the same argument as the Dutch, Swiss, and Italians. All wanted a revolution without "tears"—a humane revolution in the spirit of the Enlightenment, a free and modern republic without popular intrusion or mob violence, with order guaranteed by the French army. The Directory, however, refused to sponsor a separate Cisrhenane Republic. Many of the Cisrhenanes, doubting the viability of such a republic anyway, were equally willing to accept annexation to France instead. Petitions requesting annexation circulated throughout the Rhineland. There were thousands of signatures. Many people, in any case, saw no better alternative. The Directory began to reorganize the wonderland of a hundred-odd bishoprics, duchies, free cities, and minuscule separate dominions into four *départements*. By 1800 these were fully annexed to France, with which they remained united until 1814. The Rhinelanders proved to be amenable citizens of the Napoleonic empire, in the course of which seigneurial dues were abolished, the laws were codified, and the system of taxation, law courts, and administration brought up to date. Most of the area, thus homogenized, modernized, and liberalized, was turned over to Prussia at the Congress of Vienna.

There were agitations also on the Right Bank of the Rhine, across from Alsace. Clubs of Revolutionary sympathizers were formed by substantial middle-class persons—doctors, lawyers, merchants, government servants, and men of independent means. Some of them were connected with the conspiracy in which the French emissary Poteratz played a part, and which the Directory first favored and then repudiated in 1796. In 1798, at the time of the Swiss revolution, a handful of Germans based in Basel tried to subvert the government of Baden. At the same time, the old disputes between the estates and the duke came again to a head in Württemberg. A deputy named Baz sought French intervention, and projects for a Swabian or Danubian Republic were drawn up. In 1800 a republican conspiracy was discovered in Bavaria. None of these movements was ever supported by the French. None developed any strength of its own.

In the realm of action, in short, there is little to report for

Germany in the 1790s. Yet Germany was in fact more permanently transformed than most other parts of Europe in the Revolutionary-Napoleonic years. The Holy Roman Empire, already doomed by the agreements between France and Austria in the treaty of Campo Formio of 1797, was finally extinguished in 1806. Its hundreds of units were consolidated under Napoleon's auspices into a mere twenty states. The Left Bank of the Rhine was "revolutionized" during its annexation to France. East of the Rhine, in the new and enlarged states patronized by Napoleon— Bavaria, Württemberg, Westphalia, and others—German reformist administrators worked in close association with the French. Changes were made of the kinds prerequisite to a more modern society, but they were made by existing governments, without disrespect to proper authority, without leaving memories of a people struggling to assert its rights, without building self-confidence in the civilian middle classes, and without serious dislocation of the older aristocratic families, who generally maintained an important position until the German defeat in the First World War.

It was in the realm of thought that the Revolution had its greatest and most lasting influence in Germany. It reinforced a kind of conservatism that was not so much genuinely conservative as merely anti-Revolutionary. It contributed to a kind of nonpolitical neutralism in which revolutionary action was seen as useless or delusive. And it prepared the way for a theory of revolution in which "the Revolution" was valued as a vast phenomenon of world history, or total emancipation of the human mind or personality, rather than being seen as a passing conflict between specific groups for specific objectives.

Conservatism in Germany, as elsewhere, antedated the French Revolution. It was not, however, the conservatism of an experienced governing class, as in England, nor even the rationalization of its existing advantages in which the Parliament of Paris before 1789 had occasionally indulged. The larger German governments were by no means conservative, for many of their bureaucrats had the aims and temperament of reformers. Conservatism was a philosophy of intellectuals outside the circles of government.

After about 1770 it was developed by intellectuals who opposed the Enlightenment, or what the Germans called the *Aufklärung*. Sometimes it justified the small states and old idiosyncracies of the Holy Roman Empire, and so rejoiced in medieval institutions and in long vistas of uninterrupted continuity through time. Sometimes it was inspired by the defense of religion against the rationalist and critical spirit. Thus the Protestant H. M. Koester established his journal, the *Neuesten Religionsbegebenheiten* in 1777 to combat the freethinking tendencies of the day. He continued it in the 1790s with attacks on revolution as the mere work of secret societies. It was from this source that the Scottish Presbyterian Robison drew much of his material in writing his *Proofs of a conspiracy against all governments and religions* in 1797. Meanwhile, among German Catholics, a group of ex-Jesuits at Augsburg likewise attacked the Enlightenment, and especially the Illuminati, or "enlightened ones," who were discovered and suppressed in Bavaria in 1786. The Illuminati were a secret association, some of whose members were in the service of Bavaria or other states. They hoped by persuasion or manipulation to work for a general world-renewal. Though the association really existed, it had little importance, and was soon broken up. Its importance lies more in the psychology developed against it. If for some Germans the Revolution was a gigantic phase of world history, for others it was no more than the incursion of plotters into ordinary affairs. It was from sources going back to the Augsburg Jesuits that the French émigré Barruel seems to have developed his conspiratorial version of the Revolution, as set forth in his *Memoirs on the History of Jacobinism* of 1798.

In 1790 the government of Electoral Saxony, shaken by the peasant revolt, already mentioned, requested the librarian of the duke of Saxe-Gotha, H. A. O. Reichard, to edit a journal against revolutionary ideas. He complied willingly in his *Revolutions-Almanach*, which lasted until 1801. He filled its pages with an abundance of material, ranging from Luther's diatribes against the great Peasant Rebellion to praises for John Reeves's society founded in England in 1792, the Association for the Protection of Freedom and Property against Republicans and Levellers. The Levellers in Reichard's translation became *Aufklärer*; the Enlightenment was to be discredited not only as irreligious but because it led to demands for equality. Meanwhile in Vienna L. A. Hoffmann, in his *Wiener Zeitschrift*, carried on a campaign against secret societies as the authors of revolutionary disturbance. The Austrian government, which preferred to have no public discussion of revolution at all, closed down Hoffmann's paper in 1793. Men like Hoffmann, Reichard, and others then formed an anti-Revolutionary secret society of their own, the Eudämonists. They published a journal called *Eudämonia*. Some of them were former Freemasons who claimed special knowledge of conspiratorial activities over many years. They accused, denounced, exposed, and reported upon various men in the German governments and universities as Illuminati or Jacobins in disguise. They got up campaigns of letter writing, one of which forced Fichte out of his professorship at Jena. Wild charges eventually went too far. When the censor at Vienna found himself denounced for Illuminism, he forbade *Eudämonia* in Austria. Other German states took similar steps, so that the paper ceased publication in 1798.

Among Germans opposed to the Revolution, there were of course other explanations for it than the merely conspiratorial. Burke's *Reflections* were widely read. His warnings against the errors of individual reason, his faith in the inherited wisdom of the species, his sense of national differences and traditions, his scorn for tradesmen in politics, and his idealization of the virtues of chivalry and loyalty—all struck sympathetic chords across the Rhine. Burke's translator, Friedrich Gentz, became one of the most active writers in Germany against the French Revolution, which he began to characterize as a *Total-Revolution* in 1793. He repeatedly contrasted the American and French Revolutions, seeing the former as constructive, limited, and conservative—and so a good thing—the latter as boundless, aimless, and insatiable, a blind force with no obtainable goals. The better to arouse the European powers against it, as one by one except England they dropped out of the Coalition, he magnified it into a colossal and superhuman manifestation of destructive power. Actually, after 1794 the governments of France and the sister republics were middle-class regimes that might have accepted a peace in which their own existence and territories were recognized. Their problems, difficult but not superhuman, were to control their own generals and extremists. But for Gentz the French Revolution would "favor other revolutions into infinity . . . lead to a succession of revolutions, and turn human society into a theater of never-ending civil war." Gentz, with a different evaluation, thus echoed the Babouvist, Sylvain Maréchal: "The French Revolution is but the forerunner of another revolution, far greater, far more solemn, which will be the last." The mystique of an ongoing and all-devouring "total" revolution had many sources, not all of them on the Left. Maréchal was silenced by the Directory, Gentz subsidized by the British.

A great many Germans neither raged against the Revolution, nor saw much in its favor. Some were neutral in that while disliking the French Revolution they distrusted a movement against it led by England, the "modern Carthage" or monopolist of the sea, and cared nothing for the Bourbons, the French émigrés, or the French Catholic church.

Nonpolitical attitudes were very common, in which politics was felt to be a low occupation at best. There was a good deal of moralism, which held that true liberty was a spiritual and internal quality, or that no political program would succeed unless conducted by high-minded men. As the Pietist Jung-Stilling said, reform would come only from a pure and obedient Christianity, not from "the spirit of revolt and revolution." Some felt that the Revolution was good in principle, but had miscarried in the hands of the French. "Paradoxical as it may seem," wrote Rebmann, who hoped for a revolution in Germany, "the truly republican spirit, enlightenment and sound philosophy are infinitely more widespread in Germany than in France." Some of the Cisrhenanes, in particular, believed that the French Republic would enormously benefit from the annexation of the Rhineland, since the Germans would bring to it a degree of moral earnestness and philosophical profundity in which they thought the French sadly deficient.

Among literary figures, Klopstock penned an Ode to the French Revolution when war began in 1792. Young Tieck longed to fight with Dumouriez, and compared the French to the Greeks at Thermopylae. What Goethe really felt at Valmy is not known;

he was present in the entourage of the Prussian king, and saw
the famous Prussian army turn and retreat before Kellerman's
sans-culottes, but it was many years later that he remembered,
or recorded, his famous pronouncement: "Here and on this day
begins a new era in world history." The oracular detachment of
this statement is to be noted. What he said was that the event
was historically momentous, not that the French had succeeded
in a great effort under adverse conditions, or that they had the
better cause. There came to be a great disillusionment with
"liberty." Schiller by 1801 could see no refuge for it on earth
or in public life—"freedom exists but in the world of dreams,/
And beauty blossoms only in song." Goethe, Schiller, Wieland,
and Wilhelm von Humboldt never engaged in counterrevolutionary polemics, but they found the violence and fanaticism engen-
dered by revolution distasteful. They feared that so much pre-
occupation with political issues would have a debasing effect on
the higher culture in which they were interested. They thought
that liberty had been betrayed in the French Revolution, especially
since it was not civil or even intellectual liberty that concerned
them, so much as the creative liberty of the artist on which the
newly rising romantic movement set so much importance. As for
equality—whether of legal rights, political participation, career
opportunities, education, or wealth—they cared very little about
it, considering the values of civilization or of highly cultivated personalities to be more significant. They were willing, like lesser
men in Germany, to trust the authorities in matters of state.

The great trio of philosophers, however—Kant, Fichte, and
Hegel—were all warm advocates of the French Revolution in the
1790s. Kant, though he never left Königsberg, followed events
in France very closely in the newspapers. He attributed the violence of the Terror to the threats of the counterrevolution, and
he distrusted the British. His project for *Perpetual Peace*, written
in 1795, was used as an argument for Prussian neutrality. In the
ideal of equality he saw an application of his own ethical doctrine,
that each man should live in such a way that the principle of his
conduct might become a universal law. Above all, he saw the
Revolution as a moral act, the assertion by man of his freedom,
the attempt to create a society in which all men could live and

be respected as moral beings. Some of his philosophical followers put his ideas to conservative uses, arguing that no revolution could achieve anything unless the leaders were unselfish and the citizenry morally well advanced. Kant himself meant something more nearly resembling the doctrine of Robespierre, that "virtue" should be the result of the Revolution, not a precondition to it. Kant's theory did not claim to be realistic, or to see the Revolution as an interplay of contending interests or forces. It furnished no cues for political behavior. It did relate the Revolution to the demands of justice, and to the world as seen by Immanuel Kant.

Fichte himself believed that his metaphysical system was directly inspired by the French Revolution. In 1793 he wrote a long tract in defense of the embattled French Republic. In 1794 he published his *Theory of Knowledge.* "It was in the years," he wrote in 1795, "when the French were fighting for political liberty against external forces . . . that there came to me . . . the first inklings and intimations of my system." And he added that, where the French only "liberated man from external chains," his philosophical system, "the first system of liberty," liberated man "from the chains of the Thing-in-Itself, or of external influence, and sets him forth in his first principle as a self-sufficient being." Fichtean liberty was a total and integral freedom, a cosmic self-sufficiency, in which the Self, far from conforming or adjusting to any outer reality, made use of the Not-Self to build up a universe of its own. It was more an anticipation of the romantic revolutionaries of the 1830s than a codification of what the actual French Revolutionaries really wanted. The French Revolutionaries in the 1790s were at war with declared and identifiable enemies, over difficulties which political and legislative action might relieve. They talked much of the "law" and of civic obligations, and even the sans-culottes, for whom mere bourgeois liberty was insufficient, were more concerned with an adequate livelihood, social respect, the education of their children, and the fall of aristocrats than with the emancipation of human consciousness from an alien world. Fichte, however, believed that his doctrine expressed the inmost meaning of the French Revolution. He even hinted that the French should officially adopt it and offer him appointment in France as an authorized spokesman of the Republic. Like the Cisrhenanes, he believed that the French Revolution would be strengthened and ennobled by an infusion of the German philosophical spirit.

Fichte became professor of philosophy at Jena in 1794. He soon gained a following of fascinated students. He lectured on Sundays, preached the liberty and equality of all men, threw himself into student affairs, and engaged in public disputation on the nature of God. So much opposition developed against him that he was obliged to resign. Since many other German professors had equally unorthodox ideas on the divine nature, Fichte was perhaps right in believing that he was pursued not as an atheist but as "an infamous democrat." He became disgusted with Germany. "Only the French Republic," he wrote in 1799, "can be considered by a just man as his true country." There would be no freedom in Germany, he said, unless the French influence came to predominate in it. Then he had hopes for Prussia. It was to the reforming Prussian minister Struensee that he dedicated his *Closed Commercial State* in 1800, in which he argued that a "closed" state, by reducing outside connections, would best develop the moral character and purity of its citizens. Later, when the French did in fact dominate Germany under Napoleon, he turned to the extreme nationalism of his *Addresses to the German Nation*. True liberty was now to be obtained through immersion in the collective Self of the German people, and all influence from the French or other foreigners was to be avoided as a source of corruption.

It was Hegel, more than Kant or Fichte, who forged the link between the actual French Revolution and the most significant revolutionary philosophy of the nineteenth century, by formulating the ideas of historical necessity and continuity, the "dialectic," for utilization by Karl Marx. Hegel was a close observer of real events. In his youth, beginning in 1792, he spent four years at Bern in Switzerland, where he became critical of the Swiss oligarchy and sympathetic to the revolutionary agitation in the Pays de Vaud. In 1797 he went to Württemberg, where he observed the conflict between the duke and the diet. In a vehement pamphlet (which he did not publish), dedicated to "the people of Württemberg," he denounced the duke for his absolutism and the diet as no more than a hereditary privileged class. Mainly he was excited by the French Revolution. He hoped that some such modernization and liberation from ancient trammels could be accomplished for Germany, and hence for several years, like many other Germans, he favored Napoleon. In his later years he became a convinced monarchist, and upholder of the Prussian monarchy in particular. He never turned against the French Revolution. He did not have to repudiate it, since in his dialectical philosophy it could be seen in retrospect as a "stage" in human development, which, even though superseded, had been a necessary and forward step in its own time. When he delivered his *Lectures on the Philosophy of History* at Berlin in the 1820s, he still held that "world history is nothing else but the development of the concept of freedom." The French Revolution provided the climax to his final lecture. Hegel, when he wished, could think in ordinary political terms. If the Revolution broke out in France in 1789, he said in his lectures of the 1820s, it was because "the Court, the Clergy, the Nobility, the Parliaments themselves were unwilling to surrender the privileges they possessed." But he could not be content with such an empirical diagnosis.

The French Revolution, for him, was more than a conflict between tangible persons or social groups in a particular time and place. It embodied the concept of Right, the march of Liberty, the movement of Mind. "Never," he said, meaning never until 1789, "never since the sun has stood in the heavens and the planets moved about it, had it been seen that man relies on his head, that is on thought, and builds reality correspondingly." The liberty of the French Revolution, in short, signified the triumphant emancipation of Mind, not merely of the French mind, nor the bourgeois mind, nor anyone's mind in particular, but of Mind itself, the human if not the Absolute Mind. Possibly he was right (in a philosophical sense); possibly this was the significance of the eighteenth-century Enlightenment. In any case, with this heady doctrine, and despite the conservatism of his later years, Hegel gathered up the ideas of Kant and Fichte and put them into movement as a philosophy of history, as an ongoing process through time and hence into the future, of which future revolutionaries, with a few modifications, could make such use as they wished. That Marx eventually claimed to derive "mind" from material circumstances was only a variant of the Hegelian vision.

As Georg Forster, the Mainz Jacobin put it, "The lava of revolution flows majestically on, sparing nothing." As Gentz said, the revolution was "total." Unless stopped from outside, it would never stop. Actually, the French Revolution began to stop itself after 1793. The Revolutionary Government itself curbed the sansculottes. Robespierre stopped Hébert. The Convention stopped the Terror. The Directory crushed not only Babeuf, but the more general demand for more political democracy. Militants became fatigued or discouraged. Bonaparte stopped the Revolution; if he promoted changes, especially outside France, it was not under pressures of popular revolution. Even most of the Jacobins still alive during the Restoration, with conspicuous exceptions, were no longer revolutionary. France as a whole, in the nineteenth century, became a conservative country. Having finished the business of 1789, the Revolution came to a halt.

The idea of the Revolution lived on. It drew its force as much from a philosophy generated in Germany as from the memory of what had really happened in France.

[10]

The Explosive Inheritance:
Myth and History

THE REVOLUTION QUIETED DOWN AFTER 1800, but it could not be forgotten. It became lodged in the collective memory, a past event with which each succeeding generation had to come to terms. Some lived in fear, and others in hope, that the giant was only sleeping and might be rearoused. Whether looking backward or forward in time, some thought of the Revolution with awe, some with loathing; some saw in it a means of salvation, others the work of diabolical forces, whether retrospectively in the years before 1800, or prospectively as a possibility of the future. The Revolution became a subject of both myth and history. The two were not opposites; each contributed to the growth of the other.

"Myth," be it said, is not merely erroneous or infantile history. It is of no importance whether prototypes of Prometheus, Oedipus, or Ulysses ever existed; the fall of Adam preserves its meaning after removal from the biological record; and even the historicity of Jesus Christ is no longer considered the most significant issue presented by the Gospels. Myth aims at some truth which may or may not be higher than history, but which in any case is detached from the existence of particular persons and events in

251

particular times and places. It reflects a belief about the human predicament or human behavior. Some myths may provide incentive for historical research and lead to historical knowledge, as the Homeric stories led to the unearthing of Mycenean civilization; and the same is true of some "myths" about the French Revolution. Others prove barren, both of historical and moral content, and remain mostly as evidence of the superstition of those who created them. The story of the rape of Europa by Zeus disguised as a bull may be an example. Some "myths" about the French Revolution may be put in this category. There are good myths and bad myths, and men are known by the myths in which they find meaningful lessons.

A persistent lesser myth held that the French Revolution was somehow "un-French." This was a favorite idea of Charles Maurras in the twentieth century. It went back to the most extreme of the original French counterrevolutionaries, and could be found in Edmund Burke, who observed in 1793 that some 30,000 émigrés were the real people of France, and the Revolutionaries only burglars who had broken into the house. For Maurras, who was condemned to perpetual seclusion in 1945 for collaboration with the Germans, after half a century of writing against the Republic, the Revolution had been the work of "metics," Jews, Protestants, Freemasons, and other aliens to the true spirit of French civilization. Similar ideas were held by the most ardent partisans of the Bourbon restoration after 1814. The refutation of this myth produced the first serious histories of the Revolution in the 1820s.

Another long-lived myth held that the French Revolution had been a failure. One version contrasted it to the American Revolution, which was said to have been successful because it was limited in its aims. This idea, which went back at least to Friedrich Gentz, reappeared in the 1960s in the writings of Hannah Arendt, an American of German philosophical background, who thought that the French Revolution had "failed" because it was disoriented by a blind and futile mass revolt against poverty. A version on the Left held that the Revolution had been "betrayed" by the bourgeoisie. In the allegation of failure there was at least some spark of truth. The Revolution did not fulfill all the claims that it made or all the expectations that it aroused. The middle-class leaders did not satisfy, and in a sense "betrayed," their working-class allies of 1793. They did not thereby betray the actual Revolution, which was mainly a middle-class or bourgeois movement, as the most judicious Marxists have always insisted. The Revolution that they "betrayed," if any, was a timeless Revolution aimed at total emancipation, or a later Revolution carried on in the name of the workers in an industrialized society. The Revolution succeeded in dislodging the monarchy, the nobility, the church, and the sociolegal structures of the Old Order. It introduced a new and modern form of state. It had its failures, its compromises, and its deceptions; but to call it simply a "failure" is to judge by utopian standards, to be more visionary than Condorcet or Robespierre, to complain, like Fichte, that the French Revolution broke only "external" chains, or, like Babeuf, that it did not provide everyone with "equal enjoyments."

A related myth, and a less empty one, is the idea that the Revolution was not worth the effort and suffering that it involved. In half a century after 1789, according to this idea, conditions in France would have been much the same, no worse, or possibly even better, if there had been no revolution at all. It is pointed out that the people of Paris, plagued by early industrialism, irresponsible capitalism, inhuman working conditions, mounting population, and increasingly congested and unsanitary streets and lodgings, had more to suffer in 1840 than in 1780. It is noted that the Revolution left wounds and divisions that were not yet healed over a century later, that warring camps were bent on each other's extermination, that every regime into the twentieth century proved unstable, that the national consensus was irreparably broken. Even granting the force of such observations—which are exaggerated, since France remained essentially satisfied, or indeed too satisfied (being the only European country in the nineteenth century to have no mass emigration)—they are not altogether relevant to the question of whether the Revolution was worth the cost. The only way to answer this question is to think in terms of alternatives to the 1780s, to employ that "retrospective calculation of probabilities" in which Raymond Aron, thirty years ago, saw the necessary instrument of historical judgment. What else could or should have been done, given the breakdown of the royal finances in 1786, the demands of the privileged orders in 1789, the invasion as announced in the Brunswick Manifesto of 1792, the restoration as called for in the Declaration of Verona of 1795? Would the Estates General in three houses, as desired by the nobility and by Louis XVI in June, 1789, have known how to govern wisely, or been still governing in 1840? If so, would the estates have softened the class conflict which their mere convocation had accentuated? If they could not govern, or if the country would not accept so great a role for nobles and clergy, by what gradual and peaceful means could they have been liquidated or transformed? No positive answer can be given to such questions. All we know is that such questions received an answer in the Revolution. It is possible to see the Revolution as a tragedy. It is not possible to see it as merely foolish, useless, or vain. That the cost was high is a matter of history. The worth of the outlay touches on the realm of myth. For some, it was an appalling waste. For others, the very cost of the Revolution enhanced its value.

There was an element of myth also, or at least of gross exaggeration, in the memory of the Revolution as having been most especially an attack on Christianity and on all religion. It was forgotten that many Catholic priests had been actual revolutionaries in France, Italy, Poland, and Ireland, and that Protestant ministers in America had refrained from condemning the French Revolution, and in Ireland had joined the rebellion. That both Pope Pius VII himself, and the New England pontiff Jedidiah Morse, had expressed sympathy for revolutionary republicanism disappeared into the "non-facts" of history. What had been a conflict among Christians was seen as a struggle between Christians and infidels. This view went back to the polemics not only of the Counterrevolution but of the Counter-Enlightenment. It was reinforced by the actual deaths, deportations, and sufferings of priests during the Revolution. It was enlarged in the nineteenth century, when the continuing conflicts between clericals and anticlericals, the more aggressive materialism of many revolutionaries, and the open hostility of the papal Syllabus of Errors to all forms of liberal civilization projected a simplified image back into the 1790s.

By the same backward projection, anything disliked in later times could be supplied with an "origin" in the French Revolution. The growing seriousness of historical studies gave an appearance of science to such undertakings. Thus, in the mid-twentieth century, Gerhardt Ritter drew a kind of straight line from the *levée en masse* of 1793 through Napoleon to Adolf Hitler, and J. L. Talmon drew a straight line from Rousseau to Robespierre to Babeuf to Josef Stalin. Totalitarianism of either the Right or the Left was thus "explained." If such views have a mythic quality, it is because the truth in them is fragmentary, indemonstrable, and didactic, and because contrary truths are at least equally probable. Almost everything in the modern world can be somehow ascribed to the Enlightenment and the French Revolution. Whatever else they were, Robespierre, though briefly a kind of dictator, was a figure in the history of democracy, and Napoleon, though a conqueror, was in the authentic stream of the enlightened organizers of Europe.

There were also myths more favorable to the Revolution. Against the idea of the Revolution as "un-French," current during the Restoration, liberal historians pictured it as the most essentially French thing in the long history of France. For them it was the revolt of the "nation" against the privileged classes. This view went back at least to Sieyès' famous pamphlet of 1789 in which the third estate was identified with the nation, and the nobles were dismissed as a useless minority. Liberal historians saw it also as the outcome of a conflict extending over centuries, from the rise of towns and an urban, or burgher, culture in the Middle Ages. In this view, set forth with lucidity and eloquence by Guizot in the 1820s, the whole history of France, for centuries before 1789, was a struggle between two classes, the people and the nobility, a class war of which the Revolution had been the final battle. Somewhat the same had been said, with elegant brevity, by the young Revolutionary, Barnave, guillotined in 1793 at the age of thirty-two, in a history of the Revolution not published until 1843.

In the "myth" of Guizot, as of other liberals and defenders

of the Revolution, the Revolution became a point in a long con-
tinuum, the result of causes reaching far back in time and accumulating over the centuries. Many generations of French history had
gone into producing it. Given French history, it had been inevitable. Possibly this myth was mistaken; possibly more immediate
and short-run causes offer a better explanation; possibly the
Revolution need not have happened. The matter has been touched
on in the early pages of this book. On the whole, the myth of
continuity, or insistence on deep-seated and long-run causes, rests
upon strong evidence and weighty arguments. More "mythic" in
Guizot's view, constituting a kind of bourgeois myth, was his
belief that no further revolution was probable or desirable—that
the Liberty and Equality won in 1789 should be enough to satisfy
everybody.

But if the Revolution was only a point in a long process, why
should the process stop? Was it possible to believe, in the 1820s
and 1830s, that the whole people of France or any other country
had been liberated? If not, who had been liberated, and who
remained to be liberated in the future? Such questions gave
rise to the troubled liberalism of Alexis de Tocqueville. It was
answers given to such questions that also produced the most
potent myth of all, the myth of the continuing or permanent
revolution.

Some of the activists of the 1790s were still alive thirty years
later, and some of these were still militant. Such a thing as the
professional revolutionary had developed, the man who makes a
career of planning and working for revolution, in a way hardly
known in the actual French Revolution, when the participants
had improvised roles which they had not foreseen and for which
they were unprepared. Among the survivors of the real Revolutionaries was Filippo Buonarroti, who had been the companion
of Babeuf in 1796. In 1828 he published a book, part history,
part recollection, in effect a narrative of the French Revolution,
but entitled *La conjuration de l'égalité dite de Babeuf*. The book
argued that Robespierre had meant to introduce a kind of socialism or social democracy in 1794, that he was cut down and put
to death for that reason, and that Babeuf and his followers, seizing
the torch thus struck from Robespierre's hand, had proposed to

carry Liberty and Equality to their natural conclusion by the abolition of property and the equalization of wealth. Buonarroti's work had a great influence. It was widely read by the rising generation of socialists in France. It was immediately translated into English, and became known to the Chartists. Even those who rejected its "communism" formed the impression that a true democracy had once almost been realized, only to be betrayed, that the great Revolution had been rudely interrupted, and that it ought to continue.

These were the worst years, in both France and England, of misery and hopelessness for the victims of economic change. The Revolution of 1830 in France, while it put the Bourbons to final flight, and confirmed the principles of 1789, only brought in the Orleanist monarchy of Louis-Philippe, under which working-class demonstrations and strikes were violently repressed, and the more idealistic upholders of the republican memories of 1793 were wholly unsatisfied. The 1830s saw an explosive mixture of genuine social distress with rediscovery of the great events of 1789 and 1793. To Buonarroti's book were soon added the first reprints of the speeches of Robespierre and the huge compilation published by Buchez and Roux, *L'histoire parlementaire de la Révolution française*, a 40-volume work full of historical sources. Socialists, republicans, workers, and intellectuals formed their conception of recent history from such readings. A favorable idea of Robespierre spread among German republicans, and could be found in Russia, at the very beginning of the Russian revolutionary movement, in the writings of Belinski as early as 1842. If there had been a great Revolution a generation ago, and a small one as recently as 1830, it seemed reasonable to expect that there might soon be another.

The creation of a whole new social vocabulary, unknown in the French Revolution, revealed that a new revolutionary mentality was being formed. From Saint-Simon came the word *avant-garde*, to signify a small elite who would guide a phlegmatic mass into a regenerated world of the future. The word soon caught on both in revolutionary politics and in the arts. With Blanqui's first insurrectionary attempt of 1839, the Babouvist idea of social revolution by a small militant elite was launched in a form that Lenin would develop later. Others, including the youthful Marx, used "alienation" as a more up-to-date term for slavery or lack of freedom; it removed the problem of liberty from the supposedly superficial plane of law and politics to the presumably higher levels of psychology and philosophy, for which Marx eventually concluded that the main basis was economic. "Left" and "Right" came into use, signifying positive and negative attitudes toward continuing movement in a revolutionary direction. Above all, the indispensable new words were "bourgeois" and "proletarian." What Barnave had called a democratic revolution in 1792, what Guizot and Michelet saw as a liberation of the people, was now seen as a bourgeois revolution leading only to bourgeois democracy in which the bourgeoisie had been liberated but not the working man. Louis Blanc was one of the first to formulate the new conception in France. The German Ludwig Börne said the same in the 1830s: "The French Revolution only benefited the bourgeoisie."

"Proletarian" was an accurate term for the working class of the 1840s, the time of Disraeli's "two nations" in England, and of similar social estrangement in France, with the urban and industrial wage workers in both countries being virtually outcasts from the cultures of their own countries. The word "bourgeois" was ambiguous from the beginning. It was a useful term, when used to designate a social stratum that belonged neither to the aristocracy nor to the common people, a stratum of persons in the professions, in trade or government employment, men of education and accepted position, with more or less secure incomes from personal earnings or profits or annuities or the rental of land. Such persons had in fact been the main supporters of the Revolution of the 1790s in all European countries.

But "bourgeois" had other meanings when launched in the 1830s. One might look "down" on the bourgeois as philistine, vulgar, or lacking in the sensibilities of a true upper class. One might look "up" to him as a boss, or person enjoying undue economic advantages and hence a superior way of life. Or, for Karl Marx, the bourgeois was anyone, vulgar or refined, noble or plebeian, who owned capital goods as his private property and made a profit from the employment of labor. Briefly, the bourgeois was the designated target of the next revolution.

The coming revolution was announced in the *Communist Manifesto*, which Marx and Engels published just before the actual Revolution of 1848. Although followed almost accidentally by these revolutionary events, the *Communist Manifesto* heralded a much greater revolution which never came—or which came only in Russia, much later and under different conditions. In form a summons to a grand final Revolution, in substance the *Communist Manifesto*, like Marx's later work, was an analysis of existing or bourgeois society. It reflected Engels' knowledge of the condition of the working classes in England, and Marx's observations of France in the 1840s, reinforced by his studies of the French Revolution. It incorporated Guizot's view of the history of France as a long history of class struggle; but Marx was not concerned with the revolution in France alone, and drew on German philosophy, on theories of world history, and especially on Hegel, to show that a more universal revolution was being inevitably generated by the forces at work in existing society. After the bourgeois revolution a proletarian revolution must surely follow.

Whatever other valid message it might contain, the myth of a continuing or proletarian revolution was awkwardly related to historical fact. The supposedly coming revolution was to be made by a beaten-down and oppressed class, virtually excluded from civilized society, but instructed and led by an alert vanguard or elite, who at the proper moment would take power, perhaps peacefully, from the enfeebled hands of a disappearing bourgeoisie, proclaim the public ownership of the means of production, and introduce real liberty and equality while dispensing with political authority, the state itself eventually withering away. The course of the actual revolution, the Revolution of 1789, had been very different. A strong and confident class (the "bourgeoisie" in a non-Marxist sense), having no need of a revolutionary vanguard, and sharing abundantly in the advantages of civilization, was suddenly called upon by a government in distress. It collided head-on with a noble or privileged class that was far from declining and showed no tendency to vanish. It received strong assistance from the peasantry (for whom the coming proletarian revolution could find no place), and under circumstances of war and invasion it worked with an aroused common people, the sans-culottes, whose excitement was as much patriotic as social. The Revolutionaries, far from aiming at anarchy, or the general emancipation of human personality favored in German and romantic philosophy, produced a more effective and equitable form of public authority, a more modern state. Both the *Communist Manifesto* and the *Social Contract* spoke of "chains." But where Marx promised to break them, Rousseau, more realistic, had only proposed to make them "legitimate." However realistic as a social analyst, Marx was utopian as a prophet.

What continued in the nineteenth century was less the Revolution than the idealization of the Revolution. There were indeed the revolutions of 1848 in many countries, and in France the Paris Commune of 1871. All soon succumbed; but the very triumph of counterrevolution, the ferocity with which desperate workingmen and eager republicans were suppressed, kept alive a revolutionary frame of mind. The extremes of Left and Right reinforced each other. Revolutionary threats, predictions, and outbursts alarmed all who had a stake in the existing order, who therefore reacted more violently against such attempts at revolution as were made. The violence of the reactions confirmed those who were not favored by the existing order in their hatred and disaffection. Gradually, by the close of the nineteenth century, with the development of industry, the rise of wages, the softening of the worst social dislocations, and the admission of the working classes to a more or less democratic electorate, the forces making for a real revolution became weaker than ever. Marx and Engels were hardly dead when "revisionism" and "opportunism" appeared among Marxists. The revolutionary mentality, by the turn of the century, signified less an actual expectation of revolution than an inveterate hostility to bourgeois society. It showed itself in the tendency to see everything as an aspect of the class struggle, in a kind of negativism or social alienation, a proud outsider's psychology, an attitude of suspicion, a dislike of conciliation or compromise, a scorn for mere reforms or half-measures or improvements of detail, a contempt for institutions which the Revolution ought to eradicate—though it never did. Even so, the supposedly Marxist or revolutionary workers rallied to their respective governments in the First World War. The myth of a coming proletarian revolution proved less strong than the appeals of national solidarity and self-defense.

In 1918, a few months after the October Revolution in Russia, a statue of Robespierre was erected near the Kremlin. Made of temporary materials, it soon fell to pieces, and was not replaced. The absence of a more permanent statue suggests that, once the Russian Revolution was clearly established as a reality, it had less need to celebrate distant predecessors in far-away countries. That Robespierre was thus commemorated at all, in 1918, signifies Lenin's belief that his own movement, mediated through Marxism, was descended from the great French Revolution of 1789. Undoubtedly the real causes of the Russian Revolution were to be found in Russia. That Leninism and Bolshevism were even genuinely Marxist, let alone Robespierrist, could be endlessly debated in Marxist and other circles. Yet the memory or myth of the French Revolution contributed to the form taken by the revolution in Russia. Without it, Lenin might have become discouraged in the twenty years preceding 1917. With it, he could believe in a long-continuing Revolution, a wave of the future drawing strength from the past—a cause, which however suppressed or deflected by its enemies or betrayed or weakened by its friends, must yet prevail because it embodied the true meaning of history.

Lenin's success, on the other hand, and the establishment of the Soviet Union, revived belief in the Revolution in Western Europe. While some Marxists, rejecting first Leninism and then Stalinism, remained merely socialists or social democrats, not at all revolutionary except in being negatively oriented toward bourgeois society, others accepted the Russian Revolution as legitimately Marxist and so became Communists. They approved of it the more readily, especially in France, because they saw it as a modern continuation of a glorious movement initiated in 1789. Communists were seen as the Jacobins of the twentieth century, the differences being overlooked. In this formidable identification the extreme Left was sometimes joined by the extreme Right. Counterrevolutionary as well as revolutionary myths were rejuvenated. That the French Revolution might have somehow led to the Russian Revolution was a final exposure of the destructive forces it had unleashed.

The response to Communism and to the revived revolutionism of the Left was the totalitarian revolutionism of the Right, in its various fascist forms, all of which deliberately undertook to discredit the French Revolution as well as the Russian. There was a sinister symbolism in the destruction of the European Jews, who had received equal rights and the protection of equal citizenship from Revolutionary France, as from its sister republics. Even the milder of these Rightist regimes were afraid of the French Revolution. Vichy France, in 1940, suppressed all copies of a new book by the eminent French historian, Georges Lefebvre, his *Quatre-vingt-neuf*, published the year before to mark the sesquicentennial of 1789.

For all these "myths" had their counterparts in the writing of history. The best history, of course, was never merely ideological. But any history reflected the mind and spirit of its author, and no historian of any spirit could be indifferent toward the Revolution, or even merely impartial. Thus Guizot was the great upper-middle-class liberal Protestant; Michelet the rhapsodist of democracy, the soaring eulogist of the "people"; Louis Blanc a founder of French socialism and the first historian to present the upheaval following 1789 as the "bourgeois revolution" in twelve volumes. Tocqueville, in the 1850s, was the anxious aristocrat who believed democracy to be inevitable, providential, morally just, and yet pregnant with lurking dangers; who feared that his country was ungovernable because it suffered from a chronic internal division, but who attributed the disease less to the Revolution than to the Bourbon monarchy and the Old Order. Taine, in the 1870s, enraged by the Paris Commune, made his history almost into an ideology of Counterrevolution. Aulard, in the 1890s, became the first "scientific" historian of the subject, but his fervent republicanism, in the days of the Dreyfus affair, kept breaking through the science. His younger rival, Mathiez, an indefatigable scholar and an excitable human being, saw the Revolution climaxed by social democracy in the person of a much misunderstood Robespierre. He revived, with more substance, the view publicized by Buonarroti in 1828. Mathiez's successor, Lefebvre, a deeper and more balanced man than most of his predecessors, able to see the Revolution from the point of view of its many conflicting participants, brought to it a highly modified Marxist interpretation, and was widely respected as the greatest historian of the French Revolution produced in the twentieth century.

Yet even Lefebvre was drawn into polemics on so explosive a theme. After the Second World War a New Left made itself heard. Daniel Guérin, in a book on the working-class Revolutionaries of the years 1792 to 1795, represented Robespierre as no more than a bourgeois and false friend of the workers, and disdainfully classified Lefebvre, along with Mathiez, as a mere apologist for the bourgeoisie. Lefebvre, much offended, responded with dignity, affirming his own working-class origins and his lifelong admiration for Jean Jaurès, the great democratic and nonrevolutionary Marxist of the years before 1914, who had incidentally written an *Histoire socialiste* of the Revolution and obtained government support for organized historical research on Revolutionary problems. In 1954 Alfred Cobban, on assuming the chair in French History at the University of London, delivered a provocative inaugural lecture entitled "The Myth of the French Revolution." Cobban thought it a myth, in the sense of a fallacy, to see the French Revolution as the triumph of a "bourgeois" over a "feudal" order. Without saying so, he questioned the use of Marxist categories in the interpretation of the French Revolution. He gave the impression of believing that the importance of the French Revolution had been exaggerated anyway. If the Revolution was bourgeois, he remarked, it was because the holders of lesser government offices managed to get rid of a nobility which blocked their advancement to more distinguished positions.

Lefebvre wrote a brief rejoinder. He noted the wide array of meanings of liberty and equality in the French Revolution, which Cobban had neglected to mention, and he insisted that the Revolutionaries, while not consciously working to promote capitalism, had, "for the first time in Europe," proclaimed freedom of economic enterprise without restriction except for public order. The French Revolution, said Lefebvre, had therefore opened the way, or broken the barriers, to the rise of a capitalist and bourgeois society. Going further, Lefebvre declared that the French Revolution of 1789–93 was indeed a "myth," in the sense meant by Georges Sorel. That is, it was an emotionally charged belief, an energizer or stimulus to further action, whether action was realizable or not. As such, he said, it remained alive as a continuing myth into the present.

In general, the thinking of historians of the French Revolution, in all countries in the 1960s, is dominated by the conception of the "bourgeois revolution" as applied to the events of 1789 and the following years. One group, whose sympathies generally lie to the Left, while insisting that the Revolution was bourgeois, are in fact most interested in the working classes, partly because the subject is newer and relatively more unknown, partly because the working classes during the Revolution were opposed to or exerted pressure upon the bourgeoisie. While including Rudé, Cobb, and Hobsbawm in England, the group is led by Albert Soboul of Paris. For similar reasons there is much interest in Babeuf, his ideas, his "communism" and his conspiracy of 1796, especially on the part of historians in France, Italy, the German Democratic Republic, and the Soviet Union. In 1960, at the Historical Congress at Stockholm, a special conference was devoted to the bicentennial of Babeuf's birth. It is not asserted that Babeuf was a central figure of the French Revolution. A distinction is drawn between the true mass movement in France in 1792–93 and the more secret and less popular character of Babeuf's short-lived organization, in which revolutionary elitism was more definitely foreshadowed. The satisfaction in these studies, apart from the new discoveries that are actually made, seems to lie in the thought that the bourgeoisie, even at the height of its revolution against "feudalism" and aristocracy, was already challenged by spokesmen of the working classes, even though these were not yet "proletarian." It lies, that is, in the detection of a later or continuing or preproletarian revolution in embryo within the bourgeois revolution itself.

Others, less ideologically involved, pursue statistical inquiries to find out exactly what kind of people, in terms of income, occupation, marriage habits, or social mobility, the "bourgeoisie" of the eighteenth century really were. Still others, like Cobban, and including many Americans, express doubt that class analysis is the most useful tool for understanding the French Revolution. Or they think that the social classes active in the Revolution were not classes in an economic sense, distinguished from each other, as Marxism and the ideas of a continuing revolution seem to require, by differences of economic interest or by the kinds of property they owned. It is widely agreed, in all schools, that capitalists were not the actual initiators, agents or leaders of the French Revolution. Since the term "bourgeois" implies capitalist, some argue that the terms "bourgeois," "bourgeoisie" and "bourgeois revolution" should be abandoned altogether, since they cannot be used without suggesting mistaken ideas. It is natural that anyone attached to the Marxist tradition should resist such a proposal. It would seem that the proposal should be easy to carry out, since the term "bourgeois" was not used during the very Revolution it purports to describe. It is nevertheless not easy even for a non-Marxist to dispense with the concept of a bourgeoisie, which, however, need not be the bourgeoisie of Marxist dialectic. A parallel is suggested by the Reformation. The word "Protestant" was not current until long after the break with Rome, yet the word remains useful. Technically anachronistic, and hence calling for caution, such terms may still serve a purpose.

There remains one more myth, which is especially pertinent to the present book, and which may throw light on these questions. It is the opposite of the conservative myth that the Revolution of 1789 was un-French. This myth holds that the French Revolution was not only French, but French alone. It asserts that there was nothing worth calling a revolution in any other country. It denies the reality of an all-European revolutionary movement in the eighteenth century. It rejects what the French historian Jacques Godechot has called the "Atlantic" revolution, and looks with suspicion on the idea of the present book, that is, on the conception of a revolutionary disturbance common to Europe and America, or to what then constituted Western civilization. In this myth, it is feared that the French Revolution may lose its significance, or be reduced or not seen in its true dimensions, if represented as part of a wider upheaval or allowed to evaporate into a vague international agitation. Like the other myths that have now been surveyed, this one contains its element of historical truth. The French Revolution, like all human events, had its unique features. It was far more revolutionary than the revolutions or attempted revolutions in other countries. But the myth of the purely or exclusively French Revolution is restrictive and confining. The French Revolution becomes greater, not smaller, when seen as part of a larger whole. And the wave of excitement that swept through Europe and America is more understandable when seen as more than a reaction to French events.

Contemporaries were keenly aware of the more than national character of the Revolution. Even Babeuf once attributed the French Revolution of 1789 to "seeing the Revolution in North America and the attempts at popular movements in Holland and Brabant." Conservatives such as Burke and Barruel saw a universal contagion. The Revolutionaries in France, beginning with the Declaration of Rights, and as good pupils of the Enlightenment, thought in terms of humanity itself. From Camille Desmoulins through Brissot and the Jacobin orators to the advanced democrats of the Directory, including the handful of Babeuf's extremists, the recurrent cry was for a war of all peoples against all kings. In all countries, as this book has shown, there were men who wanted revolutionary change along the line of the French Revolution, while hoping to avoid its violence. That the Revolution was purely French would have been an astonishing idea in the 1790s.

Yet somehow the belief arose that no significant revolution had occurred except in France. This became the dominant recollection, or "myth," of later times. It arose from many sources, one of which was among the Revolutionaries themselves.

In 1793, when the French were beset by the Coalition, no other people offered any support. There might be objection to the war, as there was in Britain, Holland, Prussia, and the Austrian empire, but nothing happened; the French were isolated in their crisis, and many of them, including Robespierre, developed a scorn for so-called revolutionaries and sympathizers in other countries, and a pride in the French as the only people who had the power,

courage, or stamina to repel the combined forces of the Old
Order of Europe. Many revolutionaries elsewhere, notably in the
sister republics after 1795, disillusioned by the demands of French
military occupation, by the plunder and requisitions, or by the
moderatism or diplomatic maneuvers of the Directory, turned
against the French while continuing to favor great changes in
their own countries. The idea grew up that each people must rely
on itself to make its own revolution. The Revolutionary idea
of the "nation" itself promoted this tendency.

Where revolution failed, or where the older institutions maintained themselves against radical opposition, it was convenient
not to keep certain memories alive. A failed revolution was not
a revolution. What had happened in Ireland in 1798 was a
Rebellion. What had happened in Poland in 1794 was an Insurrection. As feelings of nationality and national loyalty became
stronger in the nineteenth century, it became a matter of shame
and embarrassment, or of actual disbelief, that one's ancestors
should have collaborated with foreigners, or even expressed enthusiasm for a French Revolution. Even the democrats of later
times suppressed such memories. That there had been many angry
"Jacobins" in England and Scotland was forgotten. The enthusiasm in the United States for the French Republic was
recalled as a mere passing craze. Only a few hotheads or firebrands,
among the Dutch, Belgians, Germans, Swiss, and Italians, could
have ever collaborated with the French or invited them into
their countries. The sister republics had been imposed by the
French; or, at most, they showed the "expansion" of the French
Revolution, not the merging of revolutionary forces that already
existed throughout many parts of Europe. If the French annexed
Belgium and the Left Bank of the Rhine, they did so simply
as conquerors, as Louis XIV would have done if he had had the
power. The myth of a continuing revolution was countered by a
myth of continuing indifference to revolutionary temptations, by
a myth of a solidarity of separate nations which had hardly existed
at the time of the French Revolution.

The labors of historians, as history became more serious and
professional, had the same effect. Even when not positively nationalistic, historians who increasingly worked with printed sources

and manuscript archives used materials in their own languages and concentrated on the history of their own countries. Or, if they aimed more widely, they dealt with diplomatic history and international relations, by which was meant the relations among governments or "powers," not among peoples or individual human beings. History became divided into separate national compartments. The French historians had their French Revolution. Others had the respective tribulations of their own countries at that period, or, more often, thought the period of little importance in their own national histories, and wrote very little about it. There were of course always exceptions, and by the mid-twentieth century a good deal of historical work on a general eighteenth-century revolution had accumulated, of which the present book is an example, and on which indeed it depends.

The more the idea of a geographically extensive movement is emphasized, the more it is seen as primarily a "bourgeois" revolution, in a certain sense of the confusing term "bourgeoisie." It is not enough, and not even accurate, to see the Revolution as primarily an episode in the rise of capitalism. Indeed it may have retarded the growth of capitalism in France. It was, however, a decisive episode in the history of property and the property-owning classes. Wherever the Revolutionary ideas took effect, which is to say in France and its sister republics, and in the Napoleonic empire later, one of the things that happened was a redefinition of property. The "feudal" features were removed from the ownership of land, along with such aristocratic embellishments as primogeniture, *fidecommessi*, and family trusts. The separation of property right on the one hand, the sphere of the individual, from public authority and jurisdiction on the other, which became the sphere of the state, was the hallmark of the Revolution. It was part of the "abolition of feudalism." In addition, a good deal of property was redistributed, through the secularization and resale of church lands, in France and elsewhere, so that a good many people of all classes, including the peasants, owned more real property after the Revolution than before it. Here was the economic basis for the real conservatism of France, beneath its apparent turbulence, throughout the nineteenth century. Here also was a foundation for bourgeois society in much of Europe.

In some countries, as in Italy, as has been seen in the preceding pages, noblemen could be active as revolutionary leaders. In some, where a national or antiforeign purpose predominated, as in Poland or Ireland, persons of all classes might take part. Many of the clergy likewise adopted revolutionary ideas. The United States was peculiar in that the agrarians were more inclined than townspeople to favor the Revolution. France was unique in having a popular mass upheaval, especially in 1792–93, which was precipitated by war and invasion but aimed also at a wider measure of social equality. For this reason, as well as because of the great size and population of France, the French Revolution was in fact different from the disturbances elsewhere. The success of other revolutionary movements depended on the French; without French aid, none was successful; and only in France can significant beginnings of a later revolutionary movement against the bourgeoisie be detected. In this sense the French Revolution was the only "real" revolution of the period. But there is no conflict between the ideas of a "distinctively" French Revolution and a wave of revolution throughout Europe and America at the same time.

The main sympathizers with the Revolution everywhere were of the middle classes, those free from the demands of daily menial labor, enjoying the benefits of education and income, yet outside the privileged, aristocratic, patrician, religious, or other favored categories of the Old Order. Often joined by individual noblemen, and often supported by lesser people, they were lawyers and government employees, doctors and pharmacists, merchants and sometimes bankers, men of scientific or technical interests, shopkeepers and manufacturers, professors and teachers, writers and miscellaneous intellectuals, journalists and publishers, occasionally agriculturists and frequently men drawing income from landed rents, together with the sons of those too busy, too elderly, or too prudent to engage in risky agitations themselves. They were, in fact, a revolutionary bourgeoisie.

They not only rebelled; they projected a new form of state and society. They brought the Enlightenment into practical politics. They desired a world that would look more to the future than to the past. In this world, constitutional government would be more than the rule or consultation of ancient estates. Against the claims of monarchy, or any other hereditary or self-chosen governing body, was set up the sovereignty of the people. In place of the subject, the Revolutionaries envisaged the citizen, and indeed they created the very idea of national citizenship. They wanted freedom of thought, expression, religion, association, and of enterprise of all kinds, including economic. Against older restraints they affirmed the value of liberty, against old forms of discrimination they made an ideal of equality, and in solidarity with each other, and with all who would join them, they were generous enough to dream of fraternity. They recognized their own program in the great Declaration of Rights of 1789. New rights, for more people, have been demanded ever since. Resistance to new rights has also been a continuing story. The waves set in motion in 1789 have sometimes been stormy, sometimes more tranquil, but never quite calm—nor does it seem likely that they will ever wholly subside.

Additional Readings

Books on the Revolutionary era have been accumulating for generations, in many languages and at all levels from wide popularity to extreme specialization. Many can be identified in the concluding chapter of the present volume. The following is a selection of relatively recent works of general interest in English. Those marked with an asterisk are available in paperback.

For the Old Order it is always wise to read Alexis de Tocqueville, *The Old Régime and the Revolution*, first published in 1856. For more recent works see C. B. A. Behrens, *The Ancien Régime* (London and New York, 1967), useful for its brevity and its illustrations; also, M. S. Anderson, *Europe in the Eighteenth Century, 1713–1783* (London and New York, 1961). For the intellectual revolution see Peter Gay, *The Enlightenment: An Interpretation* (London and New York, 1966 etc.), and Norman Hampson, *A Cultural History of the Enlightenment* (London and New York, 1968). A collection edited by William F. Church, *The Influence of the Enlightenment on the French Revolution* (London, 1964), reprints the views of a dozen persons, from Edmund Burke to a modern American professor, on the question whether ideas "cause" events, or the Enlightenment should be "blamed" for the Revolution.

On the French Revolution proper, with some attention to events in other countries, there have recently been translations of many of the works of Georges Lefebvre. The most respected authority on the subject in the twentieth century, Lefebvre died in 1959. See his *Coming of the French Revolution* (Princeton, N.J., 1947), on the year 1789 alone; his *French Revolution from Its Origins to 1793* (London, 1962) and *French Revolution from 1793 to 1799* (New York, 1964); and his *Thermidorians and the Directory* (London, 1964). Among prominent living French historians of the Revolution there are Albert Soboul, whose main work has been abridged as *The Parisian Sans-culottes and the French Revolution, 1793–1794* (Oxford, 1964), and Jacques Godechot, two of whose works have appeared in English: *France and the Atlantic Revolution of the Eighteenth Century* (London, 1965), and *The Taking of the Bastille* (London and New York, 1970). For the theme of the present volume, it is to be hoped that his *La Grande Nation: l'expansion révolutionnaire de la France 1789–99* (2 vols., Paris, 1956) and his *La Contre-Révolution: 1789–1804* (Paris, 1961) may soon appear in English also.

There are new standard histories of the Revolutionary era by the British

271

writers George Rudé, Norman Hampson, and M. J. Sydenham. See also, on working-class participation, Rudé's *The Crowd and the French Revolution* (London and New York, 1958). Of great interest are Alfred Cobban, *Social Interpretation of the French Revolution* (Cambridge, 1964), and his *Aspects of the French Revolution* (London, 1968), a collection of stimulating and sometimes provocative articles made shortly before Cobban's death. An older book, in narrative vein, is R. R. Palmer, *Twelve Who Ruled: The Year of the Terror in the French Revolution* (Princeton, N.J., 1941, 1958).

For the "wave" or "world" of the French Revolution, the subject of the present volume, the literature in English is very sporadic. R. R. Palmer, *The Age of the Democratic Revolution: A Political History of Europe and America, 1760–1800* (2 vols., Princeton, N.J., 1959 and 1964), gives further references. There is Steven T. Ross, *European Diplomatic History 1789–1815: France Against Europe* (New York, 1969). On the difference between two very important countries and cultures see Hans Kohn, *Prelude to Nation-States: The French and German Experience 1789–1815* (Princeton, N.J., 1967). The writings of Godechot and Hampson, cited above, stress the revolutionary movements outside of France.

For particular countries there are Carl B. Cone, *The English Jacobins* (New York, 1968); Thomas Packenham, *The Year of Liberty: The Great Irish Rebellion of 1798* (London, 1969); Klaus Epstein, *The Genesis of German Conservatism* (Princeton, N.J., 1966), essentially on the impact of the French Revolution in Germany; and Ernst Wangermann, *From Joseph II to the Jacobin Trials: Government Policy and Public Opinion in the Habsburg Dominions in the Period of the French Revolution* (Oxford, 1959). See also on a timely subject C. L. R. James, *The Black Jacobins: Toussaint l'Ouverture and the San Domingo Revolution* (New York, 1938, 1963).

There are many collections of readings. For excerpts of eighteenth-century sources see Philip Dawson, *The French Revolution* (Hemel Hempstead, 1967); Leo Gershoy, *Era of the French Revolution: Ten Years That Shook the World* (London, 1958); Alfred Cobban, *The Debate on the French Revolution* (London, 1950), selections from British books and pamphlets; and John H. Stewart, *Documentary Survey of the French Revolution* (London, 1951), for the French constitutions, legislation and other public papers. George Rudé, *Robespierre* in "Great Lives Observed" (Hemel Hempstead, 1967) combines both source materials and historiography since it contains excerpts from speeches by Robespierre, observations of him by his contemporaries, and estimates of him by later historians. For collections of writings by historians, often technical or argumentative, there are F. A. Kafker and J. M. Laux, *The French Revolution: Conflicting Interpretations* (New York, 1968); Jeffry Kaplow, *New Perspectives on the French Revolution: Readings in Historical Sociology* (Chichester, 1965), with translation of articles by a dozen French scholars; Ralph W. Greenlaw, *The Economic Origins of the French Revolution: Poverty or Prosperity?* (London, 1958); and Peter Amann, *The Eighteenth-Century Revolution: French or Western?* (London, 1963). This last item reproduces arguments for and against the theme of the present volume, on the idea of a general revolutionary movement beyond the French Revolution itself; but it appeared in 1964, before the case had been fully heard.

Index

273